"In *Zoë Bakes Cookies*, Zoë brings her inimitable style, and joy, to baking cookies! She continues to inspire us with her creativity and passion as she teaches us with flawless technique and a wealth of helpful hints. Zoë warms our hearts with charm that flies off every page and delivers a delightful dose of nostalgia with every craveable cookie!"

—**CLAUDIA FLEMING**, executive culinary director for Daily Provisions-USHG and author of *Delectable*

"A flawless baking guide to the cookie classics, *Zoë Bakes Cookies* offers up a master class on combining passion with precision to make perfection. Mixing love and creativity with science and tradition, this instant baking go-to will raise your game and is the only cookie book you'll ever need . . . for life!"

—**ERIN FRENCH**, *New York Times* bestselling author and founder of The Lost Kitchen

"When Zoë François writes a book about cookies, I hope everyone knows to drop what they're doing to buy it. Zoë's recipes always work, and *Zoë Bakes Cookies* might be her best collection yet."

—**DEB PERELMAN**, author of *Smitten Kitchen Keepers*

ZOË
BAKES
cookies

everything you need to
know to make your favorite
cookies and bars

ZOË BAKES COOKIES

Zoë François

TEN SPEED PRESS
California | New York

To my aunt Kristin and her legendary love of shortbread cookies!

And

to my two poodles: Rafman, who is my constant companion
in the kitchen, and his late brother, Miles, who *loved* butter.
RIP my sweet pood! Here's a treat for all the dogs, to distract
them from the butter as you bake cookies.

Dog Biscuits

½ cup / 130g peanut butter

½ cup / 124g mashed ripe banana

1 cup / 100g rolled oats

¼ cup / 60g peanut flour (or oat flour)

¼ tsp ground cinnamon

¼ tsp ground turmeric

Line a baking sheet with a silicone mat or parchment paper.

In a large bowl, mix together the peanut butter, banana, oats, peanut flour, cinnamon, and turmeric with a wooden spoon, until well combined.

Place the mixture on the prepared baking sheet, cover with plastic, and spread evenly using your hands to a thickness of ¼ inch / 6mm.

Freeze until firm, about 15 minutes. Preheat the oven to 350°F / 175°C.

Use a 3½-inch / 9cm bone-shaped cookie cutter to shape the dough. If it gets sticky, return it to the freezer until firm, about 5 minutes. Gather any scraps and use for training treats (see Baker's Note).

Spread the cut cookies on the same baking sheet and bake for about 15 minutes, or until golden brown.

BAKER'S NOTES

Roll the extra dough into tiny balls, about ¼ inch / 6mm thick, and bake for 8 minutes. These make excellent training treats for your puppies.

Check with your veterinarian to make sure this is a healthy snack for your pup.

Contents

Recipe List

Introduction

Cookies started my wonderfully wild voyage into baking. I got hooked as a child, and it's easy to see why: They're pretty simple to make, and they require less equipment, specialty ingredients, and know-how than cakes and other intricate pastries. But I didn't realize what moved me to bake in the first place until I started writing this book. As the cookies formed into chapters, I realized this wasn't just a collection of delicious cookies, but also an ode to my ancestors who baked before me. This group of incredibly strong and determined women all baked for different reasons—some to create moments of joy in a hectic life, others to express love at the holidays, and a few for survival. All the reasons my grandmothers and great-great-grandmothers baked have become a part of me and my cookie DNA.

One of my earliest and fondest food memories involves me buying cookies with my mom, Bubbe (my mom's mom), and my two great-aunts, Sylvia and Rose Berkowitz, in Brooklyn. It was the 1970s and I was about five years old. I still remember walking into a tiny Jewish bakery where the rows of steamy glass cases were overflowing with poppy seed–speckled mohn kichel, triangle-shaped hamantaschen filled with apricot and prune (page 141), and still warm, buttery rugelach (page 135). We left loaded with bags of cookies, the sweet smell clinging to our clothes. I devoured as many as I could on our walk back to my great-aunts' apartment along the Brighton Beach boardwalk.

I recently returned to that neighborhood, hoping to step through a looking glass mirror of those sugar-dusted memories and found far fewer Jewish bakeries. But the ones that remained greeted me with those familiar aromas—the nutty-stuffs, jammy centers, and sugar crackles—and delivered that rush of sweet nostalgia. The baked goods carried a life full of stories with their tantalizing smells—in the recollections of past generations and the promise of sweet days ahead.

LOVE AND HONEY

This lovely memory stands out so strongly for me because of its contrast to my everyday life growing up in a commune with my parents, who fed me homemade tempeh, alfalfa sprouts on everything, and brewer's yeast–topped popcorn as a treat. They were earnest hippies, and "sugar" was treated like a four-letter word. While there was plenty of cooking and baking in our Vermont communal kitchen back then, it looked very different. It came with a soundtrack of Bob Dylan and loaves of sturdy, heartfelt twelve-grain bread, pans of crunchy granola, and a lot of food assembled for fuel rather than pleasure. If there were cookies on the commune, they'd be full of brown rice, wheat germ, and "mighty mush" (the name of that cereal says it all) baked into lumps that tasted way too healthful for you and resembled something closer to tree bark than sweetness and joy. Honestly, I kinda love those flavors now, but they were less exciting to the frazzy-haired wild-child (my nickname in the commune was Frazzy Bringle) that I was back then. I've since learned to bake with these healthier ingredients and create delicious cookies that are full of love and honey.

GRANNY NEAL'S CHRISTMAS COOKIE TIN

Sugary, buttery cookies—and definitely anything with candy, caramel, chocolate, or sprinkles—were reserved for rare special occasions. And these moments of sugar in my early childhood were always connected with my grandmothers. Every holiday season, we visited my dad's mom, Granny Neal, in New Jersey. I don't ever remember her baking any other time of the year, but she sure pulled out all the stops for Christmas. When we walked into her house, dozens of holiday tins perched on every surface and were filled with all of the classic Betty Crocker holiday sweets— robustly buttery shortbread, powdery Mexican wedding cookies, thumbprints with jam, zigzag spritz cookies, and layered coconut bars—plus a few Norwegian family recipes tossed in. I still have and treasure Granny's Betty Crocker cookbook from the 1950s. I know which recipes she loved most, because they are spattered with chocolate, butter, and oleo (another name for margarine). The book is falling apart, some pages are lacquered together from sticky fingerprints, and her notes are jotted in the margins, but I love it just the same. I also have her recipe box filled with a family recipe for krumkaker (page 119) from Norway and recipe clippings from the many, many newspapers and magazines she subscribed to, plus the beautifully scripted gift recipes she collected from her sister and close friends.

My Granny Neal also owned a bookstore, and I remember trays of cookies—likely pulled out of the freezer after her holiday baking extravaganza—next to the chairs and sofas set up around the store. This was the 1970s and 1980s—an era before chain bookstores—but even then, she knew that a cookie and coffee helped people linger and browse the shelves and leave with a new book and a smile. I remember sitting in an overstuffed chair with her cat in my lap, eating shortbread cookies and reading YA novels, all while watching customers do the same: They'd drop into a couch with a stack of books and then reach for the cookie tray. Granny Neal had it figured out.

BUBBE BERKOWITZ'S BAKING GENES

My Bubbe, Sarah Berkowitz, grew up in Williamsburg, a part of Brooklyn that was predominantly Jewish. By the time I was born, she had moved the family to Connecticut, where my mom grew up, far from the Jewish bakeries. Bubbe didn't have much time for or interest in baking herself, but she adored sweets. During Jewish holidays and special occasions, she had boxes of macaroons—both coconut and almond (page 131 and page 134)—wrapped in plastic that, in retrospect, did not taste awesome. (Sorry, Bubbe!) But as a kid with my commune diet, I loved them because they were sweet. One thing she did bake herself was mandelbrodt (page 147), a nutty twice-baked cookie very similar to an Italian biscotti. For her, these were essential—she dunked them in the many, many cups of coffee she drank throughout the day.

For my Bubbe's side of the family, baking cookies and other sweets wasn't only to satisfy a craving, it also sustained their family. My great-great-grandmother Shaindel Siro grew up in a Jewish ghetto in Kyiv in the late 1800s. To make enough money to survive and bring some well-needed joy to her community, Shaindel baked in her tiny home kitchen and sold her babkas, strudels, rugelach, and mandelbrodt to her neighbors.

In the early 1900s, on the eve of the Russian Revolution, it became clear that Shaindel and her children needed to flee the Pale of Settlement, where many Jews made their home. It was no longer safe for them, especially after her husband had been killed in a pogrom. They needed to create a life outside of Kyiv but doing so was difficult and expensive. So Shaindel's teenage daughter, Sonny, came up with a plan to get the family the money they needed. She started surreptitiously swiping ingredients such as flour, sugar, and salt from her mother's kitchen and sneaking them into nearby army camps to sell to the soldiers. She was fearless, tenacious, and resilient—all family traits passed down through the generations. And her plan worked.

It wasn't long before Sonny had saved up enough money from her secret operation to send one family member to the United States. Sonny was still too young to go by herself, so her older sister Zelda landed in New York City and promptly started baking in restaurants. As soon as she earned enough money, she sent for Shaindel, Sonny, and the rest of the family. These humble baked goods carried them across the sea to a new life in America. Shaindel became Shirley Sierra at Ellis Island, but in Williamsburg, she was still Shaindel. She tied on an apron and started selling cookies, cakes, and bread to her neighbors, just as she had done in Kyiv. Business as usual.

Most of my mother's memories of Zelda (my great-grandmother) are of her in the kitchen with her pet parakeet. My mother remembers the surreal image of the two of them bustling around the cramped kitchen in their tiny Brooklyn apartment, both covered with a dusting of flour. Zelda never just baked one batch but always felt compelled to bake for the entire community, which is surely something she got from her mother, Shaindel. Her baking genes may have skipped a couple generations (my Bubbe and my mom), but they landed deeply in me. I have poodles underfoot instead of a parakeet, but sometimes their curly coats have a white sprinkle of flour while I'm at the counter. We are cut from the same cloth.

MY SWEET PATH STARTED IN HOME ECONOMICS

It was in grade school, while peering into other kids' lunch boxes, when I realized my carob-studded commune world was sincerely lacking in real sweets. (If you've read my cake cookbook, you probably recall my near-religious experience with a Twinkie.) Lunch was a time for serious bartering. Unfortunately, I didn't have much trading power with my homemade twelve-grain bread slathered with hand-crushed peanut butter and honey we gathered from my dad's beehives. It's a lunch I would be so proud of today, but this was 40 years prior and what I wanted was a *Brady Bunch* lunch. I managed, through the art of persuasion, to score the odd bologna sandwich or Oreo, but that generally only worked once or twice. I needed a new game plan to get some lunchroom bargaining power, not just to satisfy my sweet tooth, but also to make some new friends fast.

I moved around a lot with my spiritually curious, wandering hippie parents. And by a lot, I mean every six months or so, so I needed to fit in quickly. (I ended up going to sixteen schools before graduating from college.) My dad is probably just finding out about this now (sorry, Dad!) but I have to confess, I pocketed loose change from the top of his dresser and used it to stock up on cookies and candy on my way to school. I shared the sweet plunder with my schoolmates on the playground or during lunchtime swaps. At an early age, I realized that cookies brought joy and a new set of friends way faster than alfalfa sprouts did.

By middle school, I was obsessed with all things sweet, and I realized that if I were going to have cookies, beyond the holidays with my grandmothers, I would have to start making them myself. In those days, we had a line of credit at the tiny, two-aisle-wide grocery store on the corner, and just by signing my name at the cash register, I could run up a tab with all the ingredients for Toll House cookies. I'd bake and happily eat the better part of a warm batch, then bring the remainders to school. The eating and baking were my joy and calm in an otherwise chaotic, albeit exciting, childhood. My cookie path was set, and I hadn't even realized it yet.

My first forays into baking anything more challenging than the recipe on the Toll House bag happened because of a French class potluck in middle school. My home economics teacher handed me the Time-Life book series, *Foods of the World*, where I discovered recipes for Florentines (page 163) and chocolate mousse and immediately went home to try them. I was transfixed by the lacy, caramelly Florentines that emerged from my oven, but less so by my mousse, which had serious issues. I didn't know to use brewed coffee and added the grounds instead. The texture was a disaster, but even through the grittiness, I knew there was a magic I'd nearly tapped. My next attempt was a success and proved to be one of the best lessons of baking: failure is where the learning happens, so embrace the opportunity to suck a bit on your way to success! I then baked my way through Lee Bailey's *Country Desserts*, Martha Stewart's cookbooks, and *Baking with Julia*, with the same voracity I'd had with that ambrosial bite of Twinkie. It was the humblest—and sometimes edible—start of my lifetime's worth of sweet discovery, and I have my middle school teachers to thank.

THE UNEXPECTED BUSINESS OF COOKIES

My baking adventure continued in college, when I worked weekends at Sneakers, a crushingly busy breakfast joint in Winooski, Vermont. That was my introduction to larger batch baking of any sort. I was responsible for making dozens of muffins, cookies, sticky buns, and simple pastries and for prepping all things breakfast. The prep kitchen, where I set up the morning cooks with trays of bacon and stacks of bread to grill into French toast, was tiny and hot. I had a big bowl for mixing, but no stand mixer (I wouldn't operate one of those until I started my own baking company). Each recipe was made with the owner's stained recipe cards and my muscle and determination. Oh, the hours I would have saved if I'd just known to ask for a stand mixer! But I made do and learned to problem solve like a boss. Simultaneously, I took a business class at the University of Vermont, solely to fulfill a math requirement, and for an assignment, I came up with a business plan for Zoë's Cookies. The plan was meant to be fictitious, but it sparked something in me that not even my art or theater classes had managed (those were two of my many majors). Six months later, I was selling cookies from a cart that my boyfriend, Graham, built for me and Zoë's Cookies was born. I pushed the cart from his apartment several blocks to Church Street in Burlington and set up between a men's clothing store and the park where people ate their lunches. Location, location! All the surrounding shop owners and their customers visited to buy cookies from me, and it felt triumphant to be paid for something I loved doing.

Cookie cart, 1986

I ran my cart during the gourmet chocolate chip cookie trend of the 1980s, when companies like Mrs. Fields, David's Cookies, and Famous Amos were making glamorous and elevated versions of the unpretentious chocolate chip cookie by adding ingredients like white chocolate, macadamia nuts, and big chunks of high-quality chocolate instead of small, waxy chips. I took the little I'd learned about production baking during my time at Sneakers, and I blissfully made a go of it out of Graham's apartment, commandeering his kitchen. He had a twenty-inch apartment-size stove that I could only fit the tiniest baking pans in, like an adult version of an Easy-Bake Oven. I stayed up all night baking tiny tray after tray to have enough cookies ready for the morning. I was still studying for school between batches, but my heart belonged to the cookie baking at all hours.

I had absolutely no idea what I was doing. Sometimes the cookies I cranked out were fantastic, and sometimes not so much. There were equal amounts of flops to successes, and that's probably being generous. One time I threw a very cold (honestly, it was frozen) block of butter into the mixer and just ground the gears to a halt. I was working so fast, I would put dough on a hot cookie sheet, and they would spread too quickly and burn on the edges. Even so, I would try to sell all the cookies, good and bad ones. (Pro tip, selling burned cookies is not a great business move.) Fortunately, I'm a quick study and I eventually figured out a decent routine to improve my recipes with each batch. I had the engine in my mixer rebuilt and I was back in business.

I did well enough that I actually picked up some wholesale accounts and took a semester off from school to focus on my cookie empire. I expanded my operation to a fraternity house kitchen with giant ovens, where I paid rent with warm cookies that I left in a generous pile on the counter. The experiment with the cookie cart was a sweet success, albeit short lived. Once the Vermont winter set in and the cookies started to freeze on the cart, I packed it up and returned to my studies. Many years later, I would find my way to culinary school and finish the dream of baking for a living, but there were a couple of life chapters still to live out.

BAKING NEW TRADITIONS IN MY MIDWESTERN KITCHEN

I married Graham, who built the cart and sacrificed his kitchen for me, and lucky for him, I'm a much better and tidier baker these days. But, some things don't change: 35+ years later, our home kitchen is still the heart of my baking domain. I've held on to a few of my original recipes from Zoë's Cookies, and although they haven't aged entirely well and make me cringe a bit looking through them, they are also a beautiful reminder of just how far I've come. Those stained index cards represent the messy passion and determination I had for baking long before I went to culinary school to learn baking chemistry and proper techniques or worked in professional kitchens. I have spent more than three decades baking, honing my craft, writing about it, and making it my mission to share my love for baking with anyone who will listen. Part of the journey has been embracing the science of baking: I now know what makes a cookie crisp or soft and chewy or how changing ingredients or temperatures can affect how much a cookie spreads. Back in the day, that may have intimidated me, because I considered myself an artist and in no way a mathematician or a scientist. (Remember, I went so far out of my way to avoid a straightforward math course that I ended up building an entire cookie business.) Now I thrive on some simple food science; knowing the basics allows for more creativity.

ABOUT THIS BOOK

When I set out to write this book, I hadn't quite realized how cookies are so woven into my family history, my own life's journey, and the everyday simple joy of baking for my friends and family. This book is more than just a collection of my favorite cookies (although it is also that!). It's autobiographical, and the different chapters touch on different periods in my life.

There are cookies based on memories and specific ingredients that were so emblematic of my early days at the commune. Over the years, I've significantly revamped the commune cookie recipes, as many were dense, stodgy, and ate like homework. After a lot of experimentation, I've come up with recipes for cookies that you can feel good about putting in your kid's lunch box. They won't even want to trade them away because they're too delicious! A number of these recipes are gluten- and dairy-free, too, because cookies are even tastier when we can share them with more friends.

Many of the holiday cookies are a nod to my Granny Neal's recipe box and Betty Crocker cookbook from the 1950s. Granny Neal baked the same cookies every year, and while I love and admire her adherence to tradition, I'm far too fickle and fond of experimentation to do the same. My cookie tray looks different every year. My aunt Kristin, whom I've dedicated this book to, has been on the other end of the phone throughout my journey of writing this book, regaling me with stories of her mom in the kitchen and her own cookie memories.

There's also a chapter with cookies my Jewish ancestors would have made. Shaindel, Sonny, and Zelda baked by feel, never really measuring ingredients, grabbed flour by the fistful, and added a pinch of salt here or a spoonful of sugar there. They were brilliant, formidable women, able to navigate war and a new life in America, but they were also unable to read and write, so they passed on their recipes orally.

The Time-Life books I was introduced to in middle school showed me a whole new world of flavors and styles of cookies I might otherwise have missed. These classic recipes were also what I learned in culinary school and became the backbone of the professional kitchens I worked in. They are fabulously delicious and can range from rustic to dainty and sophisticated, like the mighty macaron.

There's an entire chapter devoted to the chocolate chip cookies based on my college days and the Zoë's Cookies cart, but with decades of tweaking and improving all the recipes. Reworking all these recipes (and introducing a bunch of brownies) brought back so many memories and almost makes me want to revive the cart.

The last chapter, Midwestern Cookies and Bars, is inspired by Minnesota—the place I've called home now for three decades. One can't live in Minnesota without experiencing the food at the State Fair, nearly two weeks of festivities that capture the flavors and celebratory treats of this community. I leaned hard on my best friend, Jen Sommerness, and her Duluth, Minnesota, cookie traditions for this chapter. Betty Crocker was invented right here in Minnesota, so she's had a big impact on the home bakers in the community and beyond, all the way to my Granny in New Jersey.

THE COOKIE ACADEMY

The Cookie Academy is there to help you with technique and guide you deeper into the recipes. If you want to unpack a family recipe that has never quite come out the way you recall your grandmother making it, there may be some tips and tricks here you'll find useful in your pursuit of a memory. It's lightly science-based and is filled with helpful how-tos I've picked up throughout my career. It's there for you to use if you want, but all of the recipes stand alone and you can jump straight into baking delicious cookies. Some of my greatest joys, over the decades I've baked cookies, is discovering something new—and that often comes from messing with (aka messing up) a recipe! Lean into your creative instincts.

These are the recipes of my life and the generations that came before me. They've all been exactingly tested and written to give you an easy jumping-off point to all the cookie success in the world. I hope you'll use this heavily and get your own finger smudges and chocolate smears on the pages. Happy baking, enjoy all the cookies!

Ingredients

There are certain ingredients that are staples in baking and will appear in everything from cakes to cookies. If you have my cake book, *Zoë Bakes Cakes*, which I hope you do, some of these ingredients and descriptions will be familiar to you, others will be new. My philosophy is that a really good recipe starts with great ingredients. I suggest you use your favorite brands when baking these cookies. There may be a few instances when I call out a particular brand I prefer to use in a recipe. I generally only do this when I've tested with something that produced cookies far better than the rest. I try to use organic ingredients whenever possible, but they aren't always the best option. For instance, natural food coloring is not as bright as artificial coloring, which means your cookies may not have the pop of color you desire. Another example is cake flour: Organic cake flour is not as pure white as its nonorganic counterpart. The organic products will work, but the results may be slightly different.

In the Cookie Academy (page 35), I've created a guide to help you make your "perfect" cookie and that encourages you to play with the ingredients to get the flavor and texture you desire. Understanding how the various ingredients play with one another is key to getting the cookie you want without having to do endless experiments—that's my job! In the Chocolate Chip Cookie Lab (page 45), I baked dozens of batches with varying amounts of each ingredient, so you can see the results of tweaking the recipe. Purposeful substitutions are fun and will make a cookie that fits your mood and occasion. However, there are other substitutions that are trickier. Swapping out gentle cake flour with equal amounts of a hearty whole-wheat flour, or replacing all the sugar with honey, will throw off the chemical balance of the recipe in ways you may not intend. You could accidentally end up with something you love, but chances are more likely it will be a dense and disappointing experiment. I spent a long time testing these recipes, so I suggest you give them a go as I wrote them, before putting your creative spin on them.

CHOCOLATE

Chocolate is an, if not *the*, essential cookie ingredient, representative of devotion and love. People have been eating some form of cocoa for thousands of years. It has caused wars—it's just that powerful. The chocolate that we consume today is made from the beans of the cacao tree in the form of cocoa powder, bar chocolate, chunks, or chips. They're all an essential part of many cookies, imparting richness, a depth of flavor, sweetness, bitter notes, and—of course—the classic look of a chocolate chip cookie. It's in the name! You will notice a big improvement in the taste of your recipes if you use the highest-quality chocolate you can get your hands on.

Cocoa Powder

Cocoa powder is the result of drying and grinding cocoa solids. My favorite unsweetened cocoa powder is Valrhona, for the depth of flavor and deep color. Their cocoa is Dutch-processed, which means it has been alkali-treated, so it is less acidic and darker as a result. All of my recipes were tested with Dutch-processed and natural cocoa. Droste, Guittard, or other brands will also work but may vary in color from black to red, so the color of your cookies may vary depending on the cocoa. Natural cocoa is more acidic and may change the way a cookie rises or spreads, and the color won't be as dark. The recipes were also tested with Ghirardelli's natural cocoa. In some cases, the type of cocoa won't make a big difference in the results and in other cases, the difference is huge. I mention the kind I prefer to use in the recipes. If you don't have that type on hand, you can move forward with a different kind, but keep in mind that your cookies may look and taste a bit different from mine.

Solid Chocolate

Cocoa beans grow in large pods on cacao trees. Those beans are fermented, dried, and ground into a paste before being melted into cocoa liquor, which is then separated into cocoa butter and cocoa solids.

Cocoa butter gives chocolate its smooth melting mouthfeel and makes chocolate more glorious when baked into a cookie or stirred into ganache. If you want that extra luxurious taste, look for chocolate made with cocoa butter rather than other types of fats. There are plenty of chocolate chips that have a mixture of fats that make excellent cookies but have other drawbacks. The other fats, typically soy lecithin, have a longer shelf life, keep the chips in their distinct shape as they bake, which may be a desired effect, and tend to make the chocolate cheaper. The drawback to chocolate containing lecithin is it just isn't as delicious as cocoa butter and can have a waxy mouthfeel. All chocolate can be used in your cookies with great success, so pick your favorite.

Unsweetened baking chocolate is 100% chocolate with no sugar, milk solids, or anything else that dilutes the flavor. It is as close to a 50/50 ratio of cocoa solids and cocoa butter as you'll get. It is often called "baking chocolate" since people rarely eat it as a candy, but it is a great way to add intense chocolate flavor without adding more sugar to the recipe. The recipe needs to be written with this chocolate in mind or the flavor can be overwhelming and not sweet enough for most palates.

WHITE AND MILK CHOCOLATES

The only part of the cocoa bean that appears in white chocolate is cocoa butter. This is why white chocolate (cocoa butter blended with sugar and milk solids) is white or ivory in color. It also makes white chocolate behave differently from other chocolates, so you can't substitute it for other chocolate in recipes. Be sure that your white chocolate contains cocoa butter, otherwise it isn't really related to chocolate at all. White chocolate can be caramelized to create a deeper, richer flavor (see page 120 for directions).

Milk chocolate is dark chocolate with—you guessed it—milk solids, sugar, and cocoa butter added to it. The milk gives it a lighter color and creamier texture and the additional sugar makes it far sweeter than dark chocolate.

Milk and white chocolates are different beasts and will make your recipes sweeter. You can use them chopped up in chocolate chip cookies without any changes to the recipes, but don't try to sub them in ganache or in place of melted bittersweet chocolate when it's added to cookie or brownie doughs; they behave very differently from their dark chocolate cousins.

Valrhona and some other brands also offer white and milk chocolate that are flavored with raspberry, passion fruit, yuzu, dulce de leche, and many others, which give recipes a unique flavor. These are typically quite sweet and based on milk or white chocolates so swap them in place of those.

CHOCOLATE SHAVINGS

To make chocolate shavings, scrape a large bar of chocolate with a sharp chef's knife or use a vegetable peeler on the side of the bar, which results in a slightly thicker shaving. The harder you press down as you scrape the chocolate, the thicker the shavings will be.

The only chocolate to avoid when baking is "coating chocolate," which contains no cocoa butter and is meant to be melted to coat the outside of a cookie. I prefer just to use melted chocolate for that task, because "coating chocolate" can be very waxy and sweet. In my honest opinion, coating chocolate of any color should be avoided for the purposes of this book.

Cocoa solids give chocolate its distinctive flavor and color. The percentage number you see on a chocolate refers to the combined amount of cocoa butter and solids in the bar. If the chocolate says 70%, it means that 30% of that bar is some combination of sugar, milk solids, and/or other non-cocoa ingredients. In this book, I use bittersweet chocolate (about 70% cocoa), but you can replace it with semisweet (about 60% cocoa). For bittersweet bar chocolate, Valrhona is my favorite, but Callebaut, Scharffen Berger, Guittard, and other premium brands also work quite well. If premium chocolate is unavailable, try the recipes with your favorite brands of solid chocolate or chips. I even made the chocolate chip cookies with chips sweetened with stevia, and they were fantastic.

DAIRY

There are many forms of dairy products that are added to cookies. Depending on which one is called for, it can add moisture, flavor, fat, acidity, body, or all of the above.

Cream Cheese

Cream cheese is a soft, fresh, mild-flavored cheese, and I use it to create a super-tender cookie dough for my Rugelach (page 135), and there are cheesecake bars that rely on this soft cheese for its smooth texture and mild flavor. Philadelphia Original is my hands-down first choice for baking because it has a wonderful texture and lightly tangy flavor. If you can't find that brand, just avoid the low-fat or no-fat varieties and make sure the cream cheese isn't full of unnecessary gums, which aren't as nice in texture or flavor.

Heavy Whipping Cream

I use heavy whipping cream to make glorious fillings and toppings for cookies, brownies, and bars. Buy the heavy whipping cream with the highest fat content you can for best flavor and stability.

Milk

I typically use whole milk in these recipes; its fat lends a richness to cookies that helps flavor and texture. Lower-fat milks will also work, but the recipe will come out slightly different. You can also substitute non-dairy milk (almond, coconut, soy, oat, or any that you typically use) in any of the recipes. If you do use a non-dairy substitution, I recommend going with a nonsweetened variety, since the added sweetness might make the final cookie taste too cloying.

Sweetened Condensed Milk

The name really says it all: this is cow's milk with sugar added and then cooked to remove most of the water content. The result is super-thick, sweet, and creamy. You can use it straight out of the can, or you can caramelize it in the can to make dulce de leche (page 168). The consistency of the caramelized version is so thick that you can spread it onto cookies, like Alfajores (page 167), or add it to Rice Crispy Bars (page 221).

Sour Cream

The tanginess of sour cream helps to temper the sweetness of some recipes. It is also super-rich, which gives the cookies a wonderful texture without adding any greasiness from additional butter or oil. The fat and acid in sour cream act as tenderizers; the acid interacts with baking soda in a recipe to aid in the rise. If you can't find sour cream, you can replace it with crème fraîche, which is a younger, mellower version of this set cream, or use plain Greek yogurt. Avoid low-fat or no-fat sour cream for the best results.

DRIED FRUIT

I make recommendations, based on tradition, for the type of dried fruit to use in your cookies, but they are just suggestions, and you should use whatever pleases you. My eldest son won't touch anything with raisins, and one of my husband's favorite cookies is oatmeal raisin, so they rarely fight over the same cookies. I totally understand that someone's palate takes precedence over tradition, so make swaps wherever you see fit for a different dried fruit. I typically go for unsweetened dried fruit since the recipes already have all the sugar I desire. Sometimes I want bright colorful fruit, like apricots in biscottini, and this means fruit processed with sulfites. It is a preservative that keeps the fruit from turning brown, but some people are sensitive to sulfites and should stick to the unsulfured fruit.

EGGS

As everyone knows, eggs have two parts. There are the whites, which are mostly protein. They offer strength and, when whipped, the rising power in a recipe. The yolks are mostly fat and help to emulsify a mixture, adding color and flavor.

How you use eggs in a recipe will give you wildly different results. Whole eggs can create a dense, smooth texture when added to a cookie. On the other hand, egg whites can be whipped into ethereal pillows of meringue that lighten a cookie dough or are baked just as is. (For more on the power of eggs in cookies, see Chocolate Chip Cookie Lab, page 49, and Meringue, page 43.)

All of the recipes in this book were tested with fresh large eggs. Check the date on your eggs; they will get thinner and lose some of their stretch and strength as they get past 2 weeks old. The most important thing to know about eggs is that they should be at room temperature when mixed into your dough, so they won't chill the room temperature butter, which seizes it and doesn't allow the mixture to trap air bubbles. Use cold eggs only if stated in a recipe. (For more information about proper temperature of ingredients, see page 36.)

Using cage-free eggs with their darker-hued, almost orange yolks really does make the color pop, but keep that in mind when making sugar cookie dough or something you want to be white in color. I'm lucky my best friend lives across the street and raises chickens, so I have a steady supply of fresh eggs for all of my baking needs. If your neighbor doesn't have a flock of chickens, try a local farmers' market or co-op.

Separating eggs is much easier when they are chilled, since the eggs are firmer; however, you then need to let them sit at room temperature for about an hour to warm up. If you forget to remove the eggs from the refrigerator before you start to bake, you can warm them in the shell in a bowl of hot water for about 5 minutes and then carefully separate them. How you separate an egg was probably taught to you by your folks when you were young. There is no right or wrong way, as long as the yolks don't break and the whites separate cleanly and completely. That said, here are two methods.

1. Tap the egg on the counter until it just cracks, face the crack to the sky, gently poke both your thumbs into the crack, and ease the shell apart. The white will start to spill out, so do this over a bowl. Rock the egg yolk back and forth between the two halves of the shell, allowing the sharp edge of the shell to cut off the egg white from the yolk.

2. Carefully crack all of the eggs into a bowl. Gently pick up the yolks with your fingertips and pinch off the whites, then put the yolks in a separate bowl. I've also seen this done by squeezing a plastic water bottle with a wide mouth to create suction and placing it directly over the yolk to gently suck it into the bottle.

Both egg whites and yolks can be stored if you find yourself with extras after making your cookies. Egg whites can be refrigerated for a couple of weeks or frozen for months, without any preparation; just put them in an airtight container. Yolks don't last nearly as long, just a few days in the refrigerator or about 1 month in the freezer. To store yolks, you'll want to stir them with a pinch of sugar to prevent them from developing a skin in the refrigerator or from being too viscous when thawed from the freezer.

As for pasteurized or frozen egg whites, I've found that they don't whip up as well as egg whites from fresh eggs, so I avoid them for meringues. They can be used for most cookie doughs—especially if you intend to be snacking on the cookie dough itself.

EXTRACTS, FOOD COLORING, AND SPICES

Flavor extracts, food coloring, and spices are the little extras that give cookies even more character. Sometimes the effects are subtle, and other times they are bold and define the cookie. I use vanilla extract in just about every recipe, so I consider it foundational. Food coloring can turn a simple sugar cookie into something absolutely festive. Spices are key to the personality of certain cookies, but you are free to play around to suit your tastes.

Extracts

Pure extracts are made with the natural essences of almond, coconut, orange, mint, or anything else you want to flavor your cookies. I recommend using pure extracts whenever you can; I even go so far as to make my own vanilla extract, which is really quite easy (see page 16). If you use imitation or artificial flavorings, you may introduce a chemical aftertaste to the recipes. If you want a flavor in your cookie or icing that demands using an artificial flavor, just add a tiny bit at a time and taste it, since these extracts tend to be very strong.

Vanilla extract appears in nearly every recipe in this book and if you find one without it, I probably just forgot it. Vanilla is like salt, meaning it heightens the flavors around it. Most of the time it is just like background music, meant to allow the chocolate, spices, or whatever is the star of the recipe to shine. When I really want vanilla to step forward, I use actual vanilla bean seeds, plus vanilla extract.

Food Coloring

Sometimes I want to add whimsy or drama to cookies by using food coloring, but most of the time I go with the natural hue of ingredients. When I do tint cookie dough, I try to use natural food coloring because the colors tend to be less garish and because they're derived from natural fruits, vegetables, or spices. Having said this, there are times when natural colors don't achieve the intensity I want.

I almost always use gel paste food coloring versus liquid, since the color is more intense and so you don't have to add as much to achieve the color you want. When adding food coloring to a cookie recipe, do it in the beginning, along with the butter and sugar. This way, you give the color time to combine thoroughly without overmixing the dough. The exceptions to this are if you are adding it to a sugar cookie dough (page 97) or the Italian Rainbow Cookies (page 177) where you want to make multiple colors. I use powdered food coloring for macarons, so that I don't add more liquid to the mixture. A drop or two won't harm the batter, but if you want a super-intense color, go with powdered coloring.

Ground Spices

Once ground, spices can lose their flavors and aromas quickly, so you'll get the most intense flavor by grinding your own whole spices as you need them. The easiest way to do this is in a spice or coffee grinder, or in a spice grater for nutmeg and ginger. You can buy ground spices, just be sure to store them in a cool, dark cabinet or freeze them.

Vanilla Extract

I use vanilla extract in almost every cookie recipe. It isn't always the starring flavor, but it is part of what makes a dough special. You can use any vanilla you typically bake with, but I highly recommend you use a pure vanilla extract. I've been making my own for decades and always have a bottle or more in the cupboard.

Making your own vanilla extract is really so easy and the result is delicious. I started my current batch in 2012, and I just keep adding more vanilla beans and vodka once it gets halfway down the bottle. The extract will keep indefinitely, and over the months, it just keeps getting better. The type of vanilla bean you use does not matter, and you can combine the various beans from Mexico, Madagascar, Tahiti, Indonesia, and beyond. They range in flavor and cost, so try many and pick your favorite. The amount needed will depend on the size of the container you use, but you want a bunch to get the best flavor. The beans can be expensive, so you may start with less and then add leftover pods after you have scraped out the seeds for another recipe. This will take longer, because you aren't adding the flavorful pulp, but it is a great way to use up scraped pods. (Don't use vanilla beans if they have been cooked in a recipe, such as custard. They'll contaminate your bottle and make the vanilla murky.)

You'll need a clean, dry glass bottle with a stopper (I recommend a 750ml bottle, but the size doesn't matter; you can make a larger or smaller amount). If you prefer a nonalcoholic version, simply scrape the seeds into food-grade glycerin instead of vodka.

Makes about 3 cups / 750ml

12 or more whole vanilla beans (the more you add the stronger the flavor)

About 3 cups / 750ml vodka (enough to cover the beans in the bottle you choose)

Slit the vanilla beans down their lengths and scrape out the seeds; this helps to better disperse the flavor in the alcohol. Put the pods and scaped seed pulp into the bottle.

Fill the bottle with the vodka, close the stopper, and shake to distribute the seeds. The vodka will remain clear for the first few days but darken over time. Shake the bottle every couple of days to break up the pulp and get the seeds distributed in the vodka. After a week, the extract will start to develop some color and flavor. After several weeks, you can use the extract, but the flavor will be very subtle. Waiting for up to 3 months for the vanilla to mature is when it gets really exciting and is at its best.

Use in any recipe that calls for vanilla extract.

FATS

Butter is fundamental to most of the cookies in this book. Not only does it make luxurious texture, but it also adds and carries flavor, so it heightens the taste of vanilla, spices, or any other flavors in the recipe. Although butter is often the main event, there are other fats that add to the flavors and textures of cookies.

Butter

Butter is delicious, period. Butter is a dairy product usually made from cow's milk. It is created by churning cream until it separates into fat (butter) and a remaining liquid (buttermilk). European butters tend to have a higher fat content than butters found in the United States, unless the US butter is labeled "European-style." Because of the higher fat content, cookies made with European-style butter may spread more and end up crisper. I tested all the recipes with American butter, so using a butter from Europe, or one of that style, may make cookies that have a slightly oily feel. But the flavor will be incredible! I always recommend starting with a half batch of cookie dough if you are going to switch a major ingredient, like the type of fat you use.

When creamed to a light, airy texture, butter will create soft, airy, almost cake-like cookies. The temperature of your butter is often the key to proper mixing. If your butter is too cold, it won't cream easily, but if it's too soft, it can create an almost greasy cookie. You'll find much more information about how to handle butter in the Cookie Academy (page 35). I always call for unsalted butter, so you can control the saltiness of your recipes.

Oil

Unless otherwise specified, I tend to use a mild oil that has little flavor, such as vegetable, canola, corn, or safflower oil, so it doesn't compete with the other flavors in the cookie. There are exceptions, where the oil is meant to be the star. Oil can make a super-moist and tender cookie. Most oils lack the deliciousness of butter, but sometimes you want the tender texture it provides. In some recipes, I combine oil to create a tender crumb and butter for its wonderful flavor, so I have the benefits of both.

Shortening

Shortening is a white, solid fat typically made from vegetable oils. In my Granny's old books, it referred to any fat that was solid at room temperature, including butter, but nowadays it's more specific to vegetable shortening, like Crisco or organic versions. The latter is what I tested these recipes with.

In the UK, shortening is sold under the brand names Trex, Flora White, or Cookeen. In Australia the best-known brand is Copha.

If you can't find vegetable shortening, you can also use the following. However, these alternate ingredients are not typically whipped—meaning they have no rising power—so the cookies may spread a touch more than with shortening:

BROWN BUTTER

This is my go-to trick for enhancing the flavor in some of my grandmother's old recipes. Some of those recipes are great in spirit but need a boost in complexity. I had the thrilling opportunity to have brunch with Ina Garten and asked her opinion about doctoring my grandmother's recipes with brown butter. She wholeheartedly agreed and said something to the effect that the old recipes often need to evolve but can still carry a spark of the original. I've never felt bad about changing a recipe since.

Brown butter is simply butter that has been cooked until the solids start to caramelize, adding a toasty flavor to the butter that is exquisite in a cookie dough. It is super-easy to make (see page 41) and I call for it in several recipes, so I typically just make a big batch and store it in the refrigerator. When the butter is done cooking, it will have no water or milk solids (the browned bits don't count), so it is oilier than regular butter and may cause your cookies to spread more than regular butter. Brown butter will last in the refrigerator for a couple of weeks.

To strain or not to strain? I like the toasty bits that settle on the bottom of the pot and use the butter without straining. If you like a cleaner-looking cookie, without the browned milk solids speckled in your batter, then strain the butter through a fine-mesh sieve.

STICK MARGARINE

COCONUT OIL (SOLID)

GHEE This is clarified butter: the water and whey are removed, and it has a nutty flavor. It is pure fat and will have a nice texture but will make the cookies *spread*.

LARD This will impart a flavor, so only use it if you like that taste.

If you can't find any of these, use all butter. The cookies will have a different consistency but will still be delicious.

FLOURS

This is a cookie book, so, of course, flour is an important ingredient. Flour gives cookies structure and is a key element in the texture. Conventional flours are made from wheat. When the proteins in wheat (glutenin and gliadin) are mixed with liquids, they form gluten, which is highly elastic and strong. Gluten development is desirable when you want a nice chewy bread. But for cookies, we are going for something slightly more delicate, so we need to keep the gluten development at bay. The flours described here have varying degrees of gluten based on what texture you want in your cookies.

All-Purpose Flour

All-purpose flour is a staple ingredient for many of the recipes in this book. All-purpose flour is made from hard wheat and has a medium protein content. Why does that matter? Some recipes require a bit of gluten for structure to hold up to a heavy ingredient, like mashed bananas or grated carrots.

Each brand of all-purpose flour has a different protein content, so if your cookies seem dry or tough, you may want to explore the protein content in your flour. The more protein, the more water the flour will absorb and create gluten. I tested all of the recipes with Gold Medal unbleached all-purpose flour or the like, which has a protein content of about 10.5 percent. King Arthur Baking Company flour has closer to 11.7 percent protein, so if you're finding your cookies are too dry with this brand, try decreasing the amount of flour by a couple of tablespoons.

Bleached and unbleached flours behave the same, but they may taste different and will have a slightly different color to them. The chemical process of bleaching the flour also changes the flavor slightly, and some people describe it as having a chemical aftertaste. I think this is pretty subtle and, when combined with other ingredients and baked, is imperceptible to anyone who isn't a super-taster (yes, that's a real thing; my husband and youngest son are both super-tasters, so they perceive flavors that I can't). Some people really like the pure-white color of bleached flour for Sugar Cookies (page 97). Other people prefer the flavor of unbleached flour; it's your call.

Cake Flour

Despite its name I use cake flour in several cookie recipes. Cake flour is made from soft wheat and has a really low protein content, so it won't develop as much gluten as all-purpose flour when added to a liquid. It is wonderful for cookies that have a delicate, tender texture. Generally, cake flour is bleached and very white. You can also source unbleached cake flour, and it can be used instead.

Gluten-Free Flour

Some of the recipes in this book use gluten-free flours or are completely flourless, so they are naturally gluten-free, but this book was not tested throughout with gluten-free flours. If you have a flour blend you've used happily in place of all-purpose wheat flour in cookie recipes, it is worth a try, and I've generally had success when I've tried them. Whenever experimenting with a recipe, I recommend making a half batch in case you want to make further changes.

Nut Flour and Nut Meal

Commercially ground nut flour is made from blanched nuts and is so finely ground, it nearly resembles all-purpose flour. It has a fine texture and is used to create a wonderful flavor and texture in some cookies, like Macarons (page 161). Almond flour is probably the most common and the one I use most because it has a subtle flavor and doesn't overpower a recipe. Hazelnut and pistachio flours are excellent as well and can be used in place of almond flour to change up a recipe. Nut flour is also naturally gluten-free. It is not a substitute for wheat flour because nut flours contain no gluten. If the recipe is not written with nut flour in mind, the cookies will likely fall apart.

You can make your own nut flour by pulverizing whole, blanched nuts in a food processor until they are powdery, but be careful not to go too far or you'll end up with nut butter. Adding a few tablespoons of the sugar or wheat flour from the recipe you are making will help prevent the nuts from turning to paste, but still keep a close eye on it. The resulting nut flour is not as fine as you can get with a commercial product, but if you are in a pinch it works well.

Blanching nuts is a simple process that just takes some time. Bring a pot of water to a boil, add the raw, natural (skin-on) nuts, and let them cook for 60 seconds (no more or they get soft), strain, rinse under cold water, and then squeeze the skins off the nuts, one at a time. Be sure the nuts are perfectly dry before pulsing in a food processor to pulverize.

Nut meal is ground unblanched nuts that have been pulverized to the point of looking like corn meal, which is a little coarser than flour. It adds richness and texture, but doesn't develop any gluten, so just like nut flours, you can't replace nut meal with the other flours called for in a recipe.

You can choose between nut meal or nut flour for most recipes, unless noted. Keep in mind that the meal (skin on) version will have dark flecks in it that may show in your cookies. Because nuts have so much oil, it is best to store nut meal in the freezer, or it can go rancid.

Pasteurized Flour

Some people love eating raw cookie dough (including me!), but it's possible you'll get sick when ingesting raw ingredients, which includes raw flour. According to the FDA, baking or microwaving flour to pasteurize it doesn't actually make it safe, so it is best to use a flour that has been commercially pasteurized if you are worried about consuming raw flour. The only product that I have found which is heat treated and safe to consume is DŌ Heat-Treated Flour and Ready-Hour All-purpose Flour. Otherwise, it's best to bake the cookies first.

Spelt Flour

Spelt is an ancient grain that when ground into flour looks and tastes just like whole-wheat flour. The difference is that it has a lower protein content, so it doesn't form quite as much gluten. It can be lovely in cookies, since you get the whole-wheat flavor without an overly tough texture.

Starches

Starches are very finely ground (powdery) grains and roots. They have no protein, so they do not create stretchy gluten, which makes them an excellent ingredient in a recipe if you want a brittle and tender cookie. The cookies may not hold together if you use only starch, so don't substitute it for flour. If you prefer, you can also use tapioca, agar-agar, or arrowroot instead of the more common cornstarch.

Whole-Wheat Flour

Whole-wheat flour contains the germ and bran of the wheat, both of which are healthful and tasty. Together they add a slightly nutty flavor, which I love, but it can also make a dense and heavy cookie. I often mix whole-wheat flour with some all-purpose or cake flour in a recipe to achieve a lighter texture, while still getting the flavor and healthful bits of the whole wheat. White whole-wheat flour is still 100 percent whole wheat, just milled from white wheat berries, so use it interchangeably. All-purpose and whole-wheat flours absorb liquid differently; swapping them in recipes will really change the texture and flavor of a cookie.

LEAVENING

Most of the cookies in this book get their rise and airy texture with the help of a chemical leaven. Baking powder and baking soda are the two chemical leavens used to create the rise in cookies, sometimes used together and sometimes used separately. But they are not interchangeable, as they work differently to help cookies become lighter.

Baking Powder

Baking powder contains both an alkali and an acid, so it is a self-contained carbon dioxide machine and needs only liquid and heat to react. On its own, it's not as powerful as baking soda, since it is made of baking soda plus a powdered acid.

Sometimes a particularly acidic or heavy cookie dough will call for both baking powder and baking soda to achieve a nice rise and the best taste. Baking powder loses its rising power over time, so be sure to check the expiration date on the can.

You can make your own baking powder by combining one part baking soda (alkali), two parts cream of tartar (acid), and a pinch of cornstarch (to keep it from clumping; this is optional).

Baking Soda

Baking soda is an alkali (base) and needs to be in an acidic environment to create carbon dioxide, which causes a cookie to rise. Sour cream, cocoa powder, honey, lemon, and brown sugar (because of the molasses) are acidic and react with baking soda. Baking soda alone is more powerful than baking powder, so it is used in smaller amounts. It can also impart a bitter, soapy flavor if overdone, so it is often used with baking powder to achieve the best rise and flavor. It can be used to give your cookies a rise with big bubbles, which will collapse at the end of baking, resulting in a cookie that is crisper. You can play with the texture of your cookie based on how much baking soda you use, but be aware that it will also affect the flavor. Check out the Chocolate Chip Cookie Lab (page 45) to see this in action.

Cream of Tartar

Cream of tartar is an acid produced by the process of making wine. It is used to create a stronger protein web when whipping egg whites. It is also used to react with baking soda in recipes, to give a dramatic rise in a cookie (see Snickerdoodles, page 205).

NUTS

Nuts add richness, flavor, and texture to some cookies. Freeze nuts if you are storing them for longer than a month or if you live in a warm climate, since the oils can go rancid and affect their flavor.

Some recipes call for toasting the nuts before using them. You can buy them toasted or easily do it yourself by spreading them out on a baking sheet and baking at 350°F / 175°C for a short time. The timing will depend on the size and type of nut (almonds are hard and require more time, about 10 to 12 minutes, while walnuts are soft and fatty, requiring less time, about 5 to 8 minutes), so keep a close eye on them.

Almond Paste and Marzipan

Both almond paste and marzipan are made from pulverized almonds and sugar. They differ only in the amount of sugar added (almond paste has less), so you can really use either one in the recipes. Both come in airtight foil or canned and should be soft, like clay. If it is dried out it will be hard and difficult to blend into a cookie dough. I haven't found a satisfactory method of reconstituting a hard lump of almond paste or marzipan, so I cut it into small cubes and add it to a batch of cookies with the chocolate or nuts.

Coconut

There are essentially two kinds of coconut that appear in the cookie recipes, sweetened and unsweetened. As you will have guessed, the sweetened has sugar added to it and retains a fair amount of moisture. I like to use Baker's Sweetened Angel Flake Coconut, because it has a great texture straight out of the bag. It can be thrown into a recipe or sprinkled on top of a cookie to add texture. Unsweetened coconut is dehydrated until it is quite dry and hard, so it should be used only in recipes that call for it or it will absorb moisture from the dough and make the cookies dry. There are finely shredded and larger flakes of coconut available; the larger it is the longer they may take to rehydrate, so keep that in mind when mixing and baking your cookies.

Nut Butter and Seed Spreads

Peanut butter and Nutella are great for flavoring cookies and icing because they are powerful flavors and have a luscious texture. For cookie recipes I like to use Skippy or Jif for the best texture, unless otherwise indicated. I love natural peanut butter on sandwiches, but it can make for a greasy, heavy cookie.

Tahini, almond butter, hazelnut paste, and any other nut or seed spread are great additional flavors and add richness, but they may have varying amounts of oil, so it is best to stick to the kind called for in the recipes. I use two kinds of tahini in my recipes. Black tahini (sometimes called black sesame paste) is made from whole black sesame seeds that are toasted and ground. It is more intense with bitter notes than the light-tan colored variety, which is made from toasted hulled white sesame seeds. They can be used interchangeably but each brings its own flavor and color.

SALT

Salt is just as key in creating the perfect balance of flavor in a cookie as it is in savory dishes. Too much salt and the cookie is obviously off, but the lack of salt can also make it taste flat and boring. For the most part I use Morton kosher salt in my recipes, unless otherwise stated. I use flaky sea salt, like Maldon sea salt flakes, to sprinkle on top of a cookie if it needs a perk of flavor on top. The flakes are too big for using in the dough, but perfect to top them off.

Here are some salt equivalents to keep handy for whatever you've got in your pantry.

1 teaspoon Diamond Crystal kosher salt = ¾ teaspoon Morton kosher salt = ½ teaspoon table salt = ½ teaspoon fine sea salt

SWEETENERS

Sweetness is the essential quality of a cookie. You want enough to make the cookie pleasing, but not so sweet that it's cloying. I try to strike that balance. Sugar also plays a role in the structure of a cookie (see Chocolate Chip Cookie Lab, page 48), so decreasing or increasing the amount will also affect the texture of your cookies.

Sugars

The recipes in my book may call for brown, confectioners' (powdered), superfine (caster), and granulated white sugars. You can use standard or organic brands for any of the recipes. All sugars obviously add sweetness to a recipe, but they are also hygroscopic; that is, they attract and retain moisture, which will soften a cookie after it is baked and cooled.

BROWN SUGAR

Like white sugar, brown sugar is made from sugarcane or sugar beets, but it has trace amounts of molasses in it to give it its distinctive brown color and caramel flavor. Brown sugar can be light or dark, and it doesn't matter which one you pick for these recipes. The color of the brown sugar is determined by how much molasses is added back to the white sugar before packaging. If you bake with cup measures, you will want to be sure to gently pack the brown sugar into the cup to get the accurate amount. Demerara, muscovado, and turbinado are three types of raw brown sugar; all have a larger grain than regular brown sugar and won't work as well in the cookie recipes unless called for. Organic brown sugars are often coarser than brands such as C&H or Crystal and don't dissolve into recipes as well. This can present problems with the texture of your cookies—the larger sugar crystals melt when baking and can cause spreading and caramelization when you don't expect or want it. If coarse brown sugar is all you have on hand, you can put it in your food processor for a few minutes and break it down.

If your brown sugar hardens, place a slice of apple inside the bag and let it sit for 12 hours to soften the sugar.

CONFECTIONERS' (POWDERED) SUGAR

Confectioners' sugar is granulated sugar that is pulverized ten times until it becomes a powder. (It is called 10X sugar in most professional kitchens.) In many cases, it has a small percentage of starch (usually cornstarch) added to prevent it from clumping in the bag. When used in a cookie dough, it will produce a fine, tender crumb. But confectioners' sugar *cannot* be used as a substitute for granulated sugar in the recipes, so use it only when it's called for. Its fine texture is perfect for making icing or dusting over a cookie as decoration.

DECORATING SUGARS

There are special sugars meant for adding color or sparkle to a cookie as decoration. The sugar is formulated not to melt, so they keep their crystalized shape when baking. These sugars come in a variety of sizes and many fun colors. The smaller crystals are often called "sanding" sugar and the larger can be labeled "sparkling" or "crystal" sugar. These sugars can be added before baking since they don't melt or can be glued on with an icing.

Dragees are decorative candies that look like little metallic balls, often in gold and silver. These are always added after baking since they will melt in the oven.

Sugar pearls and nonpareils are similar to dragees but have an opalescence to them, so they look like pearls, although they also come in other colors, besides classic white. These are meant only for decorating after baking, since they will melt in the oven. Nonpareils are just wee-little pearls.

Pearl sugar, not to be confused with sugar pearls, is a white crystalized sugar that is typically larger in size and has an opaque white color that keeps its shape and won't caramelize during baking.

Jimmies or sprinkles (depending on where you live) are slightly elongated brightly colored sugars that can be used to decorate cookies before or after they are baked. They also come in chocolate.

SUPERFINE (CASTER) SUGAR
Superfine sugar is granulated sugar that is processed to have finer crystals, but stops short of being powdered. In Europe, it is known as caster sugar; in the United States, it is often labeled as baker's sugar. I call for it in recipes when the sugar needs to dissolve quickly into the dough or eggs, such as in Meringue (see page 43). You can easily make your own superfine sugar by putting a few cups of granulated sugar into a food processor and pulverizing it until it is quite fine. You will know it is fine enough when it puffs out of your food processor like white smoke.

WHITE GRANULATED SUGAR
Granulated is the most common sugar, and we're all familiar with its pure sweetness, which doesn't conflict or compete with other flavors in a cookie. The recipes work equally well with cane and beet sugars, the two main types of granulated sugar found in the United States. You can assume that all granulated sugar in the grocery store is beet sugar unless the bag is marked as pure cane sugar. I didn't test coconut sugar or other sugar sources for these recipes, so you will need to experiment with their sweetness intensity.

Liquid Sweeteners

Some of the recipes in this book call for honey, molasses, maple syrup, corn syrup, or Lyle's Golden Syrup. In most cases, the liquid is added in small amounts for their unique flavors. Liquid sweeteners behave differently than sugar crystals, so I don't recommend substituting them in the recipes as they tend to make a cookie softer.

CORN SYRUP
I use corn syrup in this book for its invert sugar properties. That is just a fancy way of saying that it prevents crystallizing when melting or caramelizing sugar. It also makes icing shiny. By adding a bit of corn syrup to sugar while it is cooking, it is much less likely to turn to rock candy. I always use light corn syrup, which is clear and doesn't add any color to the recipe.

HONEY

Honey is more intensely sweet than sugar, so you need less of it to achieve the right balance of sweet in a recipe. Honey's flavor is determined by the type of plant nectar that the honeybees collect. Some honey is more intensely flavored, such as buckwheat honey, while others are quite mild, such as clover honey. You'll get great results with all kinds of honey, so experiment with different types and see which you prefer. Honey should be used only in the recipes where it is called for; it cannot directly be swapped out for sugar. Honey has a higher moisture content and can make cookies too dense or cakey. It is also more hygroscopic (it attracts and retains moisture) than sugar, so the cookies that call for honey will soften after they are baked and cooled.

MAPLE SYRUP

The common pancake topping is made from boiling down the sap of maple trees. This is not to be confused with "maple-flavored" or "imitation" syrup, which is corn syrup, artificial flavor, and coloring. All pure maple syrup is now labeled Grade A, but there are different colors and flavors. Golden, which is the lightest in color and mildest in flavor, is the most common and popular. Many consider it the more desirable color, but I prefer to use the darker maple syrup, which is made later in the production season and has a stronger flavor. It is great for baking because the flavor stands up to the other ingredients, but either syrup will work nicely in my recipes.

MOLASSES

Molasses is an unrefined sweetener derived from boiling sugarcane to concentrate the nutrients and iron. It is used in recipes to add color and rich flavor. There are different intensities of color and flavor depending on how processed the molasses is. Light Molasses is only boiled once, and the result is a mild flavor and light color. Blackstrap molasses has the deepest flavor, least amount of sweetness, and darkest color, making it the most intense and not for the faint of heart.

Sugar-Free Substitutes

Stevia, Swerve, and many other sugar-free substitutes have been touted as a replacement for sugar. I only mention these because I have not tested them with the recipes in this book and therefore can't officially recommend using them for my cookies. However, feel free to experiment! I once accidentally bought a bag of stevia-sweetened chocolate chips for testing, and they were excellent. If you play around with the recipes, I recommend making a half batch to make sure you love the results.

Equipment

You can bake cookies without any fancy equipment, but there are some basics that make the process a whole lot easier. Here are some of the items I find helpful. Often it comes down to what's in front of you, and how much room you have to store more. If you have my cake book, *Zoë Bakes Cakes*, you'll notice that some of the equipment is also used for cookies. In those cases, the information has not changed much, but the applications may be slightly different, like how to prepare a square cake pan for baking bars (page 28).

COOLING RACKS

Cooling racks are very helpful to prevent a soggy bottom on your cookies, and they help cookies cool quickly so they don't continue baking and dry out.

COOKIE CUTTERS, STAMPS, MOLDS, AND PRESSES

Metal and plastic shaped cutters are an easy way to create fancy cookies with ease. I have some that belonged to my grandmothers; others I picked up at garage sales and some I ordered online. To care for metal cookie cutters, wash by hand and make sure to dry well, so they don't rust. See the Cookie Academy (page 35) for tips on making sure the dough doesn't stick and other tricks for success as you are working.

Stamps and cookie molds can be used to put a decorative impression in the cookie dough. These ornate stamps and molds can be metal, plastic, ceramic, or even wood. They require special dough that won't stick in the intricate designs, and I have lots of tips for using them successfully in the Cookie Academy (page 35).

Cookie presses are used to shape soft dough, like spritz cookies. They are an easy and efficient way to get a variety of shapes and sizes from your cookie dough. Just fill the cavity of the cookie press with the dough, which gets extruded through a shaped hole in the disk at the bottom. You can switch out the disks, which changes the shape of the cookies. With some super soft cookies, like meringues and macarons, you can use a pastry bag fitted with a decorating tip (page 31).

LINERS

I almost always line my baking sheets and pans when making cookies to guarantee that bars will turn out of the pan with ease and drop cookies will come off the pan. It also reduces clean-up time. The exception is when I'm serving a bar in the pan. I am also a fan of a reusable silicone mat for both rolling dough and baking cookies.

Parchment Paper. Parchment paper is something I call for when preparing pans for baking. It makes cleaning the baking sheets a breeze and is a worthwhile piece of insurance when it comes to getting bars and brownies out of the pan after baking. You can buy cut parchment sheets for baking pans if you don't want to cut from a roll for each batch. As opposed to wax paper or butcher paper, parchment paper is coated with a super-thin layer of silicone, so it is nonstick-ish and can withstand the heat of the oven. Wax and butcher papers are coated with paraffin and, therefore, not intended to be used in a hot situation, because the wax will melt if baked.

To keep the parchment-paper sling in place in a baking pan, you can get metal clips, so the paper doesn't move around in the oven.

Silicone Mats. Nonstick, flexible silicone baking mats can be used in place of parchment paper when lining a flat baking sheet and are particularly useful when baking very sticky cookie dough or cookies you want to spread. They are convenient and can be reused hundreds of times. They are also beneficial as an insulator if your cookies tend to come out too dark on the bottom. They can be used for rolling out cookie dough to stamp, since they are nonstick and require less additional flour when rolling.

Foil. Lining a square cake pan with foil is the trick to getting ooey, gooey bars and brownies out of the pan. When you line the bottom and sides of the pan with no seams, there won't be any sticking, so the bars will slip right out. I often put a smooth layer of parchment over the foil, so the bottoms of the bars don't have any creases. It's these little steps that make baking less stressful.

MEASURERS

There are two ways to measure dry ingredients: in dry measuring cups or on a scale. I prefer to use a scale, but if you don't have one (*yet*) you can make all of these recipes using measuring cups. Glass measuring cups are reserved for liquids only.

Dry Measuring Cups. If you remain unconvinced about using a scale, invest in dry measuring cups. Pick the kind that are metal or plastic and come in 1-cup, ½-cup, ⅓-cup, and ¼-cup sizes. Just be sure to use the spoon-and-sweep method (see page 36).

Scale. If you buy anything for baking, it should be a scale. I love to weigh ingredients rather than use measuring cups, for several compelling reasons. First and most important, it's more accurate than volume measures. A cup of flour can vary wildly, depending on how you scoop up the flour, but 120g of all-purpose flour is always 120g, no matter what you do. Using a scale is also faster, and it cuts down on the amount of dishes you have to wash. Over the past decade, more recipes have appeared with both volume and weight measurements because it is common to use a scale in the rest of the world, and Americans are jumping in. Scales are particularly useful for novice bakers, because it takes the guesswork out of measuring; you can be sure each time that you have just the right amount of your ingredients. (For more on how to use a scale, see page 36.)

There are many digital scales to choose from, and they range in price, but my recommendation for a good starter scale at mid-price is the My Weigh kitchen scale.

MICROWAVE OVEN

I bought a microwave oven for my teenage boys one Christmas because they begged for it. I had never been a fan. It turns out I use it way more than they do to melt butter, chocolate, and nut spreads. Each microwave is different in how powerful it is, so be conservative when using it and start with small amounts of time until you get to know your appliance. Once you do, it is a great tool. I'm a convert!

MIXERS

Some recipes really benefit from having an electric mixer to emulsify (blend) ingredients that don't want to mix together. Sometimes you can get away with a spoon. Other times you need something with a bit more force, like a handheld mixer or a stand mixer.

Handheld Mixer. Some of the recipes in this book may be too thick to successfully complete using a handheld mixer. You can likely cream the butter or whip eggs with one and then add the flour by hand. If you do use one, just be sure to pair it with a glass or stainless-steel bowl—not a plastic one. I've had real issues whipping egg whites or heavy cream in plastic bowls, and I've had similar feedback on ZoeBakes.com from readers.

Stand Mixer. My stand mixer is the second-most-used piece of equipment in my kitchen, after my scale. It makes baking so much easier, especially when I need to whip eggs for 10 minutes or beat butter into a soft, billowy mixture. If you bake a lot and have the space and budget, I highly recommend investing in one.

PANS

PAN MATERIALS

What a pan is made of will have a huge effect on the way a cookie bakes. Thickness of the materials and even the color will all change the outcome, and possibly the baking times.

Metal Pans. Metal pans come in several colors, and they produce different results. The darker the pan, the darker the bottom of a cookie can be because the surface conducts more heat to the cookie, so watch the time if you have a really dark pan. If you want a paler cookie, try a light metal pan. Golden pans in the middle of the color range produce a cookie that is caramelized but not as dark as a black pan.

Baking pans are not all created equal, so having the right ones can make baking a lot easier and more successful. Also, the pan's material makes a difference in how a cookie or bar bakes. The following are my favorite pans, but if you have your grandmother's old pans and can't part with them, I get it. And you'll still bake delicious cookies, you may just want to keep an eye on the first batch to adjust the baking time.

Baking Sheets, Jelly-Roll Pans, and Cookie Sheets. The highest-quality baking sheets are made of heavyweight aluminum and have short rims all the way around. The size I use most are called a "half-sheet" in professional kitchens and are 18 by 13 by 1 inch. The 1-inch rim around the edge prevents the pans from warping when they go into a hot oven, especially when they are covered in frozen dough balls. When lined with parchment paper or, in some cases, a silicone mat, they are my preferred baking surface. They come in different thicknesses of metal, which may make a difference in the baking of your cookies. If the pans are too thin, they will warp, so get something that is medium to thick gauge metal. My favorite brands are Nordic Ware and the gold pans sold at Williams Sonoma. These may be slightly more expensive, but they are durable and last longer.

An "air-insulated" baking sheet can add protection from the bottom of your cookies getting too dark since it promises a more even bake—you can also achieve this by stacking two baking sheets together, which is what I do.

Square Cake Pan. Many of the bars in this book are baked in a square pan. I chose an 8-inch square pan as the default because it seems like a perfect amount for my family of four, plus a few extras to freeze or gift to neighbors. If you are going to a party and want to make a larger batch, the recipes can be doubled and baked in a 9 by 13-inch pan. You may need to adjust the baking times slightly, so keep an eye on the bars as they bake. I prefer metal pans because they have straight sides, as opposed to the rounded corners of a ceramic baker of the same size. The straight sides make it easier to line with parchment.

OFFSET SPATULAS

Metal spatulas come in many sizes and are either offset or straight. Offset spatulas are great for spreading soft dough into a pan for bars or for applying frosting. For the purposes of this book, I recommend a small size that will allow easy movement in an 8-inch / 20cm cake pan and will allow you to gently lift the edge of a small cookie.

PIPING BAGS AND DECORATING TIPS

When a recipe calls for using a piping bag to shape a cookie dough or apply a frosting, I prefer the reusable cloth bags. I suggest you get the thinnest cloth, sometimes referred to as "featherweight" bags, since they are not as stiff and are easier to use. Buy a variety of sizes so you have bags that will fit small and large projects. Flip the bags inside out and wash them with hot water and dish soap after every use and then hang to dry.

For some super-fine decorating jobs, like thin lines of royal icing piped on a sugar cookie, I use a parchment piping bag. You can buy them already cut into the triangles, which you form into a cone shaped piping bag that you cut the tip off to pipe. These parchment bags are single use, so you often need several. Clear plastic disposable piping bags are also available in several sizes.

There are large decorating tips available that fit directly into a piping bag, and small ones that require a coupler to fit into the bag. One type isn't better than another; it just depends on the project you are working on. I will indicate which decorating tips I use in each recipe.

PORTION SCOOPS

PORTION SCOOP SIZES

#12 = ⅓ cup

#16 = ¼ cup

#20 = 3 tablespoons

#30 = 2 tablespoons

#40 = 1½ tablespoons

#60 = 1 tablespoon

#70 = 2½ teaspoons

I use portion scoops in many of the recipes in this book. It is something I learned early on in my career, and I have been a strong believer in their worth ever since. One of my first jobs was to make and scoop hundreds of cookies for a catering company. All the cookies had to be the same size and shape for consistency to make baking easier. I recommend buying sturdy ones so you can have them for many years. In the recipes I give a scoop number (#), which are universal, so it doesn't matter what brand you're using. I also give the amounts to scoop in tablespoons or teaspoons, in case you haven't been convinced to get a collection of scoops (but you will!).

At left is a rundown of the most common scoop sizes and their measuring spoon equivalents. These are approximate sizes based on scooping and making sure the cookie dough is level with the edge of the scoop. Everyone scoops a little differently (see page 43 for my method), so the only way to know for sure is to weigh each dough ball and no one has time for that.

ROLLING SURFACE

The surface you use to roll out your cookie dough can be a very personal choice, one handed down from generation to generation. If your grandmother taught you to roll cookie dough on a cloth and it works every time, then there is no reason to stop now. Not only will those memories make your cookies taste better, but you likely have a surface that is well broken in and comfortable. If you are just starting out and don't have a stash of cookie rolling equipment, here are some options to consider.

Two Sheets of Wax or Parchment Paper. Using these papers to roll your dough flat is especially good for dough that is already a touch dry and that you don't want to add more flour to. Simply put the dough between the two pieces of paper and use a rolling pin to flatten. This works best with small pieces of dough. For even better control, use a sheet of plastic wrap over the dough and wax or parchment paper underneath.

Cloth Rolling Mat. This is what my Granny used and what her 1950s Betty Crocker cookbook suggested. It's a simple piece of canvas that you can rub flour into, creating a surface that the dough doesn't stick to. You need very chilled dough for this to be successful, so use small pieces and keep the rest well refrigerated. These cloths are also available in a sleeve that fits over your rolling pin.

Marble Slab. In many professional pastry kitchens, there is a slab of marble or stone used to roll dough, because it stays cooler than wood or metal and keeps the dough from warming up and getting sticky. You can get small portable ones for home kitchens.

Silicone Rolling Mat. These are larger than the similar pan liners and allow you to use a larger piece of dough. Because dough doesn't stick to the silicone, you can get away with using less flour. It doesn't move around as much as parchment paper, so it is easier to keep control of the thickness of your dough.

Wooden Board. This is an excellent surface to work on, but be sure to use enough flour to prevent sticking.

ROLLING PINS

The style of rolling pin you use comes down to comfort. There is no right or wrong, just what feels good in your hands and achieves the best results. Here are the different styles to try.

Dowel or Straight Pins. Great for rolling out even sheets of cookie dough, they come in all thicknesses, but tend to be heavier than the French pin and are suitable for larger pieces of dough.

French or Tapered Pins. Typically the smallest rolling pins, they allow you to feel the dough better than with any of the others. I like these for a soft dough, since I have more control and can use a lighter touch.

Classic or Handled Pins. Excellent for large stiff doughs. I have bony hands and sometimes a dowel pin hurts my hands when rolling a particularly stiff dough, so holding the handles on a classic pin is much easier for me. The con is that you have less control over the dough and need to be careful not to push too hard, since you can't feel the dough as well. Get one that is wide enough to roll out a good-size piece of dough, but not so huge that you can't easily control its weight.

Fixed Depth and Adjustable Pins. There is no guessing when measuring for the thickness of the dough with these pins. The pins are thick on the edges and gauged to a particular thickness in the middle. The result is an even dough with perfect thickness, in theory. I have tried these pins and find they are rarely the right size for

Wood. I like wood best. It holds on to some flour so the dough doesn't stick, it's a good weight to hold on to, and it adds the right amount of pressure to the dough.

Marble. A marble pin stays chilled, which can be a nice feature, especially when rolling sticky dough on a hot summer day. It is heavy, so the size will make a difference in how well you can handle it.

Plastic. Plastic pins are too light and don't hold the flour, so I find the dough sticks. The only time I use plastic is when I have to travel and don't want to carry something heavy. A wine bottle works, too, and there is almost always one to be found when traveling.

Metal. Dough seems to stick more to metal than to wood, and I don't like the feel as much. The nice thing about metal is that you can freeze it to work with sticky dough. Just be careful of condensation.

what I need, and if the dough is too big to fit in the center, they become unusable. There are pins that come with varying size bands that attach to a dowel pin to produce the same effect, and I find this equally difficult to navigate. I mention them because some people find it very useful to have the gauge.

Stencil Pins. A simple way to add a pattern to your cookies if you are using a dough that is made to be stamped. The pins come in many patterns. Be sure to roll the dough thicker than usual with a regular pin, then press firmly with the stenciled pin to create the pattern. Use cookie cutters to create the shapes.

THERMOMETERS

In most recipes, you can assess how something looks to know if it is finished baking. But in some cases, you'll need to be accurate and use a thermometer.

Candy Thermometer. You will need a candy thermometer for making certain recipes that require cooking sugar to a particular temperature. I like the Taylor thermometer that hangs flat against the pot I'm using. You can also use an instant-read thermometer if you don't mind repeatedly cleaning it as you take it out of the pot.

Oven Thermometer. Home ovens are often off by up to 75°F / 25°C, so an oven thermometer is an important item. An inexpensive option will help you get predictable results in your baking. For best results, place your oven thermometer right on the rack on which your cookies sit. If your oven runs significantly hot or cool, you may want to have it recalibrated by a professional. Otherwise, just compensate by adjusting your heat setting.

ZESTER

Many recipes call for citrus zest or finely grated ginger. Depending on how strong you want the flavor, you can use a Microplane grater, which produces a fine zest without getting much of the bitter pith, or a coarser zester when you want an assertive citrus flavor. I tend to use a finer zester, but you decide which suits your taste.

Smash Cookies, page 182

Cookie Academy

"The more you know, the more you can create. There's no end to imagination in the kitchen."

—Julia Child

I always wanted my books to be a collection of recipes and a resource for better baking. This is the chapter that gets me the most excited and is the place where I share the cool tricks, tips, and simple baking chemistry lessons that will make your cookies taste better, come together with ease, and give you the confidence to bake with joy. I'm putting all the helpful cookie techniques and just a bit of food science right here in case you want to refer to it while you're baking. The hows and whys of cookie baking are the kind of things I learned at culinary school, in professional kitchens, and with decades of experience baking at home. I'm a visual learner, so I've included photos of the various methods I'm using to aid you as well.

My Cookie Academy starts at the very beginning of the recipe, with organizing your ingredients and setting up the pan(s) and takes you all the way through to the decorating. Some of you will read through the whole chapter and get a fuller understanding of the techniques you'll see throughout the book, and others will refer back to this chapter as a refresher while you're making a particular recipe. Both ways of using this information are spot on. I reference this section throughout the book in Cookie Academy Review call-outs, so you can easily find your way back here. And, you'll notice the pages are even a different color to make it that much easier. I want to be sure you have the information if and when you need or want it, but you can dive right into the recipes and ignore this chapter altogether if it feels like TMI.

Let's start at the beginning . . .

GATHER YOUR INGREDIENTS

On day one of culinary school, we learned what the French call *mise en place* ("putting in its place"), or organizing a recipe (ingredients, equipment, music) before you do anything else. If you simply read through the recipe, measure everything out, and confirm proper temperatures before you start mixing, you won't have any surprises along the way to the oven. You'll need to pull butter and eggs from the refrigerator long before you start so they're at the right consistency for baking (I even have some nifty tricks in case you forgot this step). I weigh everything (more on that soon) and lay it out on a tray so it's ready to go in the mixer at the right moment. Having my *mise en place* ready to go is crucial to my timing, recipe success, and peace of mind. All of this is especially helpful when you are baking multiple recipes for the holidays or a cookie swap.

Weight versus Volume

If there is one piece of kitchen equipment you buy because of my books, I hope it's a digital kitchen scale. You can certainly bake all the recipes without one, but using weights means consistent results every time you make a batch of cookies. If you use a scale, you know you're getting 120 grams (FYI—that's how much 1 cup of all-purpose flour should weigh for this book) every time, and your cookies will be more predictable. Once you get used to it, you'll find it easier and that it makes less equipment to clean up after. Don't just take my word for it, I got my mom (the same one who never baked when I was a kid) hooked on using a scale, and she'll never go back to cup measures.

How to Use a Digital Scale. Place the mixing bowl on the scale's platform, then hit the "tare" button. This will zero out the weight of the bowl, so you are only weighing what is inside and not the bowl itself. Next, add your first ingredient to the bowl until you've reached the desired amount. (You can weigh each ingredient in separate bowls or use the same bowl, as long as those ingredients are added to the recipe at the same time.) If you're weighing another ingredient into the same bowl, hit the "tare" button again, so it reads 0, and then add the next ingredient. Repeat. It's that easy.

How to Use the Spoon-and-Sweep Method. If you do use measuring cups, fill them with the spoon-and-sweep method. Simply spoon the flour into the measuring cup and then sweep the top clean with a knife. Spooning the flour into the cup aerates it, so it isn't so densely packed. Using this method is how I get 120g per cup.

Temperature of Ingredients

In general, you want to have all ingredients at room temperature (unless the recipe indicates otherwise). If the ingredients are too cold, they won't emulsify into a smooth dough or whip up with enough air to create a good rise. But if the fat is too warm, the butter won't have enough structure to trap the steam in the air bubbles, so the dough may be dense and result in a greasy cookie. The ideal temperature is about 70°F / 20°C. Having said this, I have *never* taken the actual temperature. Here is the nonscientific way I know if the ingredients are the right temperature.

EGGS You don't want to add cold eggs to perfectly softened butter or the butter will seize, and you'll lose the fluffy texture you created. If your eggs are not at room temperature (about 70°F / 20°C) when you are ready to mix your cookie dough, warm them (in the shell) by placing them in a bowl of hot tap water for about 5 minutes before adding to the recipe. Change the water if it cools down too much.

FAT For the butter, you will know it's right if it is soft but still holds its shape when you pick it up. If the butter droops or your fingers melt right into it, it's too soft. If you can't easily press your fingers into the butter, it's too cold. Here are some ways to get your butter to room temperature fast:

1. You can warm the butter by microwaving it for a few seconds, then turn and repeat, but don't overdo this or you will have melted butter.

2. You can also heat a glass bowl and put it over the butter like a warm dome.

3. Cutting the butter into small pieces will help it warm faster.

4. Some people swear by grating butter to warm it faster, but this strikes me as too much messy work.

5. If you have rushed into a batch of cookies and your butter is close but not quite the right temperature, mix it alone in the bowl until it softens, scraping down the bowl frequently, until the butter is creamy and without lumps.

LIQUID DAIRY Adding cold milk, sour cream, or heavy cream to a perfect bowl of creamed butter will ruin the emulsion. If the dairy is too cold, heat it for a few seconds in a microwave. Too hot, and you'll melt the butter; so just go for room temperature.

THE IMPORTANCE OF PREHEATING

I remember dismantling my Easy-Bake Oven to figure out how the raw batter went in one end and came out baked on the other side. All it took was the heat of a lightbulb, which seemed like magic. Your oven is more intricate than that, but it essentially does the same job. Your work of prepping and mixing ends and the heat finishes the cookies, so it is important to get the oven set up properly and make sure it is running true to temperature, so your cookies bake as intended.

Preheating the oven is key, but when to do it? Some recipes will call for baking the cookies straight after mixing and others will have you refrigerate or even freeze the dough first. Reading the recipe through before you start and knowing the sequence of mixing and baking will help you be prepared.

Preheat

Most cookies are pretty forgiving and can wait for the preheat, but some require immediate baking, so follow the preheat instructions for each recipe. Each cookie requires a specific temperature to achieve the right texture. Some cookies need a jolt of high heat for a quick rise and a fast setting of the proteins to create a crisp edge but soft interior. Other cookies need to take it slow, so they will bake evenly throughout without getting too dark. I've had many ovens over the years and the amount of time it takes them to preheat ranged from 15 to 30 minutes. Knowing your oven is one of the greatest ways to succeed in baking.

Check the Temp

Ovens, especially older ones, can be off the mark by quite a bit. I once had one that ran 80°F cooler than the dial suggested. (It may have had something to do with the fact that I needed to prop a chair up against the door to keep it shut—true story.) By using an inexpensive oven thermometer, you can adjust your temperature and make sure your cookies bake well.

Sometimes there is a spot in the oven, typically in the back toward the top, where the temperature is hotter than the rest of the oven. Rotating your pans during the baking will help your cookies bake evenly. If the oven is off by more than 20°F, you should have it calibrated by a professional.

Use a timer, especially if you are baking a bunch of cookies at once, and use your nose. If you smell the cookies baking, chances are, they are nearly done. Check the oven and make sure they aren't burning. This leads to the bigger issue of baking times: they are always a suggestion and not a hard-and-fast rule. Every oven is different and can be hotter or cooler than the oven setting says.

Convection or Flat Heat

When I worked in professional kitchens, there were only "wind" or convection ovens, and we went to great lengths to mitigate the damage it could cause. The wind in the oven was so strong that cookies would bake on one side of the pan and be underbaked on the other, or the tops would be nicely caramelized and the bottoms needed more time. I tried blocking the fan or covering the sheet of cookies, with mixed results. Most home ovens generally provide flat heat with an option to switch to convection. My recommendation is to avoid convection heat when baking, unless the recipe specifically calls for it, for instance, if you are going for a crisp, caramelized crust on a cookie, while keeping the inside a bit gooey and chewy. If you have no choice and you have only convection, then be sure to adjust the temperature down by 20° to 25°F, which some ovens do automatically.

Which Rack

Unless otherwise noted in a recipe, always bake in the middle of the oven. Heat rises, so the top of the oven tends to be where the heat is the most intense. So, if your cookies are on an upper rack, the top will brown before the center is set. The bottom is often where the heating elements are, so cookies baked near the bottom can have burned bottoms. For the most even baking results, bake on only one rack at a time. If you have to bake several sheets of cookies at once, be sure to rotate them from top to bottom and front to back; this will create a more even bake. If your oven is particularly small, you may want to double up the baking pans, to insulate the bottoms, so they don't burn.

PREPPING YOUR PANS

Preparing the pan mostly involves lining it with parchment paper or a Silicone mat; for sticky bars and brownies. I will also grease the pan and sometimes add a layer of foil to ensure that I can easily lift them out of the pan (see below).

Grease

I haven't greased a baking sheet for cookies since I was in middle school because I discovered the ease and quickness of parchment paper. Greasing the pan can also cause the bottoms of your cookies to fry a bit and get too much color. However, if you are having issues getting a nice brown bottom, try removing the parchment paper and baking directly on a lightly greased pan. Doing so may change the baking time, so check them a couple minutes early.

For greasing the high-sided pans for bars and brownies, I like melted butter. I generally use a pastry brush to paint on a thin coat. You can also do this with a paper towel dipped into the butter. I have baked thousands of bars and brownies as I tested the recipes for this book, and as a result I've turned to the ease and speed of using a baking pan spray. If I have time, I still prefer using butter because it's delicious. Having said that, baking sprays, which contain a mix of oil and flour, as opposed to cooking spray, can be used in place of butter for greasing in most recipes. They may not be as tasty as butter, but they are super-quick and sometimes that's what wins the day.

Liners

Lining the pan with parchment paper or a silicone mat will add a bit of insurance that the cookies will release easily. The paper and silicone also provide a layer of insulation from the metal pan, so the bottom of your cookies won't essentially fry and overbake. Do not use wax paper in place of parchment paper as it is not meant for baking and will smoke terribly and burn. You can also line a pan with foil, but it does tend to result in a darker cookie bottom.

There are two ways I recommend lining a square or rectangular pan for brownies and bars:

Parchment-Paper Sling. Grease the pan and line it with a piece of parchment that has been cut to fit the dimensions of the bottom of the pan and goes up two sides to create a sling. The sides should be long enough that they hang over the edge, which will give you plenty to hang on to when you are lifting the bars out of the pan. I use metal clips to secure the sides to the pan, so they don't flop into the baking bars.

Foil. I like to use foil for gooey bars and brownies. Line the pan with a large sheet of foil, so it completely covers the bottom and all four sides. Press the foil as flat as possible and fold the top up and over the sides. Grease the inside and line with a parchment-paper sling as you would for a regular bar recipe above.

MIXING METHODS

For the most part, mixing cookies is pretty straightforward. There are really only a couple of mixing techniques you need to know in order to create great cookies. The most common is creaming ingredients together, like you would in a classic chocolate chip cookie recipe. The other is creating an egg foam, which is a go-to in some brownies. Knowing these and a few other basics will take you effortlessly through this book. They aren't difficult; there are just some tricks to make the process easier and more successful.

Creaming

Creaming involves mixing or whipping butter or other fats with the sugar, then often adding eggs and flour, and then sometimes a liquid. It is by far the most popular method of scratch-cookie mixing in the home kitchen. It's simple but knowing just a little bit more about this process can take your cookies from good to extraordinary.

Whipping air into fat plays a part in creating the texture of cookies. Unlike cakes, we don't always need the rising power created by the small bubbles whipped into the butter. We do, however, need the butter and sugar to come together smoothly and evenly, so the dough is consistent and everything blends together in harmony, which helps the baking and flavor. First, let's talk about the ingredients before we put them in the bowl to mix.

The Importance of Fats. In many cookies the fat is typically butter, because it tastes incredible. The flavor can't be beat, but butter can be finicky. It needs to be at a certain temperature when mixing to create an emulsion, and it doesn't always play well with liquids. Butter also has a low melting point, so cookies made with lots of it will spread like crazy. This is not a bad thing at all, but just something to keep in mind (see Chocolate Chip Cookie Lab, page 47, for examples). This is especially true when using brown butter (see sidebar, page 17), because the water and milk solids have been removed and you are essentially left with butter oil. It is still solid at room temperature, but it behaves more like oil in a recipe. Some of my cookies also use a bit of shortening, since it is a champ at holding on to bubbles and it has a higher melting point, so it won't spread as much in the oven. The downside of shortening is that if you use too much, you'll have a lackluster flavor. Oil doesn't have enough structure on its own to hold the air bubbles, but when mixed with butter it makes for quite a luxurious texture.

Adding Extracts and Zest. Fat is the carrier of flavor, so add your extracts and zest when you are creaming butter and not at the end of a recipe. This gives the extract time to work into the dough more thoroughly.

Brown Butter

I make brown butter in large quantities and keep it in my refrigerator for a week (or two) or frozen for months. This way I always have some at the ready. Using brown butter in a recipe is absolutely delicious, and I often add it to recipes that need just a little more oomph. If you experiment with it in your cookie recipes that aren't written specifically for brown butter, keep in mind that it behaves like oil in the recipe, and the cookies may spread more than with regular butter. You can reduce the amount by a bit if the cookies are spreading too much or seem a touch greasy.

Makes about 1⅔ cups / 350g

2 cups (16 oz) /
450g unsalted butter

In a small saucepan over medium-low heat, melt the butter. Turn the heat to medium-high and boil until the butter is frothy, about 3 minutes (longer if butter is chilled or frozen). Turn the heat to low and simmer, without stirring, until the milk solids have settled to the bottom of the pan, are dark golden brown, and smell slightly toasted, another 15 to 18 minutes, depending on how dark you like your toast (I like mine on the darker side). Once the milk solids start to caramelize, it goes quickly, so don't walk away. Remove from the heat once the butter is a deep amber color. Strain through a fine-mesh sieve, if desired.

Allow the butter to cool completely, then cover and refrigerate for up to 2 weeks or freeze for up to 2 months.

There's really only one reason to sift ingredients in a cookie recipe: If the flour, cocoa powder, confectioners' sugar, or baking soda are lumpy. These are the most frequent clumping offenders after sitting in their containers. After they are measured, these ingredients often need to be sifted or the recipe can end up with unsightly lumps—and no one enjoys biting into that.

I do *not* sift dry ingredients together to distribute baking powder or baking soda. This just doesn't work as well as whisking, and it's not nearly as quick. I'm all for quick and easy when I can get away with it. Whisking to distribute the ingredients is also key to making sure all the cookies in the batch have an equal amount of baking powder, baking soda, and salt. This will mean the cookies bake more evenly.

Flour Power. The flour helps to hold the cookies together and gives structure, but how much? Sometimes you want just a whisper of structure, so your cookie will spread and be crunchy. Other times, you want a cookie that is thick and chewy. (See Chocolate Chip Cookie Lab, page 46, for a guide on how much is right for your perfect cookie.) Once you add the flour, especially all-purpose flour, you want to mix as little as possible, so you don't get the gluten (see page 18) all excited. All of the dry ingredients should be thoroughly whisked together before they are added to the dough. This ensures that the leavening (baking powder and/or baking soda) and other dry ingredients are distributed throughout the dough evenly.

Mixing

Now that we have a fuller understanding of the ingredients, let's talk about the mixing technique. If you have a stand mixer, fit it with the paddle attachment and mix the room temperature butter and sugar until it is smooth and evenly mixed (there should be no clumps of butter or random grains of sugar left on the bowl or paddle). I wax poetic about scraping the bowl below. It is important to have the butter and sugar well blended and in a perfect union before adding the eggs or other liquid to help the mixture keep its smooth emulsion. It should be smooth, light in color, and fluffy.

Add the Eggs One at a Time. This ensures that you don't add too much liquid to the buttery mixture all at once. Remember, fat doesn't like to mix with liquids, so we have to do this gradually and let them slowly blend together before we introduce more egg or other liquids. There are a few recipes (such as Triple Almond "Biscottini," page 174) that have a high egg-to-butter ratio and the emulsion just doesn't stand a chance. The mixture will look broken and globs of butter will seem to float in the liquid. If this happens, don't panic, it will come together once you add the dry ingredients. The goal is to keep everything smooth and creamy, hence the name of the mixing technique "creaming," but staying calm and happy wins over perfection every time.

Scrape the Bowl. This technique is one of the easiest ways to make sure your cookies come out well. It seems too simple, but it's perhaps one of the keys to successful baking. I highly recommend you invest in a rubber-edged paddle attachment if you have a stand mixer. That rubber edge scrapes the bowl as it mixes, which greatly cuts down the number of times you need to stop the machine to make sure the bowl (especially the bottom) and paddle are cleaned off. If your ingredients stick to either, they are not being thoroughly incorporated into the dough. A good rule to follow is to scrape before adding anything new to the bowl. So, despite the tedium (I prefer to think of it as relaxing), scrape, scrape, scrape!

Lastly, Add the Dry Ingredients. In most recipes, you'll dump them in and gently mix until just incorporated. If there are chips, or dried fruit to go in, they will be added just before the last traces of flour have been mixed in. You want to mix as little as possible once the dry ingredients are added, so that the gluten in the flour doesn't get all excited and make the cookies tough.

MERINGUE

Whipped egg whites and sugar is called a meringue. For this book, I focus mostly on the French version, which is simply whisking raw egg whites with sugar until they are light and fluffy. Here is what you need to know to have success every time.

When Fat Is the Enemy. If there is any fat in the bowl or on the whisk attachment, it will interfere with the egg white proteins and prevent them from forming the foam we so desire. Since egg yolks contain fat, they, too, are the enemy of whipping egg whites into meringues, so be very careful when separating the eggs (see page 14). Make sure the bowl is exceedingly clean; a wipe with a paper towel soaked in vinegar can be extra insurance.

When Moisture Brings You Down. High humidity can prohibit the eggs and sugar from whipping to stiff peaks. If you live in a rainforest or somewhere ultrahumid, know that the meringues may resist whipping or get tacky once baked, so eat them quickly.

Peaks. When necessary, a recipe will indicate at what stage your egg whites should be before using in that recipe, soft peak or stiff peak. What does that look like?

> **Soft Peak.** When the egg whites are firm enough that they don't drool off the whisk when lifted out of the bowl, but they just cling and even slouch a bit.

> **Stiff Peak.** When the meringue stands straight up with no apology. It should still be glossy and smooth but very firm and may have just a wisp of a curl at the very top.

Light-as-Air Egg Foam

I'm mad for meringue and all of its fluffy, fun, and delicious qualities. The recipes may call for whole eggs or just egg whites and sugar, that's it. No matter what kind of egg foam or meringue you're making, it needs to be structurally strong, which seems like a contradiction since the foam is so light and cloud-like. A properly whipped egg foam can stand up to other ingredients being folded into it (like coconut in the brownies on page 132), albeit gently, and will hold its shape and create a lofty rise as it bakes. Typically, the foams are made by slowly whipping sugar into eggs. The sugar helps create a stretchier egg (resulting in more air bubbles forming a luxurious foam), and there are a few different ways to go about this, depending on the recipe you are making.

The egg proteins (mostly in the whites) will stretch and take on more air if they are warm when you are whipping them, so warm the eggs in the shell before you begin. If your eggs are coming straight from the refrigerator, just let them soak in hot tap water for 5 to 10 minutes. You may need to change the water a couple of times to get them warmed up quickly. Once the eggs feel warm to the touch, they are likely ready. There's no need to take their temperature, unless that's something that excites you, in which case you are going for 100°F / 40°C.

Whip It. Whip It Good! When whipping whole eggs, you want to whip the warm eggs on high speed, until foamy, about 30 seconds, then turn the speed to low and sprinkle the sugar slowly over the eggs until incorporated. Turn the machine to high speed and whip until the foam forms a ribbon when you lift the whisk out of the bowl—the ribbon should sit on top of the foam without sinking in for several seconds. To achieve the ribbon test, it will take about 10 minutes of whipping, maybe longer if you are using a handheld mixer or doubling the recipe. Then turn the speed to medium and continue to whip the egg mixture for 30 seconds. This crucial, last step will break down big air pockets and create smaller, more uniform air bubbles that are stronger and will hold up to the folding in of other ingredients.

FORMING THE COOKIES

There are several ways to shape cookies, depending on the type of dough and desired outcomes. There are drop cookies that are portioned by dropping them from a spoon or using a portion scoop. Piped or pressed cookies are made from a soft dough that's extruded from a piping bag or cookie press. Rolled cookies are made with a stiff dough that is rolled with a pin and cut into shapes with cookie cutters. Sliced cookies are stiff cookie doughs formed into a log or brick and sliced thin to bake.

Using a Portion Scoop

The brilliance of using a portion scoop for drop cookies, as opposed to a spoon, is that you can create uniform dough balls. It's important to scoop the dough, then scrape the top of the scoop along the mixing bowl to level it. This will ensure that the dough balls are all the same size and shape. Not only will your cookies look uniform, but they will bake more evenly. Squeezing the handle of the portion scoop releases the dough ball onto the prepared baking sheet and keeps the whole operation neater as well.

Setting Up and Filling the Piping Bag

A piping bag is a wonderful tool for shaping soft cookie batter (see Macarons, page 161, and Meringue Clouds, page 159) or decorating the tops of cookies with buttercream (page 61). Knowing how to handle the bag will make the process neater, easier, and more efficient.

Select a piping tip and slip it into a pastry bag. Cut the bottom of the bag to fit the tip. Start small, since you can always cut more, but if you cut the hole too big, there's no going back.

To fill and use the piping bag:

> Fold over the top of the bag so you have about a 3-inch / 7.5cm collar. Use a spatula to fill the bag, trying to keep its contents as neat as possible. Any cookie dough or frosting that ends up on the outside of the bag will be all over your hands as you work. Every time you need to refill the bag, fold over the top again.

> Unfold the top of the bag and use your fingertips to squeeze the contents to the bottom of the bag. Twist the top of the bag until it creates tight pressure inside and some of the contents comes out the bottom. It is now ready to use.

> As you are piping, always maintain the tight twist and pressure on the bag, so you'll have to stop piping on occasion to twist the top. There should be so much pressure in the bag that you can easily squeeze out the cookie dough with one hand.

> If the bag is filled with frosting or other contents that will melt, your other hand should just be used as a guide to lead the tip. So don't wrap both hands around the bag to create pressure or your hands will warm the contents and melt it.

> Once you've created the pressure in the bag, it is time to pipe the contents. Squeeze the bag over the prepared surface until you've formed the cookie or a design with icing, then let up on the pressure of the bag, so no more of the contents are flowing out and lift the bag up and away. If you continue squeezing as you lift the bag you'll end up with a tall point on the top of your cookie or a tail at the end of your icing. Practicing this technique a few times will help you get the shapes you desire.

For smaller, more delicate lines, it is sometimes easier to use a parchment paper piping bag. This is what I use for working with royal icing. To fill the cone shaped bag, set it tip down in an empty water glass and fill from the top (see page 61). If you are using a thick icing, you'll need to use a spoon. If it is thin, you can just pour it in. Make sure to just fill it halfway, so you have room to fold down the top of the bag to create the pressure. When folding the bag down, after filling, be sure to fold away from the seam, so it stays tight as you fold.

CHILLING THE DOUGH

Chilling the dough is essential when rolling or stamping cookies, otherwise it is just too soft to work with and will stick to every surface. (See more about stamped cookies on page 52.) Another chilling technique you will see often in this book is to scoop cookies with a portion scoop, line them up snug on a parchment lined–baking sheet, and refrigerate or freeze them before baking. You will space the chilled balls on another baking sheet when it is time to bake them, so they can be tightly packed while they are chilling. This is a trick of convenience and something that is essential in production baking, but it is also a way to get the best results out of certain types of cookie dough. Letting a cookie dough ball chill for even 30 minutes will give the ingredients time to marry or absorb into each other, making a better texture. It also firms up the fats in the dough, preventing a cookie from spreading as much once it hits the heat of the oven. There are exceptions to this: When the fat ratio is too high, there is no controlling the spread. You can see some of my Chocolate Chip Cookie Lab tests (pages 46 to 51) to see just what chilling can do for a cookie.

Freezing the Dough. You can also freeze cookie dough in plastic bags, as opposed to storing it in the refrigerator, which prevents it from getting stale. If I am shipping cookie dough balls, I freeze them first, as it gives them a better chance of getting to their destination without harm. Not all cookie dough likes the freezer, and I mention exceptions in the recipes. In many cases, I recommend freezing portioned out cookie dough. I often mix a big batch of cookies, but bake only a few at a time, so I always have cookie dough balls at the ready for a surprise party invitation or last-minute craving. This is an excellent way to have fresh cookies quickly. I scoop them, refrigerate until firm, then throw the dough balls into a zip-top bag and freeze. Make sure to mark the bag with the cookie type and date. I sometimes put the baking temperature and time on the bag in case my boys want to bake the cookies themselves.

CHOCOLATE CHIP COOKIE LAB

This is your chocolate chip cookie primer: the results of what I learned making the countless batches I've baked over many decades. It's helpful to understand what the ingredients do to a cookie and how baking can change them. Using this cookie guide, you can tweak your cookies to be just how *you* like them.

My testing criteria, which came straight out of my middle school science class, is based on changing only one element at a time. I kept some things the same, like scoop size, refrigeration time, baking temperature, and baking time, so the different batches would be controlled and comparable. I tweaked each ingredient to show you how it can affect the final results of the cookie. In each batch I changed only one ingredient at a time, so its influence over the recipe can be clearly seen. There are endless possibilities for tweaking the recipe, but this seemed the more profound way to show the power of each ingredient. I ended up mixing twenty-four separate batches for this lab and learned so much. I hope you do too, and conduct your own experiments based on what I discovered. (My tried-and-true version of this recipe with all of my personal favorites is on page 181.)

2⅔ cups / 320g unbleached all-purpose flour

I use an all-purpose flour that is about 10 percent protein (Gold Medal Flour). If you are using King Arthur Baking Company flour (11.7 percent protein), you will want to reduce the flour by about 3 tablespoons / 30g, or the dough will be dry. Measuring with a scale is the *only* way to ensure that every batch of cookies you make will come out consistently. If you use cup measures, you'll want to use the spoon-and-sweep method (see page 36).

Reducing the amount of flour will result in a crisper, flatter cookie. On the flip side, adding more flour to your recipe will give you a thicker cookie with a cakier texture. Add too much flour and they might become dry.

LESS — MORE

1¼ teaspoons baking soda

This is quite a bit of baking soda for a cookie, given the amount of flour. I use this much, because I want the cookies to puff up and then collapse to get the crunchy edge and soft interior. As a rising agent, baking soda needs an acid to react, and in this recipe, the acid is in the brown sugar (from the acidic molasses in the sugar). This much baking soda also helps produce a darker color on your cookie, so it isn't dull looking in the short baking time. If your baking soda seems lumpy, make sure to sift it into the other dry ingredients. There's nothing worse than getting a mouthful of baking soda in a cookie.

By reducing the amount of baking soda, your cookies will not rise as much and will come out a bit denser. By increasing the baking soda, the cookies will puff greatly in the oven and create large air bubbles, which will pop and make the cookies deflate and become flatter and crispier. It's a little counterintuitive, but more baking soda creates a flatter cookie.

LESS — MORE

¾ cup / 170g unsalted butter, at room temperature

Flavor, baby! That's why we use butter in cookies. It melts really fast, so it will cause cookies to spread if you use too much. I used American butter when testing my recipe, which has a lower fat content than European butter. If you choose to use European butter, your cookies may spread a touch more, since you have even more fast-melting fat in your butter.

By using less butter, your cookies will not spread as much, so you'll end up with a thicker, doughier cookie. Adding more will make your cookie spread quite a bit and be crunchier.

LESS   MORE

¼ cup / 57g shortening

This is 100 percent fat (unlike butter, which has some water), so it won't produce any gluten structure, which can make a cookie less tender. Shortening doesn't melt as fast as butter, so the proteins in the cookie (from eggs and flour) have time to set before you have a flat cookie. Shortening is whipped and therefore contains more air bubbles, which help cookies rise as they bake. In short, adding a bit of shortening will make a cookie more tender and help keep its shape.

By eliminating the shortening, you will end up with a cookie that has less fat, so it won't be quite as tender and rich. Increasing the amount of shortening will make a crumbly, tender cookie, but it won't spread as much.

LESS   MORE

1 cup / 200g granulated sugar

White sugar makes a crispy cookie when baked, so if you want a cookie that stays crispy, use white sugar over brown sugar. Granulated white sugar also adds to the color of the cookie; if you add more sugar, you'll get a more caramelized cookie.

With a reduction of sugar, not only will your cookies be less sweet, they also won't spread as much. Even though the sugar is a dry ingredient going into the dough, it melts in the heat, causing cookies to spread and caramelize. Adding even more sugar than the recipe calls for will make a caramelized, thinner, crunchier cookie.

LESS ← → MORE

1½ cups / 300g lightly packed brown sugar

Brown sugar is deeper in flavor than white sugar due to the molasses in the brown sugar. You can make subtle changes in the flavor by using light brown vs. dark brown sugar, but the difference is really too subtle to suggest using one over the other. Organic brown sugar tends to have a coarser grain and doesn't melt as fast, so the cookie will have a different texture when baked.

Having a lower ratio of brown sugar to white sugar will give you a crispier cookie, with less depth of flavor, and your cookie will spread slightly more. If your cookies tend to soften more than you like, consider using *less* brown sugar. Adding more brown sugar will give you a cakier texture, even brown color, deep flavor, and less spread.

LESS ← → MORE

2 eggs, at room temperature

The eggs add protein to set the cookie, which prevents it from spreading too much. Eggs also act as a leavening agent when they are whipped up with air, but in most cookies, we're not whipping them enough to really get that benefit. If your cookies end up with a shiny "crust" on the top, it's because you whipped the batter too much after adding the eggs and they developed a layer of meringue on the top. You may want this effect, but it's not typical in a chocolate chip cookie.

Cookies baked with just yolks were cakier, tinted with the yellow color, and tasted richer, which seems obvious. Cookies baked with only egg whites spread considerably and got caramelized and crunchy. I kinda love the results. This is a cool trick to hold on to if you ever find yourself with extra yolks or whites. If the recipe calls for 1 egg, I replace it with 3 yolks or 2 whites.

JUST YOLKS ← → JUST WHITES

10 ounces chocolate, chopped in largish (about ¼-inch / 6mm) chunks

I used 72% bittersweet chocolate because I like the contrast of the sweet dough and bitter chocolate, but you can use whatever kind of chocolate you want. This is the main flavor and star of the cookie, so again, I suggest you use your favorite chocolate—bittersweet, milk, white, or even flavored chips (such as butterscotch, raspberry, and so on). I save some larger chunks of chocolate for sticking into the dough after I have scooped them, so they melt on top of the cookie and look dramatic.

My husband likes a cookie with more cookie that isn't drowning in pools of chocolate. I love him anyway! Ha. You can play with the amount and type of chocolate you use. I did this test with chocolate chips, but I usually like a chunk in my cookie. There is no right or wrong answer, just preference.

1½ teaspoons pure vanilla extract

This doesn't really change the cookie's texture or shape, but adds flavor, so use a good one. Artificial vanilla flavoring is not to my taste, but some people love it, so, by all means, go for it if that's your favorite. I do recommend making your own (see page 16)—just to try it! It's so easy and tasty. Add the vanilla to the fat, not at the end of the mixing process, and you will get a more intense flavor.

1½ teaspoons kosher salt

In professional kitchens salt is often referred to as love—if a dish needs salt, a chef will say, "Add a bit of love to that!" My original recipe from 1985 was *way* too short on love. The salt is a contrast to the sweet and enhances all the flavors. If you don't have enough of it, it'll taste flat and lack that caramel flavor. See Salt, page 22, to adjust amounts according to brand and style of salt. The amount of salt in a recipe will greatly change the flavor of the cookies, but won't change the texture. If you are sensitive to the taste of salt, feel free to reduce it. Add more salt if you find your recipe is a tad dull.

Flaky sea salt

Flaky sea salt adds flavor and makes your cookie look beautiful. The contrast of salt and sweet is addictive. It is why candy bars have sooooooo much salt in them. It enhances the flavors it's combined with. I use flaky sea salt because it gives you a nice BIG hit of salt and also it looks pretty on the cookie—that does count!

For instructions on how to mix and bake the chocolate chip cookies, see page 181.

340°F
12 minute bake

350°F convection
10 minute bake

350°F
10 minute bake

350°F convection
12 minute bake

375°F
30 minute chill
10 minute bake

375°F convection
10 minute bake

350°F
30 minute chill
14 minute bake

375°F convection
30 minute chill
10 minute bake

375°F
24 hour chill
12 minute bake

375°F
frozen
10 minute bake

BETTER WITH AGE

You can mix, portion the cookie dough, and bake right away with delicious results. However, if you're not in a hurry to bake, portion all of the dough onto a parchment paper–lined baking sheet, snugged right next to each other. This way you can get the entire batch onto one sheet, and refrigerate the dough balls for at least 30 minutes. If you have the time, they really improve if you let them sit, covered in the refrigerator for 24 to 36 hours. Resting will make them taste better, be more uniform in shape, and color nicely when they bake, as all the ingredients have time to meld into a uniform dough. After the dough balls are chilled, you can bake them or freeze the dough balls for baking later (see page 45).

I tested them baked right after mixing, after a 30-minute chill, after a 24-hour chill, and after a thorough freezing. The results were very different and worthy of an experiment at your house to see which is your preferred cookie. Turns out I like a 30-minute chill or a frozen dough ball. They resulted in a crisp edge with a chewy interior, when combined with the right oven temperature (see page 56).

ROLLING THE DOUGH

There are many ways to go about rolling out cookie dough, and it just comes down to what works best for you. I've tried them all, and honestly, I like the simplest way best, with just a rolling pin (page 32) and a wee bit of flour. I dust my countertops, which are wood or stone, with just enough flour to prevent the dough from sticking. I require less flour in the winter and more in the sticky months of summer. The trick is to use as little flour as you can get away with, so you aren't adding a bunch of unnecessary flour to your dough, which can make your cookies tough. If the dough is sticking, then add more flour or try an alternative surface (page 31) that will prevent the dough from adhering.

It is helpful to keep the dough quite chilled, so use as small a piece as you can get away with and keep the rest refrigerated until you are ready to roll. You can always pop the dough back into the refrigerator to chill it again. If you are struggling to keep the dough chilled on a particularly warm, humid day, I suggest rolling on a moveable surface (page 31) that you can transfer to the refrigerator even after you've rolled it out. Freezing is a quicker way to chill the dough down, but remember that if it gets too stiff, it will be hard to roll. Be careful not to get the dough too cold or you'll have to let it warm up again!

If the dough is still sticking to the surface after you've rolled it, use a metal decorating spatula to gently unstick the dough and transfer the cookies to a prepared baking sheet. To maximize the dough, cut out the cookies as close to one another as possible. This will minimize the amount of dough that becomes scraps.

Once you've cut out all the cookies from the dough and placed them on a pan, rerolling the scraps is often just fine and will result in a great cookie. For most cookie doughs, try to reroll just one time or the dough can get too dry and can result in a tough cookie. Dust off any excess flour before gathering the scraps and pressing them together into a uniform dough. Gently knead it JUST until it comes together enough to reroll. Because you're incorporating more flour, you may not need to chill it before rerolling. If it is sticky after kneading, then chill before rerolling.

MAKING STAMPED OR MOLDED COOKIES

One of the most creative ways to get a design in your cookies without fussy piping or messy decorating sugars is to use a patterned stamp or ornate mold. When done correctly, they leave an impression in the baked cookies. Stamps are typically smaller and the pattern is shallow so it can quickly make an impression in the dough. Cookie molds are often more ornate and have a deeper pattern that you press the dough into.

There are two different ways I like to stamp the dough.

1. You can form a small, golf-ball sized piece of dough (the size will depend on the stamp. Try one and determine the size before scooping the entire batch), arrange it on a prepared baking sheet, sprinkle it with granulated or decorating sugar, and press the stamp into the dough.

2. You can roll the dough on a lightly floured surface to a rectangle about ¼ inch / 6mm thick, then cut out rounds of the dough using a cookie cutter to match the size and shape of your stamp, arrange the dough on a prepared baking sheet, sprinkle it with granulated or decorating sugar, and press the stamp into the dough.

Before you get started, there are several tricks to make stamping or molding an easy and efficient task.

Make Sure You Use the Right Dough. If the dough has too much baking powder or soda it will puff up and lose the definition from the impression. There are specific recipes in the book that I recommend for these types of cookies.

Chill the Stamps/Molds and the Dough. Having a stiff, well-chilled dough will prevent it from being too sticky. If you find it is getting soft and starting to stick, throw it back in the refrigerator until it is firm again. It is best to work in small batches of dough and leave the bulk in the refrigerator. I freeze the stamps/molds for at least 30 minutes before using; if the dough is sticking to them, I return them to the freezer.

Grease the Stamp. Using a pastry brush or paper towel, depending on the intricacy of the stamp, you can coat it with a very light film of oil. If there is too much oil the flour or starch will cake up in the design, so use a paper towel to make sure it is a thin, even coating. Baking spray can also be used but don't skip the dusting with flour or starch or your dough may stick. Avoid using butter because it can be too thick and clog the designs.

Dust the Stamp/Mold with Flour or Starch to Help the Dough Release with Ease. Apply an even layer of flour or cornstarch (other starches are equally as effective), then gently tap the stamp/mold to remove any excess, leaving the thinnest film. Be sure the design is not caked with the flour, or you will lose definition. Depending on the stamp/mold and dough, you may have to repeat this between each cookie. If there is flour left on the cookie, gently brush it off with a clean pastry brush.

Cover the Dough in Sugar, Flour, or Starch. Creating a barrier between the dough and stamp will help prevent them from sticking to each other. I use a light sprinkle of sugar or flour when stamping dough and cornstarch when molding dough. Just enough to prevent sticking, but not so much it interferes with the impression you are trying to create.

Work Quickly, so the Dough Doesn't Get Warm and Sticky. Refrigerate the dough if it does get too sticky. After the cookies are formed and arranged on the baking sheet, refrigerate the stamped/molded cookies until well chilled. This will help set the designs, so they don't lose their shape while baking.

Keep the Stamps/Molds Clean. If cookie dough gets stuck in the design, use a toothpick or a clean pastry brush to clean it out. Regrease and dust with more flour or starch before using with more cookie dough.

Speculaas, page 110

To remove the cookie from a highly detailed stamp or mold if it sticks, gently pry it out from the edges. Using a small metal spatula, paring knife, or even a skewer to gently coax the dough away from the mold can be helpful.

To use a mold, lightly brush the decorative indentation with oil, wipe it mostly out with a paper towel, then dust it with cornstarch and gently tap the mold upside down on the counter to remove the excess starch, so there is just a film left on the mold. Press the chilled dough into the mold, making sure it is an even thickness throughout, so the cookie will bake evenly. The dough should be just about flush with the top of the mold, so it isn't too thick. Turn the mold over and gently tap on the counter again to release the dough. Set on a prepared baking sheet. Clean the mold by removing any stuck dough, then start the whole process over. If you are using several molds to make cookies, be sure all the cookies are of similar size and thickness on one baking sheet, so they bake evenly.

MAKING PRESSED DOUGH CRUST

Bars are layered and often start with a crust that is baked in the pan before the other layers are added. You'll want to start by lining the pan (see page 39) and then scatter the crust layer into the pan. Use your fingers to press it into an even layer all along the bottom, and in some cases up the sides of the pan. Once it is as even as possible, which will ensure even baking, cover it with a sheet of plastic wrap and press it tightly using the bottom of a water glass or anything flat that fits in the pan. Pressing the crust in tight like this before baking will help prevent the crust from crumbling when baked and cut.

FINISHING TOUCHES BEFORE BAKING

Here are some of the tips and tricks for creating a pretty finish on your cookies and bars. Marbling flavors together is not only pretty, but a good way to add depth of flavor. Getting the pretty pools of chocolate to form on the top of your chocolate chip cookies isn't an accident, there's a trick to it. Salt can be what makes a cookie the most exciting but what kind and when it's added are crucial. These are some of the moves used on Instagram to make people stop and swoon over a baked good. Since we eat with our eyes first, it is nice to add a little flourish.

Marbling

To create a marbled top to your brownies or bars, you need to have two contrasting colors of batter. Fill the pan with one batter, then create lines over the top in the contrasting batter color. Use a knife, skewer, or chopstick to drag the batter in a zigzag pattern. As you pull through the two batters, they create fine lines intertwined like marble or a spider's web. Have fun with the patterns, but if you overdo it, the lines will get busy and less distinct.

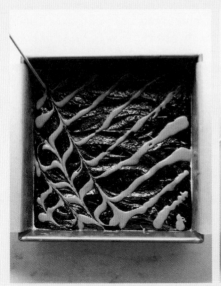  

Picture-Perfect Chocolate Pools

We've all seen the sexy chocolate chip cookie photo with the glistening pool of chocolate melted on the top. The trick to getting that perfect puddle of chocolate is to add a big chunk of high-quality chocolate to the scooped cookie dough ball. If you mix all the chocolate in with the dough, the chocolate will be encased in dough and likely not sit on top, and it will have a film of dough baked over it, so it won't be clean and shiny. Save some of the larger chunks, if you have chopped them yourself, or chips, to poke into the top.

Sea Salt Flakes

Like the pools of chocolate, you will see big, unmelted flakes of sea salt in photos. Maldon sea salt flakes are most common among food stylists. They are added just before baking, but if you want them to keep their shape and not melt into the cookie dough, then add them midway through baking. It's another step in the process, but if you want the picture-perfect cookie, you'll go to any length.

BAKING

Get to know your oven. Some ovens run hot or cold, so using an independent oven thermometer is a great idea. Just rest it on the rack you intend to bake on and see if the oven is running true to temperature (what the dial says). If it's not, adjust the setting. Some ovens have hot spots that can either be avoided (they tend to be at the top or bottom, near the heating elements), or if they can't be avoided then rotate the pans so that one side of a baking sheet isn't burning while the rest are underbaked. The baking times are always a suggestion and not a rule, since all ovens are so different.

Sometimes you'll want to play with the temperature of your oven and how long you bake the cookies to impact the results of your cookies. The lower the temperature and the longer you bake will result in a drier, more evenly textured cookie. If you bake at a higher temperature for a shorter time, you'll end up with a cookie that has a caramelized top and edges and a softer interior. The suggested baking times in the recipes are how I like the results. You can bake a batch as I indicate and then play with the temperature to get the results you want.

I tested the Perfect Chocolate Chip Cookie recipe (page 51) at varying temperatures between 340°F to 375°F, both with conventional flat heat and with convection. Again, the results were pretty different. Whether you like a light, even-colored cookie or a dark, caramelized cookie, you can get those results with the oven settings you choose. I liked the 30-minute chilled cookie baked at 375°F flat heat for 10 minutes.

Batch Baking

When baking multiple batches of cookies, you will want to have several pans or time to let the pans cool off before loading them up with more cookie dough. The hot pans will melt the dough balls as you are placing them on the pans, and they may lose their shape or start spreading in undesirable ways. Depending on the cookies, you may need to reline the pans with a fresh piece of parchment paper. You don't want any cookie remnants on the paper that can get overbaked and impact the flavor of the next batch of cookie dough.

Baking one pan of cookies at a time will result in the most even baking but that's not always practical if you have a lot of cookies to make. Baking two sheets at a time still allows for good heat flow, especially if you set up the racks in the top and bottom thirds of the oven. If the cookies are not baking evenly, then switch the position of the baking sheets from top to bottom and back to front about midway through the bake. If you are having to use three baking sheets at a time, you will want to do the switcheroo a couple of times.

BAKING AT HIGH ALTITUDES

I live in the Midwest, which is perhaps the flattest place in the country, so I am by no means the reigning expert on high-altitude baking, but I have baked in the mountains of Colorado, and this is what I learned. There can be a big difference in how cookies behave if you live above 5,280 feet / 1.6km. With less air pressure, the rising dough balloons up too quickly and then collapses abruptly, giving you a dense, sometimes flatter result. The following adjustments can help you achieve the cookie of your dreams.

Decrease the baking soda or baking powder by half.

Increase baking temperature by 15° to 25°F, which will set the proteins faster and stop the bubbles from expanding too much.

Decrease the baking time, due to the higher temperature.

Decrease the amount of sugar by just a tablespoon per cup. Sugar is a tenderizer, so it can weaken the structure of the cookie. This means it can't trap the gas as well, and too much may cause the cookie to spread.

Increase the amount of flour by a tablespoon per cup. This will lend more structure to the cookies.

Thwack, Thwack, Thwack

When should you thwack the pan and when should you leave well enough alone? If you want a flatter cookie, you can thwack the pan gently as the cookies come out of the oven. This is a trick for a crisper cookie that I first saw while working in a professional kitchen. The chef opened the door and banged the tray on the rack as she pulled them out. The cookies collapsed and ended up with a crispier texture. My friend Sarah Kieffer takes this technique even further to create ripples in her cookies by banging the pan several times while the cookies bake. It's a technique that works great for most drop cookies. It works particularly well with cookies that use a high percentage of baking soda, so the cookies puff up as they bake (see Chocolate Chip Cookie Lab, page 46).

IS IT DONE YET?

Each recipe will give you a visual cue for how to tell if the cookie is done, as well as a suggested baking time. In most cases, I go by smell, color, and feel.

First, look through the window of your oven, assuming your oven has a window. It's best not to open the oven door too often or you will disrupt the baking. The change in temperature from opening the door can cause the cookies to bake longer and may dry them out. Once the cookie looks set and is the color you want, remove them and cool as directed. If the first batch isn't exactly as you like, adjust the baking time or temperature for the next batch.

Perfectly Round Cookies Hack

I am a fan of wabi-sabi, the Japanese concept of beauty being found in imperfection. Having said that, there is a time and place for perfectly round cookies. If that is what you are going for, you can use a round cookie or biscuit cutter that is just larger than the cookie to create a more uniform shape on drop cookies. As they are coming out of the oven, still piping hot and not structurally set up, you can gently coax the cookies into perfect shape by placing the large round cutter around the cookie and move it in tiny circles, which pushes the sides of the cookie into the right shape. You are not cutting the cookie, just pushing gently against the sides. It is key to do this while they are still hot and be gentle, so you don't break the delicate cookie.

COOLING AND STORING BAKED COOKIES AND BARS

Let it be remembered that the cooling process is a continuation of baking! There is no stopping my husband and kids from reaching for a still-warm chocolate chip cookie, but until it cools, even a little, it is going to be fragile and may even break apart. Keep this in mind when you are transferring the baked cookies from the pan to a cooling rack. Some may have to sit on the pan for a few minutes before lifting them off or they will fall apart.

Cool Your Cookies

Set the sheet full of baked cookies on a cooling rack, so air can flow all the way around the pan and cool them faster. There may be a couple of exceptions to this, so follow the cooling directions for each recipe.

If you think the cookies were slightly overbaked, you can slide the parchment off of the hot pan to stop the baking process. The heavy-gauged pans retain heat, so the cookies will continue to dry out a bit.

Once the cookies have cooled enough to set the structure, you can remove them from the pan and place the cookies directly on the cooling rack. If you move certain cookies too soon, they will crumble apart. I give a warning for more delicate cookies in the recipes, but if you are not sure, gently lift a cookie. If it breaks apart, just leave it for another couple of minutes and try again. A broken cookie is not the worst thing, but it's best to not break the whole batch.

Storing Your Cookies

For most cookies, I like to bake them the day they are served, so I typically store the dough balls in the freezer and bake just as many as I want. If you are baking ahead, the best rule of thumb for keeping cookies fresh is to cool them completely and store them in an airtight container or cookie jar.

Freezing. If you have to bake way in advance or prefer to bake the batch all at once, you can also freeze baked cookies. The trick to successfully freezing baked cookies is to cool the cookies completely, wrap them up really well in plastic wrap, and immediately transfer them to the freezer to lock in the moisture for up to two weeks. The plastic wrap helps the cookies avoid picking up any flavors or odors floating around your freezer (think fish sticks). If I am shipping the cookies to my son at college or as a gift, I do it when they are still frozen and add a freezer pack to the packaging (see page 62 for more on shipping cookies). When you're ready to eat them, defrost them, still wrapped, by leaving them on the counter for about an hour.

CLEAN CUT BARS

There are a few simple tricks to achieving a perfectly clean edge on your bars for that Instagram photo.

> The bars need to be totally cooled, and if you can chill them, that's even better. This gives the bars time to firm up so when you cut them, they don't smush into a messy blob.

> The knife you use matters as well. The thinner and sharper the blade, the less it will drag as you slice, avoiding a ragged, crushed edge to soft bars. If your brownies or bars are full of nuts and other harder ingredients, then a sharp serrated blade is useful. This is especially true when slicing biscotti (page 173).

> If the bars are sticky or have a soft topping, dipping the knife into a pitcher of hot water will help the blade glide through the bars and will give you a straight, clean cut.

> Use a ruler to ensure the bars are all even sizes.

Cut off the puffed edges to give you a more uniform shape. In a professional kitchen, the scraps ("chef snacks") are shared with the other kitchen staff and make everyone happy.

Add confectioners' sugar after cutting. If you top the bars with the sugar first, the edges will be messy. Cut the bars, then spread them out slightly on a baking sheet covered with parchment, and dust with confectioners' sugar. This is also how I add a drizzle of chocolate to bars, so the chocolate drizzle doesn't shatter as I cut and adds a pretty finish to the bars.

IT'S TIME TO DECORATE

There are endless ways to decorate your baked cookies. Add caramel, chocolate in many forms, icing, frosting, intricate details, or a riot of sprinkles. No matter what you choose, here are some tips for decorating.

Chocolate

Chocolate is often the main event in a recipe and using a high-quality chocolate can take your recipe to new heights. As high-quality chocolate can be expensive, you'll want to treat it with care.

MELTING CHOCOLATE

Melting chocolate is easy and risk free with my tips. Chocolate has a low melting point, so it doesn't take a lot of heat for it to liquefy. Use low heat, so it melts slowly and evenly. If your heat is too high, the chocolate can actually get hard and become grainy. Here are a couple of options for melting any kind of chocolate:

Double Boiler. Place finely chopped chocolate or chips in a heatproof bowl and set it aside. Fill a pot that the bowl will snuggly fit over with about a ½ inch / 1.3cm of water and bring it to a boil. Turn off the heat and place the bowl of chopped chocolate over the steaming pot (the bowl should not touch the water below). The residual steam is enough to melt the chocolate. Let it sit until the chocolate looks shiny throughout, which is an indication that the fats have melted and it is liquefied. Gently stir and use in your recipe.

Microwave. Place the chopped chocolate or chips in a microwave-safe bowl. Heat for about 20 seconds, stir the chocolate and repeat until the chocolate is warm to the touch and about 80 percent melted. Allow it to sit for a minute. The rest of the chocolate should melt during this time; stir it again. If there are still chunks of unmelted chocolate, microwave for 10 more seconds.

GANACHE SOS

Ganache, which is made of chocolate and cream, is a gorgeous and tasty way to put a finishing touch on a baked cookie, bar, or brownie. But if your ganache is not smooth, it loses its luster. Depending on the chocolate you use (every brand is different), the temperature of the ingredients, or if you are reheating a ganache, it may break (this is when the chocolate and fat start to separate) and look oily.

Reheating Ganache. If the ganache is too cool to whisk easily, you'll want to heat it slightly over a double boiler or in a microwave for a few seconds (chocolate has a very low melting point, so it really only takes a little bit to soften). Once it is soft, you can whisk it. If it is smooth, carry on with the recipe, but if it separates, don't panic! It can be fixed in several ways. I have placed these in order of easiest fix to most drastic.

CREAM Drizzle in more cream as you are whisking, a tablespoon at a time, whisking in the center of the container, until the ganache is emulsified and smooth. Warming the cream slightly is also helpful.

CORN SYRUP This is similar to adding more cream, but you'll end up with a ganache that tends to be a touch shinier, so it is nice if you are using the ganache to finish a cookie.

BLENDER If your ganache won't come back together by whisking in one or both of the above, place the warm ganache in a blender or food processor or use an immersion blender and pulse until it all comes together. Remember that you are aerating the cream in the ganache as you blend it, so it will get thick if you go too far.

Making Royal Icing

I decorate Sugar Cookies (page 97) and Gingerbread Cookies (page 103) with Royal Icing (page 97) made with fresh lemon juice, which is tasty in small amounts, quite stunning, and strong enough to hold up as the glue for a cookie constructed house (page 100). I'll admit that I love the fussy work of intricate piped decorations on sugar cookies. It is the closest I will come to ever using my BFA from college. If you don't share my enthusiasm for piping, then sprinkling colored decorator sugar on as the cookies go into the oven is a quick and festive alternative. These techniques are great for any holiday, special occasion, or just a random Tuesday when you celebrate with cookies.

What Is Royal Icing? It is a meringue-based icing with loads of confectioners' sugar that has the consistency of buttercream or a thin icing, depending on how much liquid you add, and then hardens at room temperature, making it quite durable. I used to make it with raw egg whites and confectioners' sugar but switched to a pasteurized meringue powder due to food safety concerns and ease. There are several brands of the powder available, and they all pretty much behave the exact same way, so use what is convenient.

Make the Royal Icing. In a stand mixer fitted with the whisk attachment, mix together the confectioners' sugar, meringue powder, water (or fresh, strained, lemon juice), and extract (use any flavor that matches your cookies) on low speed until blended, about 1 minute. Turn up the speed to medium-high and whip until light and fluffy, like meringue, about 3 minutes. It will be quite thick, and you need it this way to create glue if you are making a sugar cookie house (page 100). You can thin it with more liquid or thicken it with more confectioners' sugar to suit your needs at any point.

Color. You can add food coloring to the icing after it is mixed. If you want multiple colors, separate the icing into more bowls, keeping each one covered with a wet towel. Use food coloring pastes or gel for bolder colors, especially if you are trying to keep the icing thick. If you want pastels or a wetter consistency, use water-based food coloring. A little color goes a long way, so add a little bit at a time.

Keep It Covered. Make sure to keep the icing covered at all times, since it dries hard and will develop a skin of hard icing within minutes. I use a damp, clean kitchen towel over the bowls. If the covered icing sits for several minutes between uses, it will develop air bubbles that will make your icing sputter as it comes out of the bag, preventing a clean line of icing. If the icing sits for several hours, some of the liquid may separate, which will make the consistency uneven. In either case, use a rubber spatula to gently stir the icing well before using, to get rid of any air bubbles and to make sure the icing is smooth.

Piping. Follow these instructions if you're piping decorations on your cookies.

1. Fill a parchment paper bag or small featherweight cloth bag fitted with a small round tip (Ateco #4 or the like) with about ¼ cup of the royal icing. The consistency should be soft enough to pipe, but firm enough to hold its shape, like buttercream or soft mashed potatoes. The easiest way to do it without making a mess is to place the piping bag in a well-fitting drinking glass, so the open end is up and stabilized as you fill the bag. If using a cloth bag, fold a cuff over the top of the glass to keep it steady. After filling, cut a very small hole at the tip of the parchment paper bag (start tiny, you can always make it bigger).

2. Decorate your cookies as you desire. Refill or start with a fresh paper piping bag when you run out. As you get the hang of it, you can fill with more icing, but to begin it is easier to handle with just ¼ cup of icing.

Flooding. If you're flooding the cookie with royal icing, follow these instructions.

1. Fill a parchment bag or small featherweight cloth bag fitted with a slightly larger round tip (about a #6 Ateco) with ¼ cup of the royal icing. (See Step 1 under Piping for instructions on how to fill the bag with royal icing.) Draw an outline around the edge of the cookie with the thick icing. Let it dry for about 10 minutes.

2. Once all of your cookies have been outlined, thin out a portion of your icing in order to flood or pool in the center of the lines you just piped. The thinner icing should be the consistency of molasses. Fill another pastry or parchment bag with about ¼ cup of the thin icing. Carefully flood the area between your outlines. Go slowly so as not to go over the lines you've drawn.

3. Once you've flooded the center of a cookie with the icing, it will be shiny and wet. At this point, you can pipe contrasting colors into it and swirl them together or put sugar decorations on the icing and they will stick. You can also let the icing dry for about 30 or more minutes. After that, it will be hard enough to pipe more decorations and details on top of the icing.

The creative options are endless. Some people make paintings on their cookies and some, like my boys when they were little, just want a riot of colorful sprinkles.

SENDING COOKIES AS A GIFT

The best way to ship cookies is while they're frozen, so they are solid and will have the most possible structure as they travel. Bake them, cool them down, wrap them in plastic wrap, and then freeze them (see page 58). You can do this up to 3 weeks in advance of shipping them.

Wrap them individually in parchment paper, little decorative bags, or snugly in holiday tins. If you want to add some flair, tie a piece of ribbon or colorful twine around the cookies or tins. Choose a box that's not so big that the cookies will be moving around. Place some packing material on the bottom. Add a layer of frozen shipping ice packs or dry ice (follow directions), a piece of cardboard to create a flat barrier over the ice packs, and your wrapped cookies, stacked neatly, as flat as can be and in a single layer. Then add more packing material on top and repeat with another layer. Finish with packing paper or bubble wrap to make sure there isn't much room for them to shift around.

Delivery Service. Ship the cookies overnight, so they arrive before the ice packs melt. Another great gift is sending frozen homemade cookie dough balls that the recipient can bake fresh. I sent my son Charlie a college care package with a small baking sheet that fit his tiny apartment oven or a toaster oven, a stack of parchment paper and a box of frozen dough balls. He could bake off one cookie while studying or make a whole bunch for friends.

HEALTHY COOKIES AND TREATS

The Vermont Commune

com·mune
/ˈkä myōon/
noun
a group of people living together and
sharing possessions and responsibilities.

In 1969, my dad bought a bucolic piece of land in the Northeast Kingdom of Vermont and invited just about anybody and everybody he ever met to come live and work the land. We grew all our own food, cooked together, and baked together. The food was wholesome and earnest—it was about sustainability and sustenance way before pleasure. Don't get me wrong, these folks also knew how to party, and we packed up the VW bus and snuck into Woodstock for the concert of a lifetime. I was a wee, frazzy-haired, naked baby running around, but those times still defined and shaped my life and baking. The recipes in this chapter are a nod to those fascinating and enlightening days; these cookies are full of healthy ingredients but are made with rock-and-roll flavor. You'll find all kinds of joy, sweetness, and deliciousness here!

Soft Oatmeal Cookies

Even loaded with healthy ingredients, these oatmeal cookies have become a François household favorite. Oats in some form were a staple as a kid, though they were often the consistency of "Mighty Mush" or dried into tree bark. These soft oatmeal cookies have come a long way since my food-as-fuel commune days. Adding the oat and hazelnut flours, plus applesauce, adds nutritional value and a beautifully tender texture, and they also give a wonderful rich nutty flavor to the cookies. You can buy these flours in the store or make your own by blending oatmeal and nuts in a food processor for a few minutes. I throw in raisins or dried cherries for a little extra chew and sweetness.

Makes about 24 cookies

Cookie Academy Review
▨ Using a Portion Scoop, see page 43
▨ Freezing the Dough, see page 45
▨ Batch Baking, see page 56

1 cup / 120g oat flour (see Baker's Note)

1 cup / 120g all-purpose flour

½ cup / 52g hazelnut flour or meal (see page 19)

3 cups / 300g rolled oats

1 tsp baking soda

1 tsp baking powder

1 tsp kosher salt

1 tsp ground cinnamon

½ tsp ground nutmeg

¼ tsp ground cloves

1 cup / 220g unsalted butter, at room temperature

1¾ cups / 350g lightly packed brown sugar

2 tsp pure vanilla extract (page 16)

¼ cup / 60g applesauce

2 eggs, at room temperature

2 cups / 280g raisins and/or dried cherries

In a medium bowl, whisk together the flours, rolled oats, baking soda, baking powder, salt, cinnamon, nutmeg, and cloves. Set aside.

In a stand mixer fitted with the paddle attachment, cream the butter, brown sugar, and vanilla on medium speed until light and fluffy, about 3 minutes. Mix in the applesauce until incorporated.

Add the eggs, one at a time, beating on medium speed until incorporated. Add the flour mixture all at once and mix until just incorporated. Mix in the raisins. You may need to give the bowl a couple of swipes with a rubber spatula to make sure the raisins are evenly distributed.

Line a baking sheet with parchment paper. Scoop the cookie dough using a #16 (¼-cup) portion scoop onto the baking sheet. You can make the cookies larger or smaller, but it will affect the baking time.

Refrigerate the dough balls for at least 30 minutes. If you have the time, the cookies improve if you let them sit, covered, for 24 to 36 hours. After they are chilled, you can bake them or freeze the dough balls for baking later.

Preheat the oven to 350°F / 175°C with racks in the top and bottom thirds of the oven. Line two baking sheets with parchment paper.

Evenly space six chilled cookies on each sheet. Bake in the oven with one sheet on the top rack and the other on the bottom rack for about 10 minutes. Rotate the baking sheets top to bottom and continue baking for about 5 more minutes, until the cookies are golden brown, but still soft.

Allow the cookies to cool for a few minutes on the baking sheets, then move to a cooling rack.

BAKER'S NOTE

To make the oat flour, place 1⅓ cups / 130g rolled oats in a food processor and pulverize until powdered.

THE VERMONT COMMUNE

Rum Raisin Oatmeal Cookies

My husband, Graham, adores rum raisin ice cream, so I wanted to replicate it in cookie form. I love this rebellious version of oatmeal raisin cookies. Soaking the raisins in rum is a game changer. The booze serves another purpose other than just flavor—soaking the raisins in rum keeps them plump and soft when they bake. Use your favorite rum, we like spiced in my house, but dark and white rum work as well. And if rum isn't your preference you can go with your favorite alcohol. These cookies are rich in flavor and kind of a grown-up treat, but because the alcohol burns off as they bake, they're just fine for the kids, too.

Makes about 24 cookies

Cookie Academy Review
▧ Using a Portion Scoop, see page 43
▧ Freezing the Dough, see page 45
▧ Chocolate Chip Cookie Lab, see page 46
▧ Batch Baking, see page 56

1½ cups / 210g raisins

⅓ cup / 80ml rum

2½ cups / 300g all-purpose flour

3 cups / 300g rolled oats

1 tsp baking soda

1 tsp baking powder

1 tsp kosher salt

1½ tsp ground cinnamon

½ tsp ground nutmeg

1 cup / 220g unsalted butter, at room temperature

1½ cups / 300g lightly packed brown sugar

1 cup / 200g granulated sugar

2 eggs, at room temperature

In a small bowl, combine the raisins and rum. Cover and heat in a microwave for about 1 minute, or just until the rum starts to bubble. Shake the bowl to make sure all the raisins are resting in the hot rum. Allow to sit until the raisins are room temperature and plump, about 20 minutes.

In a large bowl, whisk together the flour, oats, baking soda, baking powder, salt, cinnamon, and nutmeg. Set aside.

In a stand mixer fitted with the paddle attachment, cream the butter and sugars on medium speed until light and fluffy, about 3 minutes.

Add the eggs, one at a time, beating on medium speed after each addition, until incorporated. Add the flour mixture all at once and mix until just incorporated. Mix in the raisins with any remaining rum. You may need to give the mixing bowl a couple of swipes with a rubber spatula at the end to make sure the raisins are evenly distributed.

Line a baking sheet with parchment paper. Scoop the cookie dough using a #20 (3-tablespoon) portion scoop onto the baking sheet. Flatten the cookie balls into ¾-inch disks. You can make the cookies larger or smaller, but it will affect the baking time.

Refrigerate the dough disks for at least 30 minutes; if you have the time, they improve if you let them sit for 24 to 36 hours. After they are chilled, you can bake them or freeze them for baking later.

Preheat the oven to 350°F / 175°C, with racks in the top and bottom thirds of the oven. Line two baking sheets with parchment paper.

Evenly space six chilled cookies on each sheet. Bake in the oven with one sheet on the top rack and the other on the bottom rack for about 10 minutes. Rotate the baking sheets top to bottom and continue baking for about 5 more minutes.

Allow the cookies to cool for a few minutes on the baking sheet and then move to a cooling rack.

Coconut Oatmeal Raisin Cookies

Oatmeal cookies can be controversial and can divide a family, but, in my house, we all love them. This deliciously sweet and chewy version is one of Graham's all-time favorites. He likes them so much he hides the batch from the boys when I bake them so he doesn't have to share. That's high praise. The hint of black pepper gives a little complexity and balances out the sweetness of the raisins and coconut. Because these are so popular and freeze well, I always make a big batch. Especially because the boys generally discover Graham's hidden stash sooner than he'd like.

Makes about 24 cookies

Cookie Academy Review
▥ Using a Portion Scoop, see page 43
▥ Freezing the Dough, see page 45
▥ Batch Baking, see page 56

1¾ cups / 210g all-purpose flour

3¾ cups / 375g rolled oats

¼ tsp baking soda

1 tsp baking powder

¾ tsp kosher salt

1 tsp ground cinnamon

¼ tsp ground black pepper

1¼ cups / 275g unsalted butter, at room temperature

1¾ cups / 350g lightly packed brown sugar

½ cup / 100g granulated sugar

2 tsp pure vanilla extract (page 16)

2 eggs, at room temperature

1 cup / 140g raisins

1 cup / 90g loosely packed sweetened coconut flakes

In a large bowl, whisk together the flour, rolled oats, baking soda, baking powder, salt, cinnamon, and black pepper. Set aside.

In a stand mixer fitted with the paddle attachment, cream the butter, brown and granulated sugars, and vanilla on medium speed until light and fluffy, about 3 minutes.

Add the eggs, one at a time, beating on medium speed until incorporated. Add the flour mixture all at once and mix until just incorporated. Mix in the raisins and coconut flakes. You may need to give the bowl a couple of swipes with a rubber spatula at the end to make sure the ingredients are evenly distributed.

Line a baking sheet with parchment paper. Scoop the cookie dough using a #16 (¼-cup) portion scoop onto the baking sheet. You can make the cookies larger or smaller, but it will affect the baking time.

Refrigerate the dough balls for at least 30 minutes; if you have the time, they improve if you let them sit for 24 to 36 hours. After they are chilled, you can bake them or freeze the dough balls for baking later.

Preheat the oven to 350°F / 175°C, with racks in the top and bottom thirds of the oven. Line two baking sheets with parchment paper.

Evenly space six chilled cookies on each sheet. Bake in the oven with one sheet on the top rack and the other on the bottom rack for about 12 minutes. Rotate the baking sheets top to bottom and continue baking for about 5 more minutes, or until golden brown on top.

Allow the cookies to cool for a few minutes on the baking sheets and then move to a cooling rack.

■ Dairy-Free   ■ Vegan

Morning Cookies

Of all the cookies in this book, these would have received the commune stamp of approval. They are ultrahealthy, made with whole-wheat flour, oats, and no refined sugar. Instead, mashed banana, honey, coconut, and dried fruit provide the sweetness. This is the perfect morning cookie: it has all the flavor of muesli breakfast cereal, and you can grab them on your way out the door. It's also perfect for packing in a backpack when you're heading to the gym or to soccer practice. There's plenty of room for experimentation with the fruit and nut combination. I especially love using currants and pepitas, but you can try out all kinds of combinations, depending on your taste and what's in the pantry.

Makes about 14 cookies

Cookie Academy Review
■ Using a Portion Scoop, see page 43
■ Batch Baking, see page 56

2 cups / 200g rolled oats

½ cup / 70g whole-wheat flour

⅓ cup / 40g loosely packed unsweetened shredded coconut

½ tsp baking soda

1 pinch of kosher salt

½ cup / 90g carob or bittersweet chocolate chips (mini is best)

½ cup / 60g chopped walnuts, pecans, or cashews, lightly toasted

¼ cup / 35g pepitas (shelled pumpkin seeds), lightly toasted

¼ cup / 35g craisins or raisins

2 Tbsp currants

¾ cup / 180g mashed ripe banana (1 large)

2 tsp pure vanilla extract (page 16)

⅓ cup / 126g honey (or pure maple syrup for a vegan option)

⅔ cup / 150g coconut oil, melted

Preheat the oven to 375°F / 190°C. Line a baking sheet with parchment paper.

In a medium bowl, whisk together the oats, whole-wheat flour, coconut, baking soda, and salt. Using a stiff rubber spatula, mix in the carob, nuts, pepitas, dried fruit, banana, vanilla, honey, and coconut oil until well combined. Allow to sit for 15 minutes. Line two baking sheets with parchment paper.

Scoop the cookie dough into about 7 cookies using a #20 (3-tablespoon) portion scoop and arrange evenly onto each prepared baking sheet, leaving enough room to spread and flatten them slightly into thick disks. You can make the cookies larger or smaller, but it will affect the baking time.

Bake, one sheet at a time, in the middle of the oven for about 12 to 14 minutes, until the bottoms are golden brown.

Allow the cookies to cool on the baking sheet until the cookies no longer fall apart, then move to a cooling rack.

Frazzy Bringle Bars
(Chewy Maple Granola Snacks)

This is what my young, flower-child self would have wanted for a snack on the commune. It's all the things I ate back then, when my nickname was Frazzy Bringle, but a touch sweeter and more decadent. For this bar, I baked them all together to make something that's full of granola, craisins, maple syrup, and spices. It's more a snacking cake or healthy-ish breakfast treat than a cookie.

I've included my aunt Melissa's granola recipe, which she used to make in *huge* batches to feed all the commune members, plus more to sell at the local co-op in Barton, Vermont. It's super-easy to make and is perfect in these bars or a bowl of milk. You can also use your favorite granola from the store.

Makes about 16 bars

Cookie Academy Review
▓ Parchment-Paper Sling, see page 39

1¼ cups / 150g all-purpose flour

2 cups / 200g granola, store-bought or Aunt Melissa's (recipe follows)

½ tsp baking soda

½ tsp baking powder

1 tsp kosher salt

¾ tsp ground cinnamon

¼ tsp ground nutmeg

½ cup / 110g unsalted butter, melted

1¼ cups / 250g lightly packed brown sugar

¼ cup / 88g pure maple syrup

2 eggs, at room temperature

1 cup / 140g craisins or raisins

Preheat the oven to 375°F / 190°C *convection* heat (or 400°F / 205°C flat heat). Line an 8-inch square cake pan with greased parchment paper that goes up and beyond the sides to create a sling. Clip the parchment paper to the pan.

In a medium bowl, whisk together flour, granola, baking soda, baking powder, salt, cinnamon, and nutmeg. Set aside.

In another large bowl, whisk together the melted butter, brown sugar, and maple syrup. Whisk in the eggs, one at a time. Using a wooden spoon or rubber spatula, stir in the dry ingredients until well combined. Stir in the craisins.

Pour into the prepared pan. Bake until the top looks set and golden brown at the edge, about 30 minutes.

Cool in the pan to room temperature before removing the bar from the pan and cutting into sixteen pieces.

▓ **VARIATION: FRAZZY BRINGLE COOKIES**

Preheat the oven to 375°F / 190°C convection heat and line a baking sheet with parchment paper. Prepare the dough as directed, then chill in the mixing bowl for at least 30 minutes. Scoop the chilled dough with a #40 (1½-tablespoon) portion scoop and place six balls, evenly spaced, on the prepared sheet. Bake for about 12 minutes or until deeply caramelized and puffed. They may have a slightly lighter colored center. Allow to cool completely, before removing from the parchment. Repeat with the rest of the chilled dough.

Aunt Melissa's Granola

This recipe is inspired by my aunt Melissa. The actual granola recipe was lost when my aunt passed away decades ago, but I know this one is close because the smell as it bakes transports me back to those days on the commune. She would have loaded it up with raisins, dried currants, and apricots, even dried pineapple. I also like to include dehydrated berries, which are tart and wonderful in the granola. Carob chips are an optional addition because that's what we would have had on the commune. I personally won't touch the stuff after years of being told it tastes just like chocolate; it does not! If you love carob, go for it; otherwise use chocolate chips or skip them all together.

Makes about 10 cups / 1675g

½ cup / 170g honey

½ cup / 110g pure maple syrup

½ cup / 108g safflower or vegetable oil

2 tsp pure vanilla extract (page 16)

1 tsp ground cinnamon

½ tsp kosher salt

6 cups / 600g rolled oats

¼ cup / 35g sesame seeds

¼ cup / 35g pepitas (shelled pumpkin seeds)

1 cup / 150g chopped nuts

1 cup / 100g loosely packed unsweetened shredded coconut

1 cup / 120g chopped dried fruit (such as raisins, apricots, craisins, pineapple, and/or cherries)

1 cup / 20g dehydrated raspberries or other berries (optional)

1 cup / 224g mini carob (or chocolate) chips (optional)

Preheat the oven to 350°F / 175°C. Line two baking sheets with silicone mats.

In a very large bowl, whisk together the honey, maple syrup, oil, vanilla, cinnamon, and salt.

Mix in the oats, sesame seeds, pumpkin seeds, chopped nuts, and coconut until they are uniformly coated.

Divide the granola between the two baking sheets and spread it evenly over the mats.

Bake for 20 minutes, then stir the granola. Continue baking for another 10 to 15 minutes and stir. Continue baking for another 5 to 10 minutes, then stir. Continue this process until the granola is golden brown. Depending on how thick you have it piled on the pan, it can take two or three more cycles.

Cool the granola completely on the pans. Add the dried fruit, dehydrated berries, and carob chips (if using). Use in Frazzy Bringle's Bars or serve with yogurt or milk.

Gluten-Free ▪ Dairy-Free

3-Ingredient Peanut Butter Cookies

It's late, you've had a long day at work/school/gardening/whatever, and you need a quick treat—I got you! You most likely have all the ingredients in your pantry right now, and with just three ingredients (or four if you want to add some shimmer), you can mix them up literally in the minutes it takes to preheat your oven. Nothing better than warm cookies from the oven to soothe a tired mind/body/soul. This is also a great recipe to do with your kids, as it's ideal for busy hands. Bonus: they're gluten- and dairy-free. So no excuses, get baking!

You can use any peanut butter you have in the pantry, but I have to admit, I prefer these and most peanut butter cookies made with Skippy or the like, either creamy or crunchy. I save the natural stuff for my sandwiches. If you use the natural variety, make sure it's really well stirred. You may also want to add a *big* pinch of salt if the peanut butter is salt-free.

Makes about 12 cookies

Cookie Academy Review
▪ Using a Portion Scoop, see page 43
▪ Batch Baking, see page 56

1 cup / 260g peanut butter

1 cup / 200g turbinado sugar

2 egg whites (¼ cup / 60g), cold

Raw or decorating sugar for tops (optional)

Preheat the oven to 350°F / 175°C. Line a baking sheet with parchment paper.

In a medium bowl, mix the peanut butter, turbinado sugar, and egg whites with a spoon until smooth. The dough will be quite soft.

Scoop the cookie dough using a #40 (1½-tablespoon) portion scoop and place evenly, about 2 inches apart, on the prepared baking sheet, then flatten to disks ½ inch / 1.3cm thick. You can make the cookies larger or smaller, but it will affect the baking time. Sprinkle with the sugar (if using).

Bake in the middle of the oven for 10 to 12 minutes, until golden brown along the bottom and set on top.

Cool completely on the baking sheet, then dunk in milk or eat however you please.

BAKER'S NOTE

You can use whatever sugar you have on hand. Replace the turbinado sugar with equal parts brown sugar or granulated sugar. You can also replace it with 1 cup / 120g of confectioners' sugar. If you choose a liquid sweetener, like maple syrup or honey, use 2 tablespoons.

THE VERMONT COMMUNE

Ultra–Peanut Butter Cookies

This recipe uses peanut flour instead of regular wheat flour, so it has the ultimate peanut flavor and just happens to be another tasty gluten-free option. Bonus! Note that peanut flour is not the same thing as powdered peanut butter, which has become popular in recent years, as people like to add it to smoothies. Peanut flour is made from defatted peanuts and can be found in two varieties. Dark peanut flour has been roasted and has a deeper flavor, which I prefer. The light version is made with raw peanuts and has a more subtle flavor. These cookies are great for kids—and adults, too—alongside chocolate milk or with a bowl of vanilla ice cream.

Makes about 18 cookies

Cookie Academy Review
- Using a Portion Scoop, see page 43
- Batch Baking, see page 56

¾ cup / 165g unsalted butter, at room temperature

1¼ cups / 250g lightly packed brown sugar

¾ cup / 195g smooth or chunky peanut butter (like Skippy Super Chunk)

2 large eggs, at room temperature

1 tsp pure vanilla extract (page 16)

2 cups / 200g peanut flour (see Baker's Note), sifted if lumpy

1 tsp baking soda

1 tsp kosher salt

4 oz / 112g semisweet or bittersweet chocolate, finely chopped (optional)

¼ cup crystal decorating sugar for topping

Preheat the oven 375°F / 190°C. Line two baking sheets with parchment paper.

In a stand mixer fitted with the paddle attachment, cream together the butter and brown sugar for about 2 minutes on medium speed. Scrape the sides of the bowl often. Add the peanut butter and mix well. Add the eggs, one at a time, mixing until well incorporated. Mix in the vanilla.

In a small bowl, whisk together the peanut flour, baking soda, and salt. Add to the peanut butter mixture and mix on low speed just until it is smooth. Add the chocolate (if using).

Scoop the cookie dough using a #20 (3-tablespoon) portion scoop onto the prepared baking sheets, leaving about 2 inches between the cookies, so they have room to spread. You can make the cookies larger or smaller, but it will affect the bake time. Flatten slightly, sprinkle with decorating sugar, and use a fork to create a cross-hatch pattern.

Bake, one sheet at a time, in the middle of the oven for 10 to 12 minutes. They will puff up slightly and the tops will be golden, but they should still be slightly soft in the middle. If you like your peanut butter cookies crunchy throughout, bake them for another couple of minutes.

Cool completely before removing from the pan or they will crumble apart.

BAKER'S NOTES

I tried light and dark peanut flours with great results but prefer the roasted peanut flavor of the dark. Trader Joe's had a version when I was testing that also works well. More brands can be found online.

I sometimes bake half of the cookies without the chocolate and then add 2 oz / 60g of chocolate to the rest of the dough. This satisfies the tastes of everyone in my house.

Triple Ginger Cookies

I wanted these soft cookies to be extra gingery, so I used a trifecta of ginger flavor: ground ginger, grated fresh ginger, and candied ginger. It added a very nice kick! These made it into the commune cookies chapter because my parents and the other health nuts I was surrounded by during my youth often talked about the health benefits of ginger. There are many, but let's be real—ginger just tastes amazing, especially in a cookie dough with a hint of buckwheat flour to give it more depth of flavor. I love these zippy cookies with coffee or tea for an afternoon snack or with creamy ice cream jammed between two.

Makes about 18 cookies

Cookie Academy Review
▒ Using a Portion Scoop, see page 43
▒ Freezing the Dough, see page 45
▒ Batch Baking, see page 56

1½ cups / 180g all-purpose flour

½ cup / 76g buckwheat flour

1 Tbsp unsweetened natural cocoa powder, sifted if lumpy

½ tsp baking soda

½ tsp kosher salt

1 Tbsp ground ginger

½ tsp ground cinnamon

¼ tsp ground cardamom

¼ tsp ground black pepper

½ cup / 110g unsalted butter, at room temperature

3 Tbsp unsulfured light molasses

¾ cup / 150g lightly packed brown sugar

1 egg, at room temperature

2 Tbsp fresh ginger, finely grated using a Microplane

⅓ cup / 40g finely chopped candied ginger

⅓ cup raw sugar for coating before baking

Line a baking sheet with parchment paper.

In a small bowl, whisk together the all-purpose and buckwheat flours, cocoa powder, baking soda, salt, ground ginger, cinnamon, cardamom, and pepper.

In a stand mixer fitted with the paddle attachment, mix together the butter, molasses, and brown sugar on medium speed. Scrape down the bowl and add the egg, mixing until combined. Add the fresh and candied gingers. Add the flour mixture and mix on medium-low speed just until evenly combined and no flour remains.

Scoop the cookie dough using a #40 (1½-tablespoon) portion scoop onto the prepared baking sheet. You can make the cookies larger or smaller, but it will affect the baking time.

Dip each dough ball in raw sugar and flatten slightly. Refrigerate the dough balls for 30 minutes before baking so they don't spread too much. After they are chilled, you can bake them or freeze the dough balls for baking later.

Preheat the oven to 350°F / 175°C. Line a baking sheet with parchment paper.

Evenly space eight cookie balls on the prepared baking sheet. Bake, one sheet at a time, in the middle of the oven for 10 to 12 minutes, until golden brown.

Allow the cookies to cool for a few minutes on the baking sheet and then move to a cooling rack.

■ Nut-Free ■ Dairy-Free

Raisin Biscuits

These cookies are a tribute to the Garibaldi biscuit I used to eat in the 1970s. This is one of the few store-bought cookies I remember having at home. I think my folks—who never had sugar in the house—made an exception for this raisin-crammed cracker-like cookie. The sweetness of the raisins and the tenderness of the whole-wheat dough was such a satisfying snack. I hadn't seen these on the market for decades, which is a real shame, so a while ago, I decided to make my own. When I pulled them out of the oven, the fond memories of munching on them at the kitchen table came flooding back, and they were even better than I remembered. Make sure to roll the dough to be as thin as possible so they have a cracker-like snap to them. The classic Garibaldi was made with raisins, but you can use chopped dried apricots, cherries, or craisins if you're not a fan of dried grapes.

Makes 12 cookies

Cookie Academy Review
■ Rolling the Dough, see page 52
■ Batch Baking, see page 56

½ batch / 360g graham cracker dough (page 86)

Egg wash, 1 egg lightly beaten with 1 tsp water, for brushing dough, inside and out

1 cup / 140g chopped raisins (or other dried fruit)

Preheat the oven to 350°F / 175°C. Line a baking sheet with parchment paper.

On a lightly floured surface, using a rolling pin, roll the graham cracker dough out to a rectangle 9 by 11 inches / 23 by 28cm and about ⅛ inch / 3mm thick. Brush it lightly with the egg wash. Spread the chopped raisins over half the length of the dough. Fold the other half of the dough over the raisins. Roll the raisin-filled dough to be as thin as possible, trying to get it back to the 9 by 11-inch / 23 by 28cm rectangle. Some of the raisins will poke through the dough.

Cut the dough using a pizza cutter down the center lengthwise. Then cut into six equal sections along the width, to create twelve rectangles.

Arrange the pieces evenly on the prepared baking sheet so they have room to expand slightly. Brush with more egg wash.

Bake in the middle of the oven for 18 to 20 minutes, until golden brown.

Allow to cool completely before enjoying.

Graham Crackers

These are named after the flour, not my husband, whose name is also Graham. Graham flour is a whole-wheat flour that's more coarsely ground than regular whole-wheat flour. It is what these childhood favorites were originally made with and gives them their classic flavor and texture. This unique flour is no longer so easy to find, but these are just as memory-provoking when made with regular whole-wheat flour. I added a bit of cake flour to make the texture of the cracker more tender and cookie-like. They are a terrific snacking cookie and make great s'mores. They can also be used as a base layer for some of the cheesecake bars (page 227) and the Raisin Biscuits (page 85).

Makes about 32 cookies

Cookie Academy Review
▥ Freezing the Dough, see page 45
▥ Rolling the Dough, see page 52
▥ Batch Baking, see page 56

1¾ cups / 240g whole-wheat flour

½ cup / 55g cake flour

1 tsp baking soda

1 tsp kosher salt

1 Tbsp ground cinnamon (optional)

½ cup / 100g lightly packed brown sugar

½ cup / 110g unsalted butter, at room temperature

½ cup / 170g honey

1 tsp pure vanilla extract (page 16)

¼ cup / 60ml water

In a stand mixer fitted with the paddle attachment, mix together the whole-wheat and cake flours, baking soda, salt, and cinnamon (if using) on low speed. Add the brown sugar, butter, honey, vanilla, and water and mix on medium-low speed until just evenly combined and no flour remains.

Divide the dough into two equal pieces. Form each into a rectangle ½ inch / 1.3cm thick and wrap in plastic. Refrigerate the dough for at least 1 hour or freeze for up to 1 month.

Preheat the oven to 350°F / 175°C.

On a lightly floured silicone mat or piece of parchment paper, roll each piece of the chilled dough into a 10 by 13-inch / 25 by 33cm rectangle, about ⅛ inch / 3mm thick. Transfer the mat or parchment paper onto a baking sheet.

Dock the dough with a fork all over to prevent it from puffing too much. Use a pastry or pizza wheel to score the dough all the way through, cutting the crackers to whatever size you like, so when they are baked and cooled, they easily break into neat graham crackers. Bake for about 18 minutes, or until the crackers are golden brown and dry (see Baker's Note).

Allow to cool completely on the baking sheet. Then break apart and store wrapped in an airtight container in a dry, cool place. If the crackers lose their snap, you can reheat them in a 350°F / 175°C oven for about 5 minutes.

BAKER'S NOTE

The baking time very much depends on how thick you roll the dough, so check them a bit early. If the dough is not entirely even, some of the thinner crackers will bake faster and will need to be removed. You can continue baking the rest until they are all golden brown.

Spelt Sugar Cookies

The nuttiness of spelt, an ancient grain, is such a wonderful flavor, and because it doesn't have as much gluten as regular whole-wheat flour, these cookies are still super-tender and delicious. No one will guess that you've used a more healthful grain! The color is just a bit darker than my regular sugar cookie dough. I like the earthy flavor of the flour with orange zest, but you can use lemon here or perhaps play with a spice blend that speaks to you.

Makes about 24 cookies

Cookie Academy Review
▦ Freezing the Dough, see page 45
▦ Rolling the Dough, see page 52
▦ Batch Baking, see page 56

1 cup / 120g spelt flour (or whole-wheat pastry flour)

1 cup / 120g all-purpose flour

½ tsp baking powder

¼ tsp kosher salt

½ cup / 110g unsalted butter, at room temperature

⅔ cup / 150g granulated sugar

2 egg yolks, at room temperature

2 tsp pure vanilla extract (page 16)

½ tsp orange zest

In a small bowl, whisk together the spelt and all-purpose flours, baking powder, and salt.

In a stand mixer fitted with the paddle attachment, cream together the butter and sugar on medium speed until light and fluffy, about 2 minutes. Scrape down the sides of the bowl with a rubber spatula. Add the egg yolks, one at a time, mixing well between each addition and scraping the bowl. Mix in the vanilla and orange zest. Add the flour mixture all at once and mix on low speed just until it all comes together. Scrape down the bowl, and mix the mixture once more for 15 seconds on medium speed.

Press the dough into a disk, wrap it in plastic, and refrigerate until firm, at least 1 hour. This dough can also be made a couple of days ahead or frozen for up to 3 weeks.

Preheat the oven to 350°F / 175°C. Line as many baking sheets as you need with parchment paper.

On a floured surface, roll the dough out to a rectangle about ⅛ inch / 3mm thick.

Use a cookie cutter to create fun shapes out of the dough. Place the cut cookies with enough room for them to spread slightly on the prepared baking sheet. If your dough starts to get warm and sticky, return it to the refrigerator. Warm dough will be more difficult to work with. You can gather together and reroll the scraps once before they start to get too dry.

Bake for 8 to 12 minutes, until just golden on the bottom—you don't want too much color. The baking time will depend on the size of the cookie.

Allow the cookies to cool slightly on the baking sheet for a few minutes, then move to a cooling rack.

■ Nut-Free

Carrot Cake Whoopie Pie Cookies

I hear Joni Mitchell and Neil Young in my head when I think of the carrot cake from the 1970s. Soulful and deep. Both the music and the cake were all the rage on the commune. We grew the carrots for the recipe and raised bees for the honey. Music was always playing in the kitchen as we baked away. I loved that cake, because it was a rare sweet treat. Because carrot cake with cream cheese frosting is one of my first-known loves, I wanted to create that flavor combination in a cookie. Whoopie pies seemed the perfect way to keep the cake-like texture and fill the sandwich with the sweet-yet-tangy icing I love so much. You can add more or less honey to the cream cheese filling to suit your tastes. I use healthy ingredients to make this cookie, but man is it delicious. They'll make you hum as you bake.

Makes 12 cookie sandwiches

Cookie Academy Review
■ Using a Portion Scoop, see page 43
■ Batch Baking, see page 56

1⅔ cups / 230g whole-wheat flour

1 tsp baking powder

¼ tsp baking soda

¼ tsp salt

½ tsp cinnamon

½ tsp ginger

¼ tsp nutmeg

1 cup / 100g finely shredded carrots

¼ cup / 20g loosely packed unsweetened finely shredded coconut

¼ cup / 66g crushed, drained canned no-sugar-added pineapple

½ cup / 110g unsalted butter, at room temperature

½ cup plus 1 Tbsp / 200g honey

1 egg, at room temperature

1 tsp pure vanilla extract (page 16)

½ cup / 80g currants

½ cup / 50g dried pineapple, very finely chopped

Cream Cheese Frosting

8 oz / 225g cream cheese, chilled

2 to 3 Tbsp honey

1 tsp pure vanilla extract (page 16)

¼ tsp lemon zest

1 pinch of kosher salt

Preheat the oven to 350°F / 175°C. Double up two baking sheets and line the top one with parchment paper.

In a small bowl, whisk together the whole-wheat flour, baking powder, baking soda, salt, cinnamon, ginger, and nutmeg. Set aside.

In a food processor, chop the carrots, coconut, and pineapple, until they are pulsed into fine pieces, but not pureed. Add the butter and honey, pulsing several times until uniform. The mixture may not look entirely smooth at this point, but try to get it as evenly mixed as possible. Scrape down the bowl of the food processor to make sure everything is evenly mixed. Add the egg and vanilla and pulse to combine.

Mix in the flour mixture by pulsing the machine several times until just combined. Don't overmix.

Remove the blade from the food processor bowl and use a rubber spatula to fold in the currants and dried pineapple.

Scoop the dough into six cookies using a #40 (1½-tablespoon) portion scoop onto the prepared baking sheet. Make sure there are 2 inches of space between the cookies. Dip your finger in water and gently flatten the tops of the cookies to make disks ½ inch / 1.3cm thick.

Bake, one doubled-up sheet at a time, in the middle of the oven for 20 to 25 minutes, until golden brown.

Slide the parchment paper onto a cooling rack and allow the cookies to cool completely before filling.

To make the frosting, mix together the cream cheese and honey until smooth. Stir in the vanilla, lemon zest, and salt. The filling can be made ahead and stored in the refrigerator.

Spread or pipe the frosting onto half of the cookies and use the remaining cookies to top the filling to make a cookie sandwich.

BAKER'S NOTE

The texture of the cookies will be denser when chilled, which I like, but if you want a softer texture, leave them at room temperature for about 30 minutes before serving.

THE VERMONT COMMUNE

■ Dairy-Free

Zucchini Cake-Brownies

No, these are not pot or "magic" brownies, although plenty of those made their way in and out of our commune. The star ingredient in this brownie is actually zucchini, the most prolific veg in my dad's extensive garden. We were always trying to find new ways to use zukes, and I know these brownies would have been a huge hit, with or without the "magic" added. The finely shredded squash adds moistness to this cakey brownie. No one will even know it's in there! I use spelt flour, which is naturally more healthful than white flour. In all whole-wheat flours (including spelt), the outer hull of the wheat—where all the nutrients like the germ and bran—stays intact. Using spelt flour and subbing in honey for refined sugar makes this a more nutritious but still amazingly delicious brownie, especially with that rich cream cheese swirl.

Makes about 16 brownies

Cookie Academy Review
■ Parchment-Paper Sling, see page 39
■ Clean Cut Bars, see page 58
■ Melting Chocolate, see page 59

½ cup / 75g spelt flour (or whole-wheat pastry flour)

¼ cup / 30g blanched almond meal or flour (see page 19)

⅓ cup / 30g natural cocoa or carob powder, sifted if lumpy

¼ tsp baking powder

¼ tsp kosher salt

¼ cup / 55g safflower or vegetable oil

1 oz / 30g unsweetened (baking) chocolate, finely chopped

1 egg, at room temperature

1 egg yolk, at room temperature

½ cup / 85g finely shredded zucchini, tightly packed (see Baker's Note)

¾ cup / 255g honey

2 tsp pure vanilla extract (page 16)

½ cup / 60g toasted chopped walnuts (optional)

⅓ cup / 60g carob or chocolate chips (optional)

Cream Cheese Swirl

4 oz / 112g cream cheese, at room temperature

1 Tbsp honey

1 tsp pure vanilla extract (page 16)

1 pinch of kosher salt

Preheat the oven to 350°F / 175°C. Grease and line an 8-inch / 20cm square cake pan with greased parchment paper, so it goes up the sides like a sling.

In a small bowl, whisk together the spelt, almond meal, cocoa powder, baking powder, and salt. Set aside.

In a saucepan, bring the oil to a simmer, turn off the heat, and add the chopped chocolate. Swirl the pan to cover the chocolate and allow it to sit for 2 minutes. Whisk until smooth.

In a large bowl, whisk the egg, egg yolk, zucchini, honey, and vanilla until well combined. Whisk in the melted chocolate mixture, then fold in the dry ingredients with a rubber spatula. Stir in the walnuts and carob chips (if using). Spread in the prepared pan.

Make the cream cheese swirl: In a small bowl (I reuse the one I used for the dry ingredients), combine the cream cheese, honey, vanilla, and salt. Using a spoon, drizzle lines of the cream cheese mixture over the brownie layer, then use a knife to swirl the two layers together.

Bake in the middle of the oven for 20 to 22 minutes, until a tester comes out with wet crumbs and the brownies are still a bit wobbly in the center. *Do not overbake*, or the brownies will be too dry.

Cool completely in the pan, then cut into squares.

BAKER'S NOTE

There's no need to peel or squeeze the excess liquid from the zucchini; you want the moisture for the brownies. Use the finest grater you have, so the squash bakes through in the quick baking time.

HOLIDAY COOKIES

Granny Neal's Christmas Cookie Tin

There were always two things on the table when we came into Granny Neal's living room on Christmas morning: a full set of Norman Rockwell books—as if to instruct us on how that holiday was meant to look—and tins of homemade Christmas cookies. When I was little in the 1970s, I looked forward to all those cookies on Christmas morning. My well-intentioned hippie parents raised me on a commune, and for them—raisins and carob were considered candy. I ended up a pastry chef, so you can see how I responded to their dietary restrictions. The only time of year I was permitted to eat sugar, and as much as I wanted, was at my Granny's house on Christmas.

Granny Neal had rituals she never strayed from on that Rockwellian holiday. Every year, all the kids in the house would line up at the top of the stairs until Granny, elegantly coiffed and bejeweled, slowly drank her cup of coffee. When the anticipation at the top of the stairs had reached a frenetic crescendo, she'd announce the festivities had begun and we'd slide down the banister to find presents under the tree. Her coffee, as if by magic, would become a tumbler of white wine on ice, and she'd have a cigarette elegantly balanced between her fingers like a movie star—this was the 1970s. There were decorative tins of cookies on every table, in every room. I would search through the layers of cookies within each tin for my favorites, nibbling at the Sugar Cookies (page 97) to find the Maple Coconut Bars (page 127). I couldn't get enough of them; I knew the next day I'd be back on the commune eating carob!

Sugar Cookies

They may seem like a holiday cliché, but making cut-out cookies and building cookie houses are some of my favorite parts of the holiday season. Amid all the hustle and bustle of holiday preparations, I savor the evening when I can put on some music, grab a cup of tea, and settle in for a few hours of cookie decorating. When my boys were young budding cookie "artists," the experience was less meditative but full of love and always entertaining. So when December comes around, I usually need a big stockpile of sugar cookie dough on hand, and this recipe makes a good-sized batch. I like adding both lemon extract and zest to give the cookie dough a bright flavor, but feel free to sub in almond extract and cinnamon if you like a warmer flavor. Decorating the cookies with royal icing made with meringue powder makes a beautiful finish that dries hard and stays intact even if you are sending them to a loved one.

Makes about 48 cookies

Cookie Academy Review

- Freezing the Dough, see page 45
- Rolling the Dough, see page 52
- Batch Baking, see page 56
- Making Royal Icing, see page 60

Cookie Dough

4½ cups / 540g all-purpose flour

2 tsp baking powder

½ tsp kosher salt

1 cup / 220g unsalted butter, at room temperature

1⅔ cups / 332g granulated sugar

2 eggs, at room temperature

2 tsp pure vanilla extract (page 16)

¾ tsp lemon extract (or add any extract you like)

Zest of ½ lemon (optional)

Royal Icing

4 cups / 480g confectioners' sugar, plus more to thicken

¼ cup / 30g meringue powder

¼ cup / 60g cold water or fresh lemon juice, plus more to thin

½ tsp lemon extract (or any other flavor)

Food coloring (optional)

Make the cookie dough: In a large bowl, whisk together the flour, baking powder, and salt.

In a stand mixer fitted with the paddle attachment, cream together the butter and sugar on medium speed until light and fluffy, about 2 minutes. Scrape down the sides of the bowl with a rubber spatula. Add the eggs, one at a time, mixing well between each addition and scraping the bowl. Mix in the vanilla, lemon extract, and zest (if using). Add the flour mixture all at once and mix on low speed just until it all comes together. Scrape down the bowl, increase the speed to medium, and mix for 15 seconds.

Press the dough into a disk, wrap it in plastic, and refrigerate until firm, at least 1 hour. It can be made a couple of days ahead or frozen for up to 3 weeks.

Preheat the oven to 350°F / 175°C. Line baking sheets with parchment paper.

Roll the dough out on a floured surface to a rectangle ⅛ inch / 3mm thick.

Use cookie cutters to create fun shapes out of the dough. Place the cut cookies on the prepared baking sheets, leaving enough room for them to spread slightly, about 1 inch apart. If your dough starts to get warm and sticky, return it to the refrigerator, until firm, about 10 minutes. Warm dough will be difficult to work with.

CONTINUED

Bake, one sheet at a time, in the middle of the oven for 8 to 12 minutes, until just golden on the bottom—you don't want too much color on them. The baking time will depend on the size of the cookie. Let them cool on the baking sheets completely before decorating.

Make the royal icing: In a stand mixer fitted with the whisk attachment, stir together the confectioners' sugar, meringue powder, water, and lemon extract on low speed until blended. Turn up the speed to medium-high and whip until light and fluffy, like meringue, about 3 minutes. It will be quite thick, and you need it this way to create glue if you are making a sugar cookie house. You can thin it with more water or thicken it with more sugar to suit your needs.

Add food coloring (if using) to the icing at this point.

Make sure to keep the icing covered at all times, since it dries hard and will develop a skin of hard icing within minutes. I use a damp clean kitchen towel over the bowl. If the icing sits for several minutes between uses, gently stir the bowl well before using, to get rid of any air bubbles, and to make sure the icing hasn't separated.

Decorate the cookie as you see fit and leave out for about an hour so the icing can harden. The drying time will be determined by the humidity in your kitchen.

▥ VARIATION: FUNFETTI SUGAR COOKIES

If you're short on decorating time (or gusto), whip up funfetti sugar cookies by just folding ½ cup festive sprinkles into the dough. Drop spoonfuls of the dough on a parchment paper–lined baking sheet and sprinkle some extra sprinkles on top before baking.

Stained Glass Holiday Cookies

Adding stained glass to your holiday cookies is a brilliant way to dress up your cookie tins and a fun way to use up leftover sugar cookie or gingerbread dough. The cookie contrasts with the bright candy glass, and they are so pretty if you can hang them on your tree or in a window where they can catch the winter light. Adding this bit of shimmer to a cookie house just brings it all to the next level. If you have littles around doing cookie decorating, this project will keep them plenty busy. They can simply cut out a small hole in the cookie dough using a small cutter and fill the hole with candy. They will love witnessing the candy emerge from the oven magically transformed into brilliantly colored panes of glass. Jolly Ranchers, fruit-flavored Life Savers, or any hard candy will work for this project. Do a test with one cookie to make sure your candy will melt and become smooth before doing a full batch.

Makes about 48 cookies

Cookie Academy Review
▒ Rolling the Dough, see page 52
▒ Batch Baking, see page 56

Sugar Cookie dough (page 97) or Gingerbread Cookie dough (page 103)

48 hard candies (fruit-flavored Life Savers, Jolly Ranchers, hard cinnamon candies, or your favorite hard candy), one for each cookie

Preheat the oven to 325°F / 165°C.

Follow the directions for rolling and cutting out sugar or gingerbread cookies. Lay the cookies on a prepared sheet, as directed. Use a smaller sized cookie cutter to cut a smaller hole in the larger cookie, removing the cut dough to form a window.

Bake the cookie dough for about 3 to 5 minutes, until just set and the dough looks dry. Allow the cookie dough to cool completely before adding the crushed candy. Leave the oven on.

Crush the candy into small pieces using a knife or mortar and pestle.

Fill up the hole you stamped out in the parbaked cookie dough with the crushed candy. Use enough candy to come up to the top of the dough border.

Bake the cookies with the crushed candy for about 5 minutes, until the candies have melted and are smooth. They will be very sticky when hot, but as soon as the candy cools, they will peel right off the parchment and will harden again.

BAKER'S NOTE

Once the windows are filled with candy glass, they cannot be frozen. If you want to bake ahead and freeze them, do so without the candy. You can defrost the cookies, add the candy, and bake as directed.

Sugar Cookie House Instructions

When I moved into my house, it reminded me of a brick wedding cake or confection found on the banquet tables in Elizabethan times. I wanted to re-create it in sugar. I found the original blueprints of the house, and the fate was sealed. I scaled down the drawings and traced it onto parchment, which acted as a stencil for cutting out the dough. I went with sugar cookie dough, instead of the classic gingerbread, because my house is golden yellow, and the sugar cookie was a better match. You can use the gingerbread cookie dough (see page 103) for this project as well. My house has all kinds of fussy details that I re-created with cut-out cookies and piped royal icing. You can also make a simple little house from cookie cutters designed for that purpose, and use pretzels to make an old-world-looking roof. There really are no rules for how these cookie houses look! Baking a bunch of the house pieces and letting your guests build their own version is a terrific holiday party activity for youngsters and grandparents alike.

Cookie Academy Review
- Setting Up and Filling the Piping Bag, see page 44
- Rolling the Dough, see page 52
- Batch Baking, see page 56
- Making Royal Icing, see page 60

Sugar Cookie dough (see page 97)

Royal Icing (page 97)

Make the sugar cookie dough and chill as directed.

Trace the shape of the house onto parchment paper and cut out all the pieces for your template.

Roll the cookie dough to a rectangle about ⅛ to ¼ inch / 3 to 6mm thick. The larger the house, the thicker the cookie dough walls should be to create more stability.

Use the parchment templates of the house to cut out the pieces of dough. Once you have all the sections cut out, carefully transfer them to parchment paper–lined baking sheets. It will require a few sheets and you want to keep cookies of similar sizes on one sheet so they bake evenly.

Use a paring knife or cookie cutter to cut out the windows and doors. Fill windows with hard candy to create glass (see page 99). Bake the cookies as directed.

Once baked, allow to cool completely.

Use royal icing to decorate the details (page 61). I created swirls and flourishes with mini round (Ateco #3 and #4) and star (Ateco #13 and #16) tips. I find this much easier to do while the pieces of the house are lying flat, as opposed to after you have glued them all together and they are upright.

Glue the sides together using thick royal icing. Once you've glued the walls together, allow it to set for several hours so it's strong enough to hold up the roof. I often put heavy cans around the perimeter to hold the pieces in place as they dry.

Use the royal icing to add more flourishes and details around your house. I use a tiny round tip (Wilton #3) to pipe out the filigree from the porch roof railing onto parchment paper. I add flourishes with the star tip (Ateco #13). Let the icing dry completely on the paper and very carefully use a small offset metal spatula to lift the icing off the paper and then use more royal icing to glue it in place.

Once the walls of your house are solid, glue the roof panels on. Decorate with your desired details and cake decorating pearls.

If you have gaps where the pieces come together, simply decorate with royal icing icicles!

Light up the sugar cookie house by lighting a tea light candle and setting it on a plate, then place the house on top. Dust with confectioners' sugar.

Gingerbread Cookies

Cookie stamps and cutters are hands down the best thing ever for busy holiday baking. They come in so many beautiful patterns these days, and it takes just minutes to cut out or stamp fun or even elegant cookies that look like you spent more time on them than you did. I often use cookie stamps when making gingerbread cookies, so this is a gingerbread dough that holds up well and won't spread too much. The details are then accentuated by the maple glaze. Cold dough also helps maintain the pretty pattern, so chill your cookie stamp and your dough before stamping them, and freeze the stamped cookies for 10 to 15 minutes before baking to help set the design. The dough also works perfectly for making gingerbread people. Use the same royal icing you'd use for the sugar cookies (page 97) to decorate them.

Makes about 24 cookies

Cookie Academy Review
- Setting Up and Filling the Piping Bag, see page 44
- Rolling the Dough, see page 52
- Making Stamped or Molded Cookies, see page 52
- Batch Baking, see page 56
- Making Royal Icing, see page 60

Gingerbread Cookie Dough

1¾ cups / 210g all-purpose flour

1 tsp baking soda

2 tsp pumpkin pie spice (or 1 tsp ground cinnamon + ½ tsp ground nutmeg + ½ tsp ground ginger)

1 pinch of kosher salt

¼ cup / 55g unsalted butter, at room temperature

⅓ cup / 65g lightly packed brown sugar

¼ cup / 80g light or dark molasses (not blackstrap)

2 Tbsp water

Maple Glaze (optional)

½ cup / 60g confectioners' sugar

1 Tbsp unsalted butter, melted

¼ cup / 60ml pure maple syrup

2 Tbsp heavy whipping cream, plus more if needed

Royal Icing (page 97; optional)

Make the cookie dough: In a small bowl, whisk together the flour, baking soda, spice, and salt.

In a stand mixer fitted with the paddle attachment, cream the butter, brown sugar, molasses, and water on medium speed until well blended and smooth, about a minute. Scrape the bowl with a spatula to ensure everything is mixed together.

Add the dry ingredients and mix just until it forms a uniform dough.

Wrap the dough and refrigerate for at least 2 hours. This can be made 2 days ahead or frozen for up to 1 month.

IF MAKING STAMPED COOKIES

Preheat the oven to 350°F / 175°C. Line baking sheets with parchment paper.

Form the stamped cookies according to the directions on page 52. Transfer the cookies to the prepared baking sheets. If using different sized cookie stamps, make sure all the cookies on one sheet are the same size so they bake evenly. Leave a bit of room around them so they can expand in the oven without touching. Freeze the cookies for at least 15 minutes.

Bake, one sheet at a time, in the middle of the oven for 8 to 10 minutes, until the cookies look dry and slightly puffed. The timing will vary depending on how thick your cookie dough ends up being.

Leave them on the baking sheet to cool. Bake the remaining cookies. Keep the oven on if you intend to bake again after the cookies are glazed.

Make the glaze: In a medium bowl, whisk together the confectioners' sugar, butter, maple syrup, and cream (an additional tablespoon of cream may be needed to make it spreadable, but it should be thick enough to cling to the cookies).

Using a pastry brush, lightly brush on the glaze and return the cookies to the oven for about 3 minutes so the glaze is slightly absorbed.

CONTINUED

GINGERBREAD COOKIES, CONTINUED

IF MAKING GINGERBREAD PEOPLE

Preheat the oven to 350°F / 175°C. Line baking sheets with parchment paper.

On a lightly floured surface, roll the dough to a rectangle ⅛ inch / 3mm thick and cut out the figures.

Place the cutouts on the prepared pan, leaving a bit of room around them so they can expand in the oven without touching.

Bake, one sheet at a time, in the middle of the oven for 8 to 10 minutes, until the cookies look dry and slightly puffed.

Let them cool on the baking sheets completely before decorating.

Using a piping bag fitted with a small round tip (Ateco #3 or Ateco #4), decorate with the royal icing.

■ Nut-Free   ■ Dairy-Free   ■ Vegan

Ginger Snaps

A regular in Granny Neal's Christmas cookie tins. They aren't the fanciest, but they pack so much flavor and are a family favorite. This ginger cookie really brings the snap. I count on the molasses to provide much of the sugar, so these are not overly sweet and have a nice kick from the ginger—exactly how I like them! They're always great dunked into a glass of milk or a cup of tea, but are also terrific as a crust for Chocolate Ginger Marbled Cheesecake Bars (page 227).

Makes about 60 cookies

Cookie Academy Review
■ Freezing the Dough, see page 45
■ Batch Baking, see page 56

1½ cups / 180g all-purpose flour

½ tsp baking soda

1 tsp unsweetened natural cocoa powder, sifted if lumpy

½ tsp kosher salt

⅓ cup / 105g light or dark molasses (not blackstrap)

2 Tbsp granulated sugar

¼ cup / 57g coconut oil

1 Tbsp plus 1 tsp ground ginger

1 tsp ginger extract (optional)

BAKER'S NOTE

If the cookies lose their snap, you can reheat them in a 350°F / 175°C oven for 5 minutes.

In a large bowl, whisk together the flour, baking soda, cocoa, and salt.

In a small pot, heat the molasses, sugar, coconut oil, ginger, and ginger extract (if using) over medium heat until melted. (This can also be done in the microwave.) Let it cool slightly, about 10 minutes, then pour it over the flour mixture and mix to combine.

On a sheet of plastic wrap, shape the cookie dough into a log 1½ inches / 4cm in diameter.

Refrigerate for at least 1 hour. The dough can also be made 1 day ahead or frozen for up to 1 month.

Preheat the oven to 350°F / 175°C. Line baking sheets with parchment paper.

Using a sharp serrated knife, cut the cookie dough into slices ⅛ inch / 3mm thick and arrange on the prepared baking sheets, leaving about ¾ inch / 2cm of space between them.

Bake, one sheet at a time, in the middle of the oven for 8 to 12 minutes, until golden brown and set. If they are underbaked, they won't have the snap.

Cool completely on the baking sheets; they will get their snap as they cool.

Soft Molasses Cookies

These are the edgy, intensely flavored cousins to the ginger snaps and one that my husband always requests at the holidays. These are soft and chewy, with a sensational spice combination and just a tiny crunch of sugar crust. They get their richness from blackstrap molasses; don't use regular molasses or they lose their edge. But what really gives these a little extra zing is the freshly grated ginger and black pepper. Make sure to watch these in the oven carefully and bake until they are just set. They are easy to overbake, and if you do, you won't get that chewy softness that is essential to this cakey cookie. Dust with a bit of sparkling sugar, if you want a little extra fancy.

Makes about 24 cookies

Cookie Academy Review
- Using a Portion Scoop, see page 43
- Freezing the Dough, see page 45
- Batch Baking, see page 56

4⅔ cups / 560g all-purpose flour

2 tsp ground cinnamon

1 tsp ground ginger

½ tsp ground cardamom

2 tsp baking soda

1 tsp kosher salt

1 cup / 220g unsalted butter, at room temperature

1 cup / 200g granulated sugar

1 cup / 320g blackstrap molasses

2 eggs, at room temperature

1 Tbsp very finely grated, peeled fresh ginger (use a Microplane)

½ tsp ground black pepper

½ cup / 100g clear sparkling decorator sugar or granulated sugar for rolling

Line a baking sheet with parchment paper.

In a bowl, whisk together the flour, cinnamon, ginger, cardamom, baking soda, and salt.

In a stand mixer fitted with the paddle attachment, cream together the butter, sugar, and molasses on medium speed until light and fluffy, about 2 minutes. Scrape down the sides of the bowl with a rubber spatula. Mix in the eggs, one at a time, until well incorporated, scraping down the bowl with a rubber spatula as needed. Mix in the fresh ginger and black pepper. Add the flour mixture all at once and mix on low speed just until it all comes together.

Scoop the cookie dough using a #40 (1½-tablespoon) portion scoop, roll the dough balls in sparkling sugar, place onto the prepared baking sheet, leaving about 1½ inches of space between them to spread and flatten the balls slightly. Refrigerate the cookie dough balls for at least 30 minutes. The dough can also be made the day before or frozen for a few weeks. You can make the cookies larger or smaller, but it will affect the baking time.

Preheat the oven to 375°F / 190°C.

Bake, one sheet at a time, in the middle of the oven for 10 to 12 minutes, until the cookies are puffed, look slightly dry, and are golden brown just on the bottom. Don't overbake or they lose their soft texture.

Cool completely on the baking sheets.

Linzer Cookies

If you've seen my show, *Zoë Bakes*, you'll know this recipe went through a bit of a journey before I got the stamp of approval from my family. I adore traditional Linzer cookies, which draw their inspiration from the Austrian *Linzertorte* pastry. It is a rich cake made with finely ground nut flour and is layered with raspberry preserves. The cookie version of the famous pastry is crisp and smaller in size. The first batch I made was with almond flour, and my boys thought the flavor was good but that it needed some pow! I switched to hazelnuts, added chocolate ganache along with the raspberry, and dusted the cookies with a shower of confectioners' sugar. This combination was the winner with the boys, and I think you and your family will love it, too. I've also made the cookies with pecan flour, which is super-delicious. The takeaway is to experiment with a variety of nut flours and fillings. Not only can you play with the flavor, but these look great in a variety of shapes and sizes, so express yourself.

Makes about 24 sandwich cookies

Cookie Academy Review
- Freezing the Dough, see page 45
- Rolling the Dough, see page 52
- Batch Baking, see page 56
- Ganache SOS, see page 59

1⅔ cups / 212g hazelnuts or whole almonds, toasted

1½ cups / 180g all-purpose flour, divided

1½ tsp ground cinnamon

½ tsp baking powder

½ tsp kosher salt

¾ cup / 170g unsalted butter, at room temperature

⅔ cup / 130g granulated sugar

1 egg, at room temperature

1 tsp pure vanilla extract (page 16)

¼ tsp lemon zest

Filling

Bittersweet Chocolate Ganache (page 213), cooled to room temperature (optional)

¼ cup / 75g raspberry preserves (any flavor works)

Confectioners' sugar for dusting

In a food processor, pulse the hazelnuts and ½ cup / 60g of the flour until the nuts are finely ground. Pulse in the remaining 1 cup / 120g of flour, the cinnamon, baking powder, and salt.

In a stand mixer fitted with the paddle attachment, cream the butter and sugar on medium-high speed until light in color and texture, about 3 minutes. Add the egg, vanilla, and zest, mixing on medium-low speed until well combined. Add the flour mixture and mix on low just until combined. The dough will be soft. Wrap the dough in plastic wrap and refrigerate for about 2 hours. This dough can also be made a couple of days ahead and frozen for up to 1 month.

Line two baking sheets with parchment paper. Remove half the dough and roll it out on a lightly floured silicone mat to a rectangle about ⅛ inch / 3mm thick. Using a cookie cutter dipped in flour, cut out the cookies. Use a 2-inch cookie cutter for the cookies and a ¼-inch to ¾-inch cookie cutter for the small holes. Transfer to the prepared baking sheets, leaving at least a ½ inch / 1.3cm of space between them. You can press the scraps together, chill, and reroll, up to two times. Refrigerate the cookies after they are cut for at least 30 minutes before baking. They can also be made the day before, covered, and refrigerated or frozen for 1 month.

Using a small round cookie cutter or large round piping tip, stamp out the centers of half the cookies to create holes in the middles.

Preheat the oven to 350°F / 175°C.

Bake, one sheet at a time, in the middle of the oven for about 15 minutes, until lightly browned. Cool on the baking sheets completely before filling and decorating.

Separate the cookies with holes stamped out and dust them with confectioners' sugar.

Spread a thin layer of ganache (if using) over the cookies without holes. Spread a small amount of raspberry preserves on top of each. Sandwich together the cookies with holes stamped out on top of the ones without holes. Press lightly so the filling just starts to come through the hole in the top.

GRANNY NEAL'S CHRISTMAS COOKIE TIN

Hazelnut Spice Speculaas

In the Netherlands, Belgium, and nearby European countries, heavily spiced speculaas cookies and other treats have been made for centuries to celebrate the feast of St. Nicholas. Intricately carved wooden cookie molds were traditionally used to shape the cookies. You can sometimes find vintage molds in a variety of shapes online, or modern reproductions. I have found that both ceramic and plastic molds work as well, as do metal stamps. No matter the molds or stamps you use, make sure to dust them with plenty of cornstarch and to keep your dough chilled to ensure a nice clean impression. The results are stunning, and you'll have cookies that are almost too pretty to eat—but they're too tasty not to! These are delightful plain or with a very thin icing that's scented with amaretto.

These holiday speculaas cookies are a little different from the speculoos cookies (page 169) in the Worldly Cookies: My Home-Ec Cookie Evolution chapter. Along with the slightly different spelling, these cookies are amped up with spices, hazelnuts, and a bit of cream to soften them up some.

Makes about 12 cookies, depending on your mold size

Cookie Academy Review
▓ Rolling the Dough, see page 52
▓ Making Stamped or Molded Cookies, see page 52
▓ Batch Baking, see page 56

½ cup / 110g unsalted butter, at room temperature

¾ cup / 150g lightly packed brown sugar

1 egg yolk, at room temperature

1 Tbsp heavy whipping cream, at room temperature

1½ cups / 180g all-purpose flour

¼ cup / 35g hazelnut meal or flour (see page 19)

¼ tsp baking powder

¼ tsp kosher salt

¾ tsp ground cinnamon

½ tsp ground nutmeg

½ tsp ground cloves

Icing (optional)

½ cup / 60g confectioners' sugar, plus more as needed

1 Tbsp / 15g unsalted butter, melted

¼ cup / 60ml amaretto (or your favorite liqueur)

2 to 3 Tbsp heavy whipping cream, plus more as needed

In a stand mixer fitted with the paddle attachment, beat the butter and brown sugar at medium speed until creamy, about 3 minutes, stopping to scrape the bowl. Add the yolk and cream and beat until it is thoroughly combined, about 1 minute.

In a medium bowl, whisk together the flour, hazelnut meal, baking powder, salt, cinnamon, nutmeg, and cloves.

With the mixer on low speed, gradually add the flour mixture to the butter mixture, beating until just combined. Wrap the dough in plastic wrap. Refrigerate for at least 2 hours, or up to overnight.

Line baking sheets with parchment paper.

▓ IF MAKING MOLDED COOKIES

Generously brush the cookie molds with cornstarch. Quickly knead a small amount of the chilled dough on a lightly floured surface.

Roll it out to a thickness of about ¼ inch / 6mm, dust the surface with flour, and press it into the prepared mold. Work quickly, so the dough doesn't become warm and sticky. Gently pry the dough from the mold and place it on the prepared baking sheet. Repeat with the remaining chilled dough.

Refrigerate the sheets of cookies until well chilled, about 30 minutes.

CONTINUED

▒ IF MAKING STAMPED COOKIES

Roll out all the dough to a thickness of ¼ inch / 6mm and use a cutter that matches the size of your stamp. Place the rounds on the prepared baking sheets, leaving enough space for them to spread when stamped and baked.

Brush the stamp with cornstarch or dust with granulated sugar and press the individual dough circles with the stamp. Work quickly, so the dough doesn't get warm and sticky. Refrigerate the dough if it does get too sticky. Once all the cookies are stamped and on the prepared baking sheets, refrigerate them until well chilled, about 30 minutes.

Preheat the oven to 350°F / 175°C.

Bake, one sheet at a time, in the middle of the oven for 8 to 12 minutes, until the edges are golden. The baking time will vary depending on how thick the cookies are. Allow the cookies to cool on the pan completely before decorating.

Make the icing: In a small bowl, whisk together the confectioners' sugar, butter, amaretto, and 2 tablespoons cream, until smooth. The consistency should be thick enough to coat the cookies, but thin enough to see the details of the mold or stamp. If it is too thick, add more cream. If it is too thin, add more confectioners' sugar. Using a pastry brush, lightly brush on the glaze and return to the oven for about 2 minutes so the glaze is absorbed slightly.

Granny's Espresso Shortbread

My Granny Neal always made this espresso shortbread around the holidays. It's studded with hunks of walnuts, and the specks of espresso give the shortbread a rich bold flavor and an elegant look. I remember my aunt Kristin, who is a huge fan of shortbread, always munching on these. But, in recent years, she admitted to me that she always thought Granny Neal could have used a little more sugar in her shortbread. So in Kristin's honor, I upped the sugar content, and it was a great idea, as it balances out the espresso and brings out the richness of the butter even more. This cookie always makes me nostalgic and brings up memories of the holiday season, but it's wonderful any time of the year.

Makes about 75 cookies

Cookie Academy Review
▥ Freezing the Dough, see page 45
▥ Batch Baking, see page 56

1 cup / 220g unsalted butter, at room temperature

¾ cup / 150g lightly packed brown sugar

1 tsp pure vanilla extract (page 16)

1½ tsp espresso powder

2¼ cups / 270g all-purpose flour

½ tsp kosher salt

2 cups / 240g walnuts pieces

In a stand mixer fitted with the paddle attachment, cream the butter, brown sugar, vanilla, and espresso powder on medium speed until just uniform, about 1 minute. Add the flour and salt and mix on medium-low speed until it just comes together. Stir in the walnuts.

Form the dough into a 2-inch / 5cm thick log. Wrap in plastic and refrigerate for at least an hour. You can do this step a couple of days in advance of baking or freeze for 1 month.

Preheat the oven to 325°F / 165°C. Line baking sheets with parchment paper.

Cut the log into slices ¼ inch / 6mm thick and arrange the cookies on the prepared baking sheets. They won't spread much but give them a little room just in case.

Bake, one sheet at a time, in the middle of the oven for 12 to 14 minutes, until golden on the bottom. Cool the cookies until firm on the baking sheet and then move to a cooling rack.

▦ Nut-Free

Lemon Lavender Shortbread Cookies

My aunt Kristin absolutely loves shortbread and requests a batch for every special occasion. It was something her mom (my Granny) made for the holidays, and Kristin would pull them out of the cookie tins to keep for herself. Luckily, I have Granny's recipe and can bake them for Kristin whenever she wants. Shortbread is just about the ultimate treat for gifting. It's super easy to bake and stack up in tins or boxes, and it freezes like a dream. The basic, buttery shortbread—the high butter content creates its dense and rich texture—creates a sublime canvas for all kinds of flavor possibilities. Granny stuck to the classic buttery flavor, but this lemon lavender version remains one of my favorites. I love how the flecks of lavender add a touch of elegance and just a hint of blossomy sweetness. Drop a batch off to a loved one to brighten their spirits on a rainy spring day.

Makes about 40 cookies

▦ Parchment-Paper Sling, see page 39

½ cup / 100g granulated sugar

Zest of ½ lemon (optional)

¾ cup plus 2 Tbsp / 194g unsalted butter, at room temperature

1 egg yolk, at room temperature

2¾ cups / 330g all-purpose flour

½ tsp kosher salt

2 tsp lavender buds (optional; try other herbs and spices if you wish)

½ vanilla bean, scraped, or 1 tsp pure vanilla extract (page 16)

1 tsp fresh lemon juice, plus more if needed

Grease and line an 8-inch square cake pan with greased parchment paper, so it comes up over the sides to act as a sling.

In a small bowl, mix together the sugar and lemon zest (if using). Rub the zest into the sugar, so it really coats the sugar crystals.

In a stand mixer fitted with the paddle attachment, cream the butter, sugar mixture, and yolk together on medium-high speed until light and fluffy, about 3 minutes. Add the flour, salt, lavender (if using), and vanilla, and mix on low speed until the dough just starts to come together. Add the lemon juice and continue mixing on low speed until the dough comes together. It will seem crumbly but should hold together when pressed. If your dough isn't coming together, add a little more lemon juice, a teaspoon at a time.

Dump the dough into the prepared pan. Pat the dough into the pan and smooth it under a sheet of plastic. Refrigerate for at least 30 minutes, but this step can also be done a day ahead.

Preheat the oven to 300°F / 150°C.

Using a paring knife, cut the chilled dough into any shape or size you want.

Use a fork to dock the tops. This is purely decorative. Make a classic pattern, or get more creative if you like.

Bake in the middle of the oven for 20 to 30 minutes, until just golden. They shouldn't take on much color and will look dry. You only want to bake them until they are just starting to turn golden on the bottom. They are traditionally very pale.

The shortbread needs to be totally cooled before they can be removed from the pan. Once they are cooled, remove from the pan and break along the scored lines.

BAKER'S NOTE

The dough can also be pressed into a log, wrapped in plastic, refrigerated until firm, and then sliced into coins. The baking time will be determined by how thick your coins are. I tend to cut them into ¼-inch-thick coins and bake for about 15 minutes.

Almond Spritz Cookies

Almond paste and cardamom are Scandinavian staples that give these cookies a beautiful flavor and texture. They have lots of body to them, which makes them a terrific addition to your holiday cookie tins. You can add colors, sprinkles, or decorating sugar to these as well, but I like them *au naturel*. These are rare cookies that I think improve over a couple of days after being baked.

Makes about 48 cookies

Cookie Academy Review
- Setting Up and Filling the Piping Bag, see page 44
- Batch Baking, see page 56

7 oz / 200g almond paste, chopped into ½-inch / 1.25cm pieces

⅓ cup / 75g granulated sugar

¾ cup / 165g unsalted butter, at room temperature

½ tsp almond extract

¼ tsp kosher salt

2 egg whites (¼ cup / 60g)

2 cups / 240g all-purpose flour

½ tsp ground cardamom (optional)

Preheat the oven to 350°F / 175°C. Double up two baking sheets and line them with parchment paper. The double sheets will prevent the cookie bottoms from getting too dark.

In a food processor, blend together the almond paste and sugar, until it breaks into tiny pieces. Add the butter a little at a time and pulse several times to blend, until all the butter is added. Scrape down the bowl after each addition. Add the almond extract and salt.

Add the egg whites and pulse to combine. Scrape down the bowl.

Add the flour and cardamom (if using), and pulse several times, until just combined. The dough will be quite thick. Be sure to mix the dough with a rubber spatula to make sure it is an even consistency.

Using a spritz press or a pastry bag with a large star tip, press or pipe out the cookies in your desired shapes and sizes onto the prepared pans, leaving about an inch between. Be sure all the cookies on one sheet are the same size, so they bake at the same rate.

Bake, one sheet at a time, in the middle of the oven for 8 to 12 minutes, until the edges are barely golden (they should still be quite pale). The baking time will vary based on the size of the cookie. Cool completely on the baking sheet.

Nut-Free

Krumkaker (Norwegian Waffle Cookies)

I made these as a tribute to my Norwegian Granny and her famous Swedish creme served at every Christmas. It always baffled me that she made Swedish creme, which I later came to realize is the same as panna cotta, for the holidays, when she was so fiercely proud of her Norwegian heritage. There wasn't a drop of Swede in her or that dessert! Such a mystery. One thing I do know is these delicate, crispy Norwegian waffle cookies are the perfect pairing for the creamy dessert and so representative of her heritage.

Makes 24 cookies

4 eggs, at room temperature

1 cup / 200g granulated sugar

½ cup / 110g unsalted butter, melted

½ tsp pure vanilla extract (page 16)

1⅔ cups / 195g all-purpose flour

2 Tbsp cornstarch

½ tsp cinnamon

½ tsp ground cardamom

¼ tsp ground ginger

¼ tsp ground anise

¼ tsp kosher salt

In a stand mixer fitted with a whisk attachment, whip the eggs with the sugar on high speed until light yellow. Add the butter and vanilla and mix until combined.

In a medium bowl, whisk together the flour, cornstarch, cinnamon, cardamom, ginger, anise, and salt. Add to the egg mixture and mix on low speed until combined.

Preheat a krumkake iron. When the iron is hot, spoon about 1 tablespoon of the batter on top of each mold and close the iron. Cook for about a minute, or until the krumkake reaches your desired darkness and crispiness. Let each krumkake cool around a cone-shaped wooden dowel or lay flat on a cooling rack before enjoying. Repeat with the remaining batter. These are best served right after they have cooled.

Caramelized White Chocolate Sablés with Sea Salt

Sablés, aka Breton cookies, are simple butter cookies that are very popular in France. They provide a great canvas for flavor experimentation, and, in this holiday-worthy version, I've added chocolate. White chocolate often leaves me wanting more flavor, so caramelizing it before adding it to the cookie batter gives it all the toasty notes of dulce de leche plus the richness of chocolate. The chocolate may go through an awkward phase as it caramelizes, but don't panic, it will melt into a golden delight by the end. I mention it in the ingredients portion of this book (page 12), and I'll mention it again here: Don't use coating chocolate! The sprinkle of flaky sea salt at the end provides a nice contrast to the sweetness of the white chocolate.

Makes about 80 cookies

Cookie Academy Review
- Freezing the Dough, see page 45
- Batch Baking, see page 56
- Melting Chocolate, see page 59

1½ cups / 255g white chocolate, finely chopped (not coating chocolate), divided

11 Tbsp / 157g unsalted butter, at room temperature

¾ cup / 150g granulated sugar

2 egg yolks, at room temperature

1 tsp pure vanilla extract (page 16)

2 cups / 240g all-purpose flour

½ tsp kosher salt

Flaky sea salt for finishing

Caramelize the white chocolate: Preheat the oven to 300°F / 150°C. Line a baking sheet with a silicone baking mat.

Distribute the white chocolate evenly over the prepared baking sheet. Bake for about 5 minutes, until they start to melt. Spread the chocolate with a spatula into a thin layer. Bake for another 5 minutes, then stir the chocolate. Repeat until the chocolate is the color of caramel. The chocolate may liquefy or it may become granular. If the chocolate is grainy, while still warm, put it in a coffee grinder or blender to smooth it out. It doesn't need to be perfectly smooth at this point. Place ⅓ cup / 57g in a small bowl and cool slightly. Place the remaining chocolate in the refrigerator to harden.

Make the cookie dough: In a stand mixer fitted with the paddle attachment, beat the butter and sugar at medium speed until creamy, about 3 minutes, stopping to scrape the bowl. Add the yolk and vanilla and mix until incorporated, about 1 minute. Mix in ⅓ cup / 57g of the softened caramelized white chocolate.

With the mixer on low speed, gradually add the flour and salt to the butter mixture, beating until just combined. Chop up the remaining chilled, caramelized chocolate and mix into the dough.

Divide the dough in half and form each piece into a log 1½ inches / 4cm in diameter. Wrap the dough in plastic wrap. Refrigerate for at least 1 hour, or up to overnight.

Preheat the oven to 350°F / 180°C. Line two baking sheets with parchment paper.

Slice the cookies into coins ⅛ inch / 3mm thick and lay them on the prepared baking sheets, spaced ¾ inch / 2cm apart, so they have a little room to spread. Bake the cookies, one sheet at a time, in the middle of the oven for 8 to 10 minutes, until the edges are golden. Allow the cookies to cool completely on the baking sheets.

BAKER'S NOTE

You can swap out milk chocolate for the caramelized white chocolate in the recipe.

Nut-Free

Chocolate Crinkle Cookies

According to my Granny's 1956 edition of *Betty Crocker's Picture Cook Book*, a version of this cookie was developed by Mrs. Fredell of St. Paul, Minnesota. Her original recipe was made with spices and nuts, but the concept of rolling a cookie in sugar and letting it crackle in the oven captured the imagination and gave birth to a whole category of crinkle cookies. I love this chocolate version because the intensity of the chocolate with just a hint of coffee is in perfect balance with the crust of sugar. The trick to a properly dramatic crinkle in the sugar seems to be a double dip, once in granulated sugar and then in confectioners' sugar. The results are fudgy and crunchy at the same time.

Makes about 26 cookies

Cookie Academy Review
- Using a Portion Scoop, see page 43
- Batch Baking, see page 56

1 cup / 120g all-purpose flour

½ cup / 40g Dutch-processed cocoa powder, sifted if lumpy

1¼ tsp baking powder

½ tsp kosher salt

½ tsp espresso powder (optional)

½ cup / 110g unsalted butter, at room temperature

¾ cup / 150g granulated sugar, plus additional for rolling

1 tsp pure vanilla extract (page 16)

1 egg, at room temperature

2 oz / 56g bittersweet chocolate, finely chopped (optional)

½ cup / 60g confectioners' sugar for rolling

In a medium bowl, whisk together the flour, cocoa powder, baking powder, salt, and espresso powder (if using).

In a stand mixer fitted with the paddle attachment, cream together the butter, sugar, and vanilla on medium speed until light and fluffy, about 2 minutes. Scrape down the sides of the bowl with a rubber spatula. Mix in the egg until well incorporated. Scrape down the bowl again.

Add the flour mixture all at once and mix on low speed just until it all comes together. Scrape down the bowl. Turn the speed to medium and mix for 15 seconds. Turn the speed down to low, add the chopped chocolate (if using), and mix until just incorporated.

Line a baking sheet with parchment paper.

Scoop the cookie dough using a #70 (1-tablespoon) portion scoop onto the prepared baking sheet. Roll each dough ball in the palm of your hand to make a round sphere. Roll the cookies in granulated sugar. Freeze the dough balls for about 15 minutes (they should be very cold, but not frozen solid) or refrigerate for at least 30 minutes.

Preheat the oven to 375°F. Line two baking sheets with parchment paper.

Dip the cookies in the confectioners' sugar and place them onto the prepared baking sheets, leaving 3 inches between each cookie. They will spread!

Bake, one sheet at a time, in the middle of the oven for 8 to 10 minutes, until the cookies puff up, the centers no longer look wet, and the sugar coating looks crinkled. Don't overbake the cookies, or they will become crispy.

Cool completely on the baking sheet before moving.

GRANNY NEAL'S CHRISTMAS COOKIE TIN

▨ Nut-Free

Chocolate Brownie Mint Sandwiches

If you are looking for a stand-out cookie for the holiday tray, these get extra points for indulgence. Fluffy mint buttercream is sandwiched between rich dark chocolate brownies, which are then rolled in crushed candy cane for a festive look and an extra little satisfying crunch. Use a good-quality dark chocolate for these, and take care to beat the eggs and sugar together until they are light and foamy to ensure that shiny, crackly top characteristic of great brownies. The texture becomes denser and even more decadent if served chilled.

Makes about 12 cookie
sandwiches

Cookie Academy Review
▨ Using a Portion Scoop,
see page 43
▨ Batch Baking, see page 56

Brownie Cookie

12 oz / 350g dark
chocolate, finely chopped,
divided

3 Tbsp unsalted butter

2 eggs, at room temperature

¾ cup / 150g granulated
sugar

1 tsp pure vanilla extract
(page 16)

⅓ cup / 40g all-purpose
flour

¼ tsp baking powder

1 pinch of kosher salt

Mint Buttercream

½ cup / 110g unsalted
butter, at room temperature

1 cup / 120g confectioners'
sugar

¼ tsp mint extract

Candy canes, crushed
for garnish

Preheat the oven to 350°F / 175°C. Line two baking sheets with parchment paper.

Fill the bottom of a double boiler or a medium saucepan with 1 inch / 2.5cm of water and bring to a gentle simmer over medium-low heat. In a large stainless steel bowl over the double boiler, melt half (6 oz / 175g) of the chopped chocolate with the butter and stir until smooth. Remove from the heat.

In a stand mixer fitted with the whisk attachment, beat the eggs, sugar, and vanilla until light and foamy, about 5 minutes.

In a small bowl, whisk the flour, baking powder, and salt.

Stir the flour mixture into the melted chocolate. Fold the chocolate mixture into the whipped eggs along with the remaining 6 oz / 175g chopped chocolate.

Let the mixture sit for 10 minutes to allow the chocolate to set firm.

Scoop the cookie dough using a #70 (2½-teaspoon) portion scoop onto the prepared baking sheets, leaving about 3 inches between them. You can make the cookies larger or smaller, but it will affect the baking time.

Bake, one sheet at a time, in the middle of the oven for about 8 minutes, until the tops are puffed and just start to crack. Take care to not overbake them.

Allow the cookies to cool completely before peeling them off the parchment paper to fill them.

Make the mint buttercream: In a medium bowl, mix the butter and confectioners' sugar with a wooden spoon or handheld mixer until smooth and fluffy. Add the mint extract to taste.

Spread the buttercream onto half of the cookies and then top with the remaining cookies.

Dip the edges in the crushed candy cane.

Cover and refrigerate until you are ready to serve. These can also be made a day ahead.

Maple Coconut Bars

These are inspired by my Granny's holiday coconut bars, which I later realized came straight from the pages of *Ladies' Home Journal*. I took her traditional bars and gave them a modern spin. For this recipe, I brown the butter in the crust, so the cookies have a toasty, rich nuttiness. In homage to my hippie Vermont roots, I also added a bit of pure maple syrup to the sticky coconut layer to give it a more complex flavor and hit of nostalgia. They are still very much reminiscent of the delicious layered Christmas bars my Granny made, but sometimes traditions can be added to and made anew, without losing their original magic. My Granny has long passed, and with her went the wine and cigarettes, but my memory of her fondly lives on. I was just at my dad's house, and he still has her set of Norman Rockwell books prominently displayed. Every time I make these cookies, I do so in her honor.

Makes 16 bars

Cookie Academy Review
▓ Parchment-Paper Sling, see page 39
▓ Making Pressed Dough Crust, see page 54
▓ Clean Cut Bars, see page 58

Crust

¼ cup / 56g brown butter (page 41), melted and slightly cooled

1 egg yolk

½ cup / 100g lightly packed brown sugar

1 cup plus 3 Tbsp / 140g all-purpose flour

¼ tsp kosher salt

Maple Coconut Filling

¼ cup / 80g pure maple syrup

One 14-oz / 396g can sweetened condensed milk

1 Tbsp pure vanilla extract (page 16)

1 egg white, at room temperature

¼ tsp kosher salt

1 tsp pumpkin pie spice (or ½ tsp ground cinnamon + ¼ tsp ground nutmeg + ¼ tsp ground ginger)

2 cups / 200g loosely packed sweetened shredded coconut

1 cup / 170g finely chopped semisweet or dark chocolate or mini chips

1 cup / 120g chopped pecans, toasted

Make the crust: Prepare an 8-inch square cake pan with greased aluminum foil that completely covers the pan and goes up the sides, then line with a parchment-paper sling.

Preheat the oven to 350°F / 175°C.

In a large bowl, whisk together the brown butter and yolk until combined. Add the brown sugar, flour, and salt. Blend with a spoon or your fingers until it is uniformly mixed. It may be a bit crumbly, but not dry.

Distribute the dough evenly and press it into the prepared pan. Cover with plastic wrap so you can easily smooth it. Freeze until solid, about 5 minutes. Bake in the middle of the oven for 12 to 15 minutes, until the crust is golden brown. Allow the crust to cool on a rack while you make the filling. Leave the oven on.

Make the filling: In a large bowl, whisk together the maple syrup, condensed milk, vanilla, egg white, salt, and pumpkin pie spice. Stir in the coconut, chocolate, and nuts. Spread the mixture over the baked crust.

Bake in the middle of the oven for 30 to 35 minutes, until the topping turns golden brown.

Cool slightly before removing from the pan. Cool completely on a cooling rack before cutting into bars.

Bubbe Berkowitz's Cookies

Family recipes are such a gift. They pass on our history in the most delicious way. Some of the recipes in this chapter traveled with my mother's side of the family for multiple generations, and some of the recipes were inspired by my Jewish ancestors and their love of baking. So many Jewish holidays are celebrated with cookies: such as the tri-cornered Hamantaschen (page 141) served at Purim and the Coconut "Haystack" Macaroons (page 131) and Chocolate Caramel Matzo (page 151) made for Passover. When I worked in catering, the Jewish weddings and bar and bat mitzvahs were always filled with tins of cookies brought by the family of those being celebrated. The cookies meant pure love.

▦ Gluten-Free   ▦ Dairy-Free

Coconut "Haystack" Macaroons

I know, the whole macaroon/macaron thing is rather confusing. It's helpful to think of both as derivatives of a cookie that has evolved over hundreds of years with each version maintaining that base of egg whites and sugar. In this version of macaroons, almonds are subbed out with coconut.

These are one of my favorite Passover cookies. I find the commercially made ones dense and too sweet, but the homemade ones are delightful, chewy treats that are so easy to make. These cookies were inspired by Tom Gumpel, my former professor at the Culinary Institute of America (CIA). He added all kinds of dried fruits—raisins, cranberries, apricots, and cherries—for added sweetness and extra chew. Over the years, I've experimented with various flavors, such as jaggery, ground cardamom, and chocolate (see variation) to satisfy whatever cravings I have.

Makes 30 cookies

Cookie Academy Review
▦ Using a Portion Scoop, see page 43
▦ Batch Baking, see page 56

1 cup / 200g granulated sugar

½ cup / 120g egg whites (about 4 large)

½ tsp pure vanilla extract (page 16)

¼ tsp kosher salt

3 cups / 320g loosely packed sweetened angel flake coconut and/or shreds

½ tsp ground cinnamon

½ cup / 70g raisins (chopped or whole)

1 cup / 150g chopped dried fruit (raisins, apricots, cherries, and/or craisins)

½ cup / 60g finely chopped pecans or walnuts

Confectioners' sugar for dusting

Preheat the oven to 350°F / 175°C. Line two doubled-up baking sheets or insulated cookie sheets with lightly greased parchment paper or silicone mats. The doubled-up baking sheets will protect the bottoms from getting too dark.

In a large stainless steel bowl, whisk together the granulated sugar and egg whites.

Fill the bottom of a double boiler or a medium sauce-pan with 1 inch / 2.5cm of water and bring to a gentle simmer over medium-low heat. Place the bowl with the sugar mixture over the double boiler and stir the mixture with a rubber spatula until the sugar is completely melted. This can take about 5 minutes. Brush down the sides of the bowl with the spatula to make sure all the sugar is melted and no grains are clinging to the side. Feel the mixture between your fingers to check for graininess.

Remove the sugar mixture from the heat and add the vanilla, salt, coconut, cinnamon, raisins, dried fruit, and nuts. Stir well to incorporate. Allow it to sit for 30 minutes. It can also be made ahead of time and refrigerated for up to 48 hours.

Stir before portioning out the haystacks using an ice cream scoop. Be sure that the batter is tightly packed in the scoop before releasing it onto the prepared baking sheets, spacing the cookies about two inches apart. If you are using a #40 (1½-tablespoon) portion scoop, you will get about 15 per sheet.

Bake, with racks in the top and bottom thirds of the oven, for about 20 minutes until golden brown on the top and bottom, rotating the trays and switching from top to bottom halfway through baking.

Allow to cool completely on parchment paper, lift the cookies to unstick them from the paper, and then dust with confectioners' sugar.

▦ **VARIATION: JAGGERY & CHAI SPICE MACAROONS WITH PISTACHIO, DIPPED IN CHOCOLATE**

Replace the cup of sugar with 1 cup / 170g jaggery powder: ¼ tsp ground cardamom, ¼ tsp ground ginger, ¼ tsp ground nutmeg, ⅛ tsp ground clove, and ⅛ tsp ground allspice. Replace the pecans with pistachios. Add ¼ tsp orange blossom or rose water. Bake and cool as directed. In place of the confectioners' sugar, dip the bottoms in 4 oz of melted white chocolate and sprinkle with dried edible rose petals and ground pistachios.

Dairy-Free

Coconut Macaroon Brownies for Passover (or any other day)

These are two of my favorite things—rich chocolaty brownie and toasty coconut macaroon—married together into one decadent treat. Using the matzo cake meal ensures the brownie is kosher fare for Passover, but it does give the brownie a slightly different texture and can produce a dry brownie easily if you overbake it. The trick to success is to freeze the brownie layer so it doesn't dry out in the oven while the macaroon layer bakes to toasty perfection. I learned this trick from Jake Cohen in his book *Jew-ish!*, and it works brilliantly. It's a sweet worthy of the high holy days or any time you want a delicious chewy, chocolaty treat.

Makes 16 brownies

Cookie Academy Review
- Parchment-Paper Sling, see page 39
- Clean Cut Bars, see page 58

Brownie Layer

½ cup / 118ml vegetable oil

2 oz / 60g unsweetened (baking) chocolate, chopped

1 cup / 200g granulated sugar

2 eggs, at room temperature

⅓ cup / 30g matzo cake meal

⅓ cup / 30g unsweetened natural cocoa powder, sifted if lumpy

¾ cup / 135g semisweet chocolate chips

Coconut Macaroon Layer

3 large egg whites (6 Tbsp / 90g)

½ cup / 100g granulated sugar

1 pinch of kosher salt

1 tsp white vinegar

1 tsp almond extract

2 tsp potato starch (or cornstarch or tapioca starch)

1⅔ cups / 160g loosely packed sweetened angel flake coconut

Make the brownies: Grease an 8-inch square cake pan and line with greased parchment paper that goes up the sides of the pan to create a sling.

In a small pot, heat the oil over medium heat until hot—if you stick a wooden spoon in the oil, you'll see small bubbles form around it. Turn off the heat and add the chopped chocolate. Allow the chocolate to sit for 1 minute, then whisk until smooth. Add the sugar and eggs and whisk together. Sift together the matzo meal and cocoa powder to remove any lumps, then stir it into the chocolate mixture.

Spread the chocolate mixture evenly into the prepared pan and sprinkle the chocolate chips over the top. Freeze the brownie mixture while preparing the macaroon layer. If you don't freeze the brownies, they will overbake and become too dry in the oven.

Make the coconut macaroon layer: Preheat the oven to 375°F / 190°F.

In a stand mixer fitted with a whisk attachment, whip the egg whites on medium-high speed until foamy. Turn the speed down and sprinkle in the sugar, then turn the speed to high and whip until stiff peaks form. Add the salt, vinegar, and almond extract and whip until combined.

Remove the bowl from the mixer and gently fold in the potato starch using the whisk attachment or a rubber spatula. Fold in the coconut. Spread the mixture over the frozen brownies.

Bake in the middle of the oven for 35 minutes, until the top is lightly toasted and a tester comes out with moist chocolate crumbs. Allow to cool to room temperature before removing from the pan and serving. Use a sharp knife dipped in hot water to cut the brownies cleanly.

■ Gluten-Free ■ Dairy-Free

Almond Macaroons

These delicate cookies call back to those made in Italian convents in the eighth century. Made from egg whites, sugar, and ground almonds, they were the early predecessors of the airy macaron (page 161). Because they are unleavened, aren't made with flour, and are dairy-free, these cookies satisfied Passover dietary restrictions. They became so popular with the Italian Jewish population that the macaroon recipe has stayed pretty much the same for hundreds of years. My Bubbe Berkowitz always had the store-bought version of these on hand at the holidays. I liked the plastic-wrapped variety just fine as a kid, but then I had the real deal in Italy, and I can never look back. The homemade version is infinitely better; it's soft and chewy, rich with almond flavor, and is topped with a sprinkling of pearl sugar that gives it a little extra crunch.

Makes about 36 cookies

Cookie Academy Review
■ Using a Portion Scoop, see page 43
■ Batch Baking, see page 56

8 oz / 226g almond paste, broken into ½-inch / 1.3cm pieces

1 cup / 200g granulated sugar

3 egg whites (⅓ cup / 90g)

⅔ cup / 80g almond meal or flour (see page 19)

½ tsp almond extract

1 tsp pure vanilla extract (page 16)

¼ tsp kosher salt

½ cup / 55g sliced almonds

Pearl sugar for finishing

Preheat the oven to 350°F. Line two baking sheets with parchment paper.

In a food processor, combine the almond paste and sugar, until finely chopped. Add the egg whites, one at a time, and combine until a paste forms. Add the almond meal, almond and vanilla extracts, and salt, pulsing until combined.

Scoop the cookie dough using a #70 (2½-teaspoon) portion scoop onto the prepared baking sheets, leaving about 2 inches between the cookies. Sprinkle the tops with sliced almonds and pearl sugar.

Bake, one sheet at a time, in the middle of the oven for 15 to 18 minutes, until puffed and golden brown.

Cool completely on parchment paper. The cookies will be quite sticky but will peel off once they are fully cooled.

Rugelach

Rugelach are delicious little pastry-like cookies with so much tasty filling inside, it spills out as it bakes and becomes caramelized (personally, my favorite part!). I vividly recall eating them as a child when I would visit my great-aunts in Brighton Beach, Brooklyn. The cookies originated in Jewish communities in Poland and there are many variations. Using equal parts cream cheese and butter creates a barely sweet dough that yields a soft and tender cookie. Some people like their rugelach more pastry-like, so they use a puff pastry dough to create a flakier treat, sort of like a mini croissant. I've included both doughs, so you can see what tradition you connect with.

Either way, they are a delightful rolled-up treat, often filled with fruit preserves like apricot, raspberry, or cherry. They are sometimes paired with chocolate shavings or nuts—any kind will do, but make sure they are toasted for a deeper flavor. Poppy seeds are also a popular traditional filling, but you can experiment with any number of savory options, like pesto or an olive tapenade (not my great-great-grandmother's rugelach).

Makes 32 cookies

Cookie Academy Review
- Freezing the Dough, see page 45
- Rolling the Dough, see page 52
- Batch Baking, see page 56

Dough

8 oz / 225g cream cheese, chilled

1 cup / 220g unsalted butter, at room temperature

¼ cup / 30g confectioners' sugar

1 pinch of kosher salt

1 egg yolk

1½ tsp pure vanilla extract (page 16)

1 tsp lemon juice

½ tsp lemon zest

2¼ cups / 270g all-purpose flour

Filling

2 Tbsp cinnamon sugar (mix 2 Tbsp granulated sugar with 1 tsp ground cinnamon)

½ cup / 110g preserves (raspberry, apricot, or cherry)

½ cup / 60g chopped nuts, lightly toasted (pecans, walnuts, or almonds) (optional)

½ cup / 110g chocolate shavings (bittersweet, semisweet, or milk) (optional)

Topping

¼ cup / 60ml heavy cream

¼ cup / 50g granulated sugar for sprinkling on top

Make the dough: In a food processor, pulse together the cream cheese, butter, confectioners' sugar, salt, egg yolk, vanilla, lemon juice, and zest until well combined. Add the flour and pulse the dough until it just comes together in a soft ball.

Divide the dough in two equal portions (375g), wrap each in plastic, flatten into disks ½ inch / 1.3cm thick and about 6 inches / 15cm wide, and refrigerate for at least 1 hour, up to overnight. The dough can also be frozen for about 3 weeks.

Preheat the oven to 350°F / 175°C. Line two doubled-up baking sheets (the cookies will need some insulation) with parchment paper.

On a floured surface, roll one of the disks of dough to a round with a thickness of about ⅛ inch / 3mm thick. Leave the other disk in the refrigerator until you are ready to use it.

Sprinkle half the cinnamon sugar evenly over the dough. Cover with about ¼ cup of the preserves. Use a pastry or pizza wheel to cut the dough into sixteen equal wedges. Sprinkle on the nuts and/or chocolate (if using).

CONTINUED

Roll the dough up, starting at the wide end, until the pointy end is tucked under the cookie. Repeat with the rest of the pieces, working quickly, so the dough doesn't get too sticky. If the dough is sticking in spots, use a metal spatula to help release it.

Place the rolled cookies on a prepared baking sheet, leaving 2 inches between them to allow for spreading and the filling to sneak out. Brush the tops with a small amount of heavy cream. Sprinkle with granulated sugar. Bake in the middle of the oven for 20 to 25 minutes, until they are light golden-brown and set.

Remove the cookies from the sheet while they are still warm, so they will not stick to the parchment paper. Allow them to cool on a cooling rack. Repeat with the second disk of dough and remaining filling.

Call your grandmother and get all of her recipes, so they don't disappear! I'm wrapping up the rest of this batch to send to her.

VARIATION: RUGELACH WITH QUICK PUFF PASTRY

Use one-quarter of the Quick Puff Pastry dough (recipe follows). Preheat the oven to 425°F / 220°C *convection* heat (or 450°F / 230°C flat heat). Line two doubled-up baking sheets (the cookies will need some insulation) with parchment paper. This prevents the bottom from burning as they bake. Roll the quick puff pastry out into a 15-inch / 38cm square. Cover the surface of the dough with the cinnamon sugar and preserves. Using a pastry or pizza wheel, cut the covered dough into twelve triangles. The base of each triangle will measure about 2½ inches / 6.5cm. Sprinkle nuts and/or chocolate (if using). Roll the dough up, as instructed above. Place on the prepared baking sheets, leaving about 2 inches / 5cm between the cookies. Freeze the rolled cookies for about 20 minutes. Brush the frozen cookies with egg wash (1 egg beaten with 1 teaspoon water) and sprinkle with sugar. Bake in the middle of the oven for 20 to 25 minutes, until puffed and golden brown. Cool completely on the baking sheet.

Quick Puff Pastry

This is a quick version of the traditional laminated dough that can take hours to make. This one will take only 20 to 30 minutes. Use this puff pastry dough as an alternative to the rugelach dough if you want a flakier version. This version puffs up beautifully, although maybe slightly less than the traditional layered pastry. In this recipe, you'll turn the dough four times, until it is quite smooth and clean to work with. You can stop the process after two or three turns, though the less you do, the less puffing you'll get.

Makes two about 14 oz / 385g disks of dough

Cookie Academy Review
▦ Freezing the Dough, see page 45
▦ Rolling the Dough, see page 52

2 cups / 240g all-purpose flour

⅔ cup plus 1 Tbsp / 80g cake flour

¾ tsp kosher salt

1½ cups / 330g unsalted butter, cold and cut into 1-Tbsp pieces

½ cup / 120ml ice water (more or less to make dough come together)

In a stand mixer fitted with the paddle attachment, mix the all-purpose and cake flours, salt, and butter on low speed for about 30 seconds, just until the flour is coated with butter. There will still be large chunks of butter, about ¼ inch / 6mm thick or larger. Add the chilled water in a steady but slow stream while mixing, just until the dough starts to form small clumps and there is little flour left in the bowl. If you reach into the bowl and the dough comes together when you squeeze it, it's done. If it crumbles with dry powdery bits, sprinkle in a bit more water.

Turn the dough out onto a lightly floured work surface and using a bench scraper, fold and push the dough into a rectangle. It will be a bit shaggy looking and that's just right. Flour the surface as you work to prevent the dough from sticking too much. Flour the top of the dough and roll it out into a rectangle that measures 10 by 15 inches / 25 by 38cm. Brush off any excess flour with a clean and dry pastry brush. Using a bench scraper to help you lift the dough, fold one-third of the dough into the center. Fold the other one-third over the top, like a letter.

Turn the dough and roll it out again to a rectangle that measures 10 by 15 inches / 25 by 38cm, remembering to add enough flour to prevent sticking. Repeat the brushing and folding technique. The dough will start to be less shaggy and start to look like a cohesive dough.

Turn the dough and repeat all the rolling, brushing, and folding steps for the third time. If the dough is getting too sticky with butter, you can cover it and refrigerate for about 20 minutes to create a more workable dough.

Turn the dough and do the fourth and final set of rolling, brushing, and folding. The dough should now be smooth and look like a clean rectangle of dough. Divide it in two; you can use the dough right away or cover and refrigerate it for a few days. You can also freeze the dough for about 1 month.

Hamantaschen

Hamantaschen are triangle-shaped treats traditionally made during the Jewish holiday of Purim. The holiday honors a story of how the clever Queen Esther helped to foil the evil Haman's plot to destroy the Jewish population of Persia. To celebrate this deed, during Purim, "Haman's pockets" pile up on the shelves of Jewish bakeries and the kitchens of home bakers. And the filled cookies have become so sought after, now they're baked year-round. I love the traditional old-world fillings of prune and apricot or poppy, which you'll find in this recipe, but they're also made with all kinds of flavors tucked inside. Each of the fillings make about 2 cups / 600g. I like the classics, just as my grandmother made them, but you should feel free to experiment. You can also find the fillings in the baking section of many grocery stores.

Makes 50 to 60 cookies

Cookie Academy Review
- Freezing the Dough, see page 45
- Rolling the Dough, see page 52
- Batch Baking, see page 56

Dough

8 oz / 225g cream cheese, chilled

1 cup / 220g unsalted butter, at room temperature

¾ cup / 90g confectioners' sugar

¼ tsp kosher salt

1 tsp lemon juice

½ tsp lemon zest

1 tsp pure vanilla extract (page 16)

2⅓ cups / 280g all-purpose flour

Poppy Seed Filling (Optional)

1 cup / 140g poppy seeds

1 cup / 240ml water

½ cup / 70g raisins, finely chopped

⅓ cup / 75g granulated sugar

¼ cup / 85g Lyle's Golden Syrup or corn syrup

1 tsp lemon zest

1 tsp pure vanilla extract (page 16)

½ tsp cinnamon

Prune Filling (Optional)

1 cup / 160g pitted prunes, coarsely chopped

¾ cup / 105g raisins

½ orange, washed and coarsely chopped (peel and all)

¼ cup / 50g granulated sugar or honey

Hot water or black tea to cover the fruit

2 cinnamon sticks

Apricot Filling (Optional)

2 cups / 320g dried sulfured apricots, finely chopped

½ orange, washed and finely chopped (peel and all)

¼ cup / 50g granulated sugar or honey

Hot water or black tea to cover the fruit

Make the dough: In a food processor, combine the cream cheese, butter, confectioners' sugar, and salt. Add the lemon juice, zest, and vanilla, and pulse again to combine. Add the flour and pulse the dough until it comes together in a soft ball.

Divide the ball into two disks, wrap them in plastic, and refrigerate until firm, about an hour or up to 2 days. The dough can be frozen for about 3 weeks.

IF MAKING THE POPPY SEED FILLING:

In a saucepan over low heat, combine the poppy seeds, water, raisins, sugar, Lyle's Golden Syrup, lemon zest, vanilla, and cinnamon. Simmer, stirring often, until the liquid is absorbed and the mixture is quite thick, 20 to 30 minutes. Process in a coffee grinder until a paste forms. Allow to cool before filling the cookies. It will thicken even more as it cools. This filling can be made several days ahead and refrigerated, or it can be frozen for about 1 month.

IF MAKING THE PRUNE FILLING:

In a saucepan, combine the prunes, raisins, orange, sugar, hot water, and cinnamon sticks. Cover and gently simmer over low heat, stirring often, until the liquid is absorbed, the fruit is soft, and the mixture is quite thick, 30 to 35 minutes. If the fruit still isn't soft, add more water and continue to cook until it is soft. Remove the cinnamon sticks. Transfer into a

CONTINUED

food processor and pulse a few times until the fruit is chopped, but not pureed. Allow to cool before filling cookies. This filling can be made several days ahead and refrigerated, or it can be frozen for 1 month.

IF MAKING THE APRICOT FILLING:

In saucepan, combine the apricots, orange, sugar, and hot water. Cover and gently simmer over low heat, stirring often, until the liquid is absorbed, the fruit is soft, and the mixture is quite thick, 30 to 35 minutes. If the fruit still isn't soft, add more water and continue to cook until it is soft. Transfer into a food processor and pulse a few times until the fruit is chopped, but not pureed. Allow to cool before filling cookies. This filling can be made several days ahead and refrigerated, or it can be frozen for 1 month.

Make the cookies: Preheat the oven to 350°F / 190°C. Line baking sheets with parchment paper.

On a well-floured surface, roll one disk of the dough to a rectangle about 17 by 13 inches / 43 by 33cm with a thickness of ⅛ inch / 3mm. Using a 3-inch / 7.5cm round cookie cutter, cut out disks of dough. Gather the dough scraps and gently press them together and reroll to ⅛-inch / 3mm thick rectangle. If the gathered scraps are too sticky to roll, place in the refrigerator to firm. You can reroll the dough only once; any more and the dough will become too tough.

Transfer twelve of the disks to a prepared baking sheet. They may overlap slightly until filled and folded.

Fill each cookie with 1 to 2 teaspoons of desired filling. Form the dough into a triangle by folding three sides up onto the filling and pinching the three seams into points. Refrigerate the formed cookies for about 30 minutes to set the dough, which will help to keep their shape when baked. Just before baking, arrange the cookies so they have about 1½ inches of space between them. Repeat with the remaining disk of dough.

Bake, one sheet at a time, in the middle of the oven for 10 to 15 minutes, until golden brown along the bottom edge. Allow to cool slightly before serving, otherwise the pastry will fall apart when lifted.

Black & White Cookies

I'm just going to say it: I realize I'm very much in the minority here, but I've never loved black and white cookies with the passion I feel I should. The legendary cookie, popularized by Glaser's Bake Shop more than one hundred years ago, is much beloved by New Yorkers, my mom included, and versions of it are sold all over the city. In order to understand the adoration, my friend Stephen—the only one I know who feels the same as I do—and I set out on a quest. We walked the city sampling black-and-whites, whether they were found near the cash register at the corner store or in a fancy bakery on the Upper East Side. We stopped people in Central Park eating them, and they happily explained their view of the proper nibbling techniques, such as right down the middle to ensure equal parts chocolate and vanilla frosting in each bite. Though we emerged still underwhelmed—and we tried about thirty of them—I loved our hunt for the black-and-white, and it convinced me to put a version in this book. I came up with my best take on the iconic NYC cookie, albeit smaller, which one taste tester described as "a doughnut and a cookie had a baby!" Graham and my boys, the ultimate testers, love these, and honestly, so do I. I'm a convert. Now to convince Stephen.

Makes about 15 cookies

Cookie Academy Review
- Using a Portion Scoop, see page 43
- Batch Baking, see page 56

1 cup / 120g all-purpose flour

⅔ cup / 74g cake flour

¾ tsp baking powder

½ tsp kosher salt

3 Tbsp unsalted butter, at room temperature

2 Tbsp vegetable oil

⅓ cup / 65g granulated sugar

1 tsp pure vanilla extract (page 16)

1 tsp almond extract

1 egg, at room temperature

1 egg yolk, at room temperature

¼ cup / 60ml buttermilk, at room temperature

Icing

1 oz / 30g white chocolate, finely chopped

1 oz / 30g dark chocolate, finely chopped

2 cups / 240g confectioners' sugar

¼ cup / 60ml boiling hot (212°F / 100°C) water, more if needed

2 Tbsp light corn syrup

1 tsp pure vanilla extract (page 16)

4 tsp vegetable oil, divided

1 tsp black cocoa powder

Preheat the oven to 350°F / 175°C. Line two baking sheets with parchment paper.

In a medium bowl, whisk together the all-purpose and cake flours, baking powder, and salt. Set aside.

In a stand mixer fitted with the paddle attachment, cream together the butter, oil, sugar, and vanilla on medium-high speed until light in color and texture, about 2 minutes. Turn the speed down to medium-low and add the egg, scraping down the bowl with a rubber spatula after mixing. Add the yolk and combine.

Add one-third of the flour mixture, mixing on low speed, until just combined, then add ⅛ cup / 30ml of the buttermilk. Scrape down the bowl. Repeat with another one-third of the flour mixture and the remaining ⅛ cup / 30ml of buttermilk. Scrape the bowl and finish mixing in the last third of the dry ingredients.

Scoop the cookie dough using a #40 (1½-tablespoon) portion scoop and evenly space six cookie balls on each prepared baking sheet. You can make the cookies larger or smaller, but it will affect the bake time.

CONTINUED

BUBBE BERKOWITZ'S COOKIES

Using your fingers dipped in water, pat the balls into disks ¼ inch / 6mm thick. Bake, one sheet at a time, in the middle of the oven for 10 to 12 minutes, until set and just turning golden on the bottoms of the cookies. Allow to cool completely on the pan.

Make the icing: Place the white and dark chocolate in two separate medium-sized bowls, set aside. Fill the bottom of a double boiler or a medium saucepan with 1 inch / 2.5cm of water and bring to a gentle simmer over medium-low heat. In a large stainless steel bowl whisk together the confectioners' sugar, boiling water, corn syrup, and vanilla until smooth. Set over the simmering water and use a rubber spatula to stir the mixture, wiping down the sides to keep the bowl clean. Cook until the mixture is melted and hot (about 165°F / 74°C on an instant read thermometer), about 3 minutes.

Pour half the hot sugar mixture over the white chocolate and immediately cover with plastic wrap. Pour the remaining sugar mixture over the dark chocolate and cover with plastic. Add 2 teaspoons of the oil to the bowl of white chocolate and gently whisk to combine. Thin with more boiling water, 1 teaspoon at a time, if needed. The icing should be thick enough to coat the cookie with a thin, smooth, shiny layer. Cover with plastic at all times so it doesn't dry out. If the icing gets too thick while covering the cookies, add another teaspoon of boiling water.

Add the remaining 2 teaspoons of oil and the black cocoa to the dark chocolate mixture, then gently whisk to combine.

To ice the cookies, line a baking sheet with parchment paper and place a cooling rack over the parchment.

Hold the cookie over the bowl of white icing, use a spoon to ladle a line of the white icing down the middle of each cooled cookie on the flat side. Ladle more white icing over the cookie to completely cover half. Tilt the cookie slightly in your hand to move the icing away from the center line. Use the spoon to wipe away the excess icing from the edge of the cookie. Use a toothpick to gently poke any air bubbles in the icing. Set on the cooling rack to set for about 30 minutes. If the icing starts to get too thick as you are working, you can stir in a ½ teaspoon of boiling water, repeating until it is spreadable again.

Starting with the first cookie you iced, apply the chocolate icing. The white icing should be starting to set and should not move when you pick up the cookie. Use a second spoon for the dark chocolate icing and ladle a line that meets up with the line of white chocolate. Use more dark chocolate to cover the remaining bare cookie. Tilt the cookie slightly away from the center line in your hand so the dark chocolate doesn't spread into the white icing. Use the spoon to wipe off the excess icing from the edge. Set it on the cooling rack to dry completely; this can take an hour or more. Once the icing is completely dry, you can wrap each cookie in plastic wrap. It'll keep for a couple of days.

Dairy-Free

Sarah Berkowitz's Mandelbrot

My grandmother's recipe for mandelbrot, which is basically a Jewish biscotti, is one of the very few recipes she handed down to me. Though my Bubbe Berkowitz didn't bake many cookies, she did bake these. Probably because she loved her coffee (I mean 8-cups-a-day kind of love), and mandelbrot is the unrivaled complement. In fact, you really need to dip these in coffee to appreciate their true glory. Though many people use almonds—the name translates to "almond bread" in Yiddish—I like using walnuts, which, along with the orange zest and some caraway seeds (this is an acquired taste), give the biscuits a rich, rustic flavor. Dip in chocolate and sprinkles for extra flair.

Makes about 36 cookies

Cookie Academy Review
- Rolling the Dough, see page 52
- Making Stamped or Molded Cookies, see page 52
- Batch Baking, see page 56
- Melting Chocolate, see page 59

4 cups / 480g all-purpose flour

1½ tsp baking powder

1 tsp kosher salt

2 tsp caraway seeds (or anise seeds; optional)

4 eggs, at room temperature

1¼ cup / 250g granulated sugar

⅔ cup / 158ml vegetable or olive oil

1 tsp pure vanilla extract (page 16)

1 tsp orange extract

1 orange, zested

12 walnut halves, lightly toasted

6 oz / 170g bittersweet or semisweet chocolate, melted (optional)

Sprinkles for garnish (optional)

Preheat the oven to 350°F / 175°C. Line two baking sheets with parchment paper.

In a medium bowl, whisk together the flour, baking powder, salt, and caraway seeds.

In a stand mixer fitted with the whisk attachment, beat the eggs and sugar together on high speed until thick and light in color, about 5 minutes. Turn the speed to medium and drizzle in the oil, then add vanilla and orange extracts, and orange zest, whipping until combined. Switch to the paddle attachment and add the flour and walnuts to the egg mixture, mixing until it comes together in a thick dough. You may need to stir with a rubber spatula to make sure it is evenly mixed.

Form the dough into two equal logs 3 inches / 7.5cm in diameter and 8 inches / 30cm long on the lined baking sheet. Press the walnut halves into the top of the log.

Bake in the middle of the oven for 30 to 35 minutes, just until the dough is set but still soft. Let cool for 10 minutes. Keep the oven on.

Using a serrated knife, cut the logs while they are still warm into slices ½ inch / 1.25cm thick. If they cool too much, they become brittle. Keep the oven on.

Lay the slices back on the baking sheets and bake again for 10 minutes. Flip the cookies over and bake for about 10 more minutes or until crisp.

Cool completely on the pan before dipping in melted chocolate and then sprinkles (if using). Place the dipped mandelbrot back on the baking pan, and move to the refrigerator to firm up the chocolate. These cookies last for weeks. Serve with coffee as my grandmother would.

■ Nut-Free   ■ Dairy-Free

Poppy Seed Cookies (Mohn Kichel)

When I asked my Bubbe Berkowitz for family cookie recipes, she wrote them down and sent them on to me. Originally, these recipes had been passed down from her great-grandmother to her grandmother to her mother without ever being written on paper. None of those women, who baked love into these cookies for over a century, could read or write. They baked entirely by feel and taught the next generation to do the same. My grandmother wrote this recipe out for me (and now I'm crying just thinking about the significance of that gesture), and thank god she did, because otherwise it—along with all the other recipes—would be lost forever.

This is the recipe that has been in my family the longest, and this cookie is so Jewish! The Ashkenazi Jews used a lot of poppy seeds in their baking. Its cake-meets-shortbread texture is speckled with seeds and it's considered a simple peasant cookie. I think they are absolutely delicious. My grandmother's recipe didn't include lemon zest, but when I told my mom I was adding it (almost as if to ask permission to change the family recipe), she insisted that her grandmother did add lemon, so I went for it! I think Sheindel, Zelda (Jean), and Sarah would all approve and be tickled that you are baking their recipe. You can also make a variation of their recipe into thumbprint cookies with jam. The combination is fabulous, and I wish I could have shared them with my grandmother.

Makes about 36 cookies

Cookie Academy Review
■ Using a Portion Scoop, see page 43
■ Batch Baking, see page 56

---

3 cups / 360g all-purpose flour

½ tsp kosher salt

1¼ tsp baking powder

¼ cup / 36g poppy seeds

3 eggs, at room temperature

1 cup / 200g granulated sugar

½ cup / 125ml vegetable oil

1 tsp pure vanilla extract (page 16)

1 Tbsp lemon zest (optional)

Preheat the oven to 350°F / 175°C. Line two baking sheets with parchment paper.

In a large bowl, whisk together flour, salt, baking powder, and poppy seeds.

In another large bowl, whisk together the eggs, sugar, oil, vanilla, and lemon zest (if using).

Using a spoon, stir the wet ingredients into the dry ingredients and stir until combined.

Scoop the cookie dough using a #70 (2½-teaspoon) portion scoop onto the prepared baking sheets. You can make the cookies larger or smaller, but it will affect the baking time.

To make the surface perfectly smooth, roll the dough balls between your hands to create a round sphere. Place on the baking sheet, leaving about 1½ inches / 4cm between the cookies. Use the bottom of a glass to press the balls flat to create a ½-inch / 1.3cm tall disk.

Bake, one sheet at a time, in the middle of the oven for 12 to 14 minutes, until the bottoms are golden brown and tops are still pale.

Cool on the baking sheets until completely cool.

■ **VARIATION: THUMBPRINT COOKIES WITH JAM**

Once the dough is chilled and rolled into smooth balls, press your thumb into the dough, almost to the bottom, but not quite. Fill each hole with about ½ teaspoon of your preferred jam or any of the fillings for Hamantaschen (page 141). You'll need about 1 cup / 300g of your preferred filling for all the cookies. Bake as directed above.

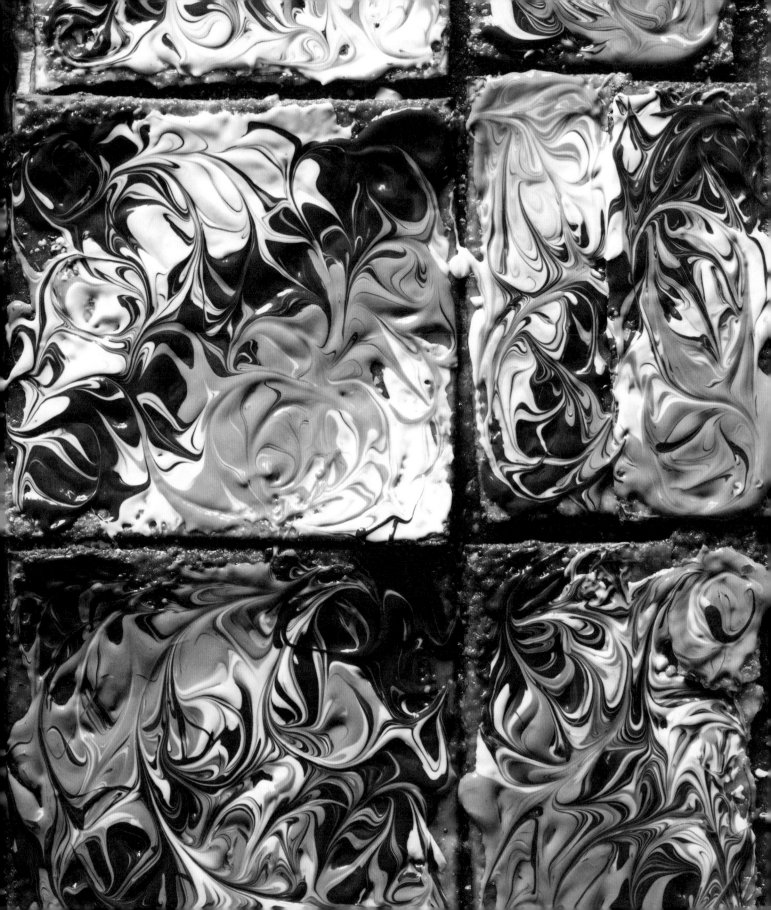

Nut-Free

Chocolate Caramel Matzo

Years ago, Marcy Goldman of *Better Baking* totally inspired me and countless others with her recipe for Chocolate Toffee Matzo Crunch, from her classic book *A Treasury of Jewish Holiday Baking*. Be warned these are crazy delicious and addictive! The crunchy matzo cracker absorbs the flavor of sweet caramel toffee and then a schmear (spread) of chocolate is added to the top. Ever since I was introduced to this recipe, I've made it every year for Passover. Experiment with various toppings, like nuts, roasted sesame seeds, and coconut flakes. I once made these for a Christmas Cookie Swap with Ina Garten and added peppermint candies, so there are really no rules. You can also sub in graham crackers or saltines for the base; either way it's delicious. Break it up into pieces and share with friends and family. They'll love and hate you for it because they won't be able to stop eating it either.

Makes about 3 dozen small pieces

Cookie Academy Review
Marbling, see page 55

4 large, whole matzo crackers (unsalted)

1 cup / 220g unsalted butter or Passover margarine

¾ cup / 150g lightly packed brown sugar

¼ cup / 50g granulated sugar

2 Tbsp sweetened condensed milk

¼ tsp kosher salt

1¼ cups / 225g bittersweet, semisweet, milk, and/or white chocolate chips

Optional Toppings

Flaky sea salt, especially if using unsalted matzo

Toasted pecans, walnuts, or almonds

Toasted sesame seeds (see Baker's Note)

Sweetened coconut angel flakes

Crushed peppermint candies

Preheat the oven to 350°F / 175°C. Line a baking sheet with aluminum foil, so it goes up the sides to catch the caramel. Position the matzo crackers flat on the prepared sheet, breaking them to fit in one even layer. Set aside.

In a medium saucepan, cook the butter, sugars, sweetened condensed milk, and salt over medium heat for 3 to 5 minutes, whisking constantly in the center of the pan, until the sugar melts and the mixture is smooth. Spread it evenly over the matzo.

Bake in the middle of the oven for about 15 minutes, until the sugar is bubbling and a deep caramel brown color. Check halfway through to make sure it is not browning too quickly. If it seems to be browning too quickly along the edges, rotate the pan and drop the oven temperature to 325°F / 165°C.

Once it is done, remove the pan from the oven, allow to sit until it stops bubbling, then top the matzo with the chocolate chips. Let the chocolate sit for 5 minutes before spreading it evenly over the matzo or creating a marble pattern (see page 55).

If you want to jazz up your caramel-and-chocolate-covered matzo, top with flaky sea salt, toasted nuts, toasted sesame seeds, coconut flakes, and/or crushed peppermint candies. Let the matzo sit for at least an hour to cool to allow the caramel and chocolate to harden. It will be easier to peel the matzo from the foil once it is cooled and set. If the chocolate is not setting up at room temperature, place the sheet of matzo in the refrigerator for about 15 minutes.

Break into strips or bite-sized pieces. Store in an airtight container and refrigerate if the chocolate is getting soft.

BAKER'S NOTE

To toast the sesame seeds, place them in a pan over medium heat and stir continuously until they turn golden brown, about 3 minutes.

My Home-Ec Cookie Evolution

"I raised to my lips a spoonful of the tea in which I had soaked a morsel of the cake. No sooner had the warm liquid mixed with the crumbs touched my palate than a shudder ran through me and I stopped, intent upon the extraordinary thing that was happening to me. An exquisite pleasure invaded my senses."

—Marcel Proust's *Remembrance of Things Past*, upon eating his first madeleine cookie

This is perhaps the most evocative cookie quote, and madeleines happen to be my husband's absolute favorite, so I make them for every special occasion or just to say I love you.

Cookies can invoke intense memories, feelings of passion, and absolute joy. This is a truth that translates around the world, in the form of recipes that delight anywhere you are. This chapter has the cookies that I've made throughout my life, starting in my middle school home-economics class, that have deep meaning or just transport me to a place.

Lemon Madeleines

On Valentine's Day, I mix up a batch of madeleines for my husband, Graham, as cookies are my love language, and these are his favorites. I also make them on his birthday, Father's Day, or any other time I want to tell him how much I appreciate him. A cookie can say way more than words. Proust made madeleines famous in his autobiographical novel when he wrote about how one dipped in tea summoned up memories of his past. For me, the little cookie, baked in its special shell-shaped pan, is connected to many joyful memories of Graham and me. The following recipe has become my go-to, and I've baked hundreds of them (maybe more) over the course of our thirty-five years together. The brown butter, almond meal, and honey are key to imparting a rich, complex madeleine. You can play with the flavor by switching out the almond meal with hazelnut, pistachio, or any other nut meal. Same goes for the zest: try orange, grapefruit, even lime.

Makes about 30 cookies

Cookie Academy Review
▥ Using a Portion Scoop, see page 43
▥ Batch Baking, see page 56

⅔ cup / 80g all-purpose flour, plus more as needed

½ cup / 60g almond meal or flour (see page 19)

¼ tsp baking powder

¼ tsp kosher salt

½ cup plus 1 Tbsp / 125g brown butter (page 41), melted

1½ tsp lemon zest

½ tsp lemon extract

1 Tbsp honey

2 eggs, at room temperature

½ cup / 100g superfine sugar (see page 24)

In a medium bowl, whisk together the flour, almond meal, baking powder, and salt.

In another medium bowl, combine the melted brown butter, lemon zest, lemon extract, and honey. Allow to cool slightly while mixing the eggs.

In a stand mixer fitted with the whisk attachment, whip the eggs and superfine sugar on medium-high speed for about 4 minutes, until thick, foamy, and light in color. Turn the speed to medium-low and slowly add the browned butter mixture. Fold in the flour, mixing until just combined.

Cover and refrigerate until well chilled, at least two hours, but overnight is best. You can let it sit in the refrigerator for up to 3 days.

Preheat the oven to 375°F / 190°C. Brush the wells of a madeleine pan generously with softened butter and dust with flour, tapping out the excess so there is just a thin coating in the pan, or coat with beeswax (see Baker's Note).

Using a #50 (4-teaspoon) portion scoop, fill each well three-quarters full of batter. Using wet fingers, flatten the batter. Place the pan in the freezer for about 10 minutes. The batter should be stiff but not frozen solid.

Bake in the middle of the oven for 10 to 12 minutes, until the edges are a caramel color and the centers are puffed and set. Let the madeleines cool for a minute. Then remove them from the pan by flipping the pan over and gently tapping. If they stick, use a small metal spatula to ease them out of the pan. Let cool completely on a cooling rack. If you are baking multiple batches, you will need to wipe the pan clean and reapply the butter and flour. The madeleines are best eaten the same day.

BAKER'S NOTES

Orange Madeleines: Swap orange zest and orange extract for the lemon.

Beeswax and butter melted together to coat the pan can prevent madeleines from sticking to old pans that don't have a nonstick surface. Just melt together equal parts food grade beeswax and butter over low heat until combined. Use a pastry brush to coat the pan. If you are doing multiple batches, you will need to wipe the pan clean and reapply the beeswax mixture.

Hazelnut Chocolate Madeleines

When I'm in the mood for decadence, these do just the trick. I love how chocolate pairs beautifully with the bold flavor of hazelnut. The finishing touch of drizzling or dipping them in chocolate and sprinkling on chopped hazelnuts can really dress them. You can also make them feel a bit more rustic with a simple dusting of confectioners' sugar. Serve these rich treats on a winter evening with a hot toddy by the fire.

Makes about 30 cookies

Cookie Academy Review
▥ Using a Portion Scoop, see page 43
▥ Batch Baking, see page 56
▥ Melting Chocolate, see page 59

⅔ cup / 80g hazelnut meal (see page 19)

½ cup / 60g all-purpose flour

2 Tbsp / 16g Dutch processed cocoa powder, plus more for dusting pan, sifted if lumpy

¼ tsp baking powder

¼ tsp kosher salt

½ cup / 110g brown butter (page 41), melted and cooled slightly, plus more for coating the pan

1 tsp pure vanilla extract (page 16)

1 Tbsp honey

1 oz / 28g bittersweet chocolate, melted, plus more for drizzling over tops

4 eggs, at room temperature

¾ cup / 150g superfine sugar (see page 24)

½ cup / 70g chopped hazelnuts for decorating

In a small bowl, whisk together the hazelnut meal, all-purpose flour, cocoa, baking powder, and salt. Set aside.

In a separate medium bowl, whisk the brown butter, vanilla, honey, and melted chocolate. Allow to cool while mixing the eggs.

In a stand mixer fitted with the whisk attachment, whip the eggs and sugar on medium-high speed for 5 minutes, until thick, foamy, and light in color. Turn the speed to low, and add the brown butter mixture. Fold in the flour mixture, mixing until combined.

Refrigerate until well chilled, at least an hour, but overnight is best. You can let it sit in the refrigerator for up to 3 days.

Preheat the oven to 375°F / 190°C. Generously butter and dust a madeleine pan with cocoa powder, tapping out the excess, or coat with beeswax (see Baker's Note page 155).

Using a #70 (2½-teaspoon) portion scoop, fill each well three-quarters full of batter. Using wet fingers, flatten the batter. Place in the freezer for 10 minutes. The batter should be stiff, but not frozen solid.

Bake in the middle of the oven for about 10 to 12 minutes, until the edges are a caramel color and centers are puffed and set. Let cool for a minute, then remove from the pan. Let cool completely on a cooling rack. If you are baking multiple batches, you will need to wipe the pan clean and reapply the butter and cocoa.

Drizzle with the remaining melted chocolate and sprinkle with chopped hazelnuts. These cookies are best eaten the day they are baked.

Gluten-Free

Meringue Clouds

I'm obsessed with meringue! I love it in every form for its magical whimsy. These "cloud cookies" are easy to make and can end up a little rustic-looking, which I love. They are crunchy, light, and a bit chewy in the middle. When mixing them, I add just a touch of balsamic vinegar to temper the sweetness. I also like to swirl in flavorful toppings, but there's a trick to it. Any fat or oil can deflate meringue, so I add in the toppings *right* before baking, swirling it in quickly so it just streaks through. Play with the flavors to create unique cookies. I've used bright fruit powders, preserves, chocolate ganache, Nutella, or, if I want something a little less sweet, I swirl in peanut butter, tahini (black tahini creates a more dramatic effect), or even wasabi powder to create a fascinating treat. For a bit of texture, sprinkle the meringue clouds with toasted sesame seeds or edible dried rose petals just before baking.

Makes 6 large meringues

Cookie Academy Review
Meringue, see page 43
Ganache SOS, see page 59

½ cup / 120g egg whites (about 4 large)

1 cup / 200g superfine sugar (see page 24)

1 tsp white or balsamic vinegar

1½ tsp pure vanilla extract (page 16)

Optional Toppings (use 1½ tsp per large meringue)

Sesame seeds (wasabi-coated sesame seeds make for a spicy and colorful alternative)

Black tahini (or use traditional white but not as dramatic)

Nutella

Peanut butter

Preserves

Half batch of Bittersweet Chocolate Ganache (page 213)

Spoon the meringue onto the prepared baking sheet in six equal-size blobs (you can make them smaller or larger, but it will affect the baking time), spaced about 3 inches apart so they have room to expand. If you are flavoring the meringues, sprinkle or drizzle your preferred topping over the meringue and swirl it in using the tip of a knife or a chopstick. Don't overwork it or the meringues may spread too much.

Bake for 1 hour, then reduce the heat to 200°F / 95°C and continue baking for 30 more minutes. Turn off the heat and leave to sit in the oven for about an hour to make sure the outside stays crisp, but the inside has a bit of chew. It may require longer depending on the oven and if you want a crispy interior.

The meringues can be stored in an airtight container for 24 hours.

Preheat the oven to 250°F / 120°C. Line a baking sheet with parchment paper.

In a stand mixer fitted with the whisk attachment, beat the egg whites on medium speed until foamy, about 30 seconds. Turn down the speed to medium-low and slowly drizzle in the superfine sugar. Once all the sugar is added, turn the speed to high and whip until it is light, fluffy, glossy, and there is no graininess left in the meringue, about 5 minutes. Add the vinegar and vanilla and continue beating at high speed for 30 seconds.

BAKER'S NOTE

If you want a more uniform and controlled look to your meringue, you can put the whipped meringue into a piping bag fitted with a large star tip and pipe them out into little kiss shapes or whatever shape inspires you. Bake smaller meringues for about 45 minutes before reducing the temperature and bake for an additional 20 minutes.

MY HOME-EC COOKIE EVOLUTION

Macarons

The macaron is having its moment. Brilliantly colored towers of them feature at weddings, and entire shops devoted to the cookie are popping up all over, way beyond Paris. These fancy little cookies made from sugar, almond flour, and egg whites had humble beginnings: They were baked in Italian and French convents as early as the eighth century. After the French revolution in 1789, nuns supported themselves by selling unadorned macaron shells. It wasn't until the early 1900s when a chef sandwiched sweet fillings between two shells that they took on rock star status—the rest, as they say, is history.

I fully support the macarons' global dominance, as they really are one of the best cookies on earth—so colorful, delicious, and fun. I know bakers are often intimidated by them, and while they can be a bit fussy to make, they just take a little practice and some helpful hints. This recipe does require a scale; there is otherwise too much variability in the measurements to come out well. Don't let the term *macaronage* intimidate you in the directions, it's just a succinct way of saying, push the batter against the side of the bowl until it's flowing and shiny. Once you get the hang of it, you'll love making them for any special occasion.

Makes about 24 sandwiched macarons

Cookie Academy Review
▦ Meringue, see page 43
▦ Setting Up and Filling the Piping Bag, see page 44
▦ Batch Baking, see page 56
▦ Ganache SOS, see page 59

Macarons

170g blanched almond flour or blanched hazelnut flour (see page 19)

120g confectioners' sugar

154g egg whites (pasteurized eggs will not work; see Baker's Note)

¼ tsp cream of tartar

150g granulated sugar

1 tsp pure vanilla extract (page 16)

¼ to ½ tsp powdered food coloring (optional)

Bittersweet Chocolate Ganache

1 cup heavy whipping cream

8 oz / 448g bittersweet chocolate, finely chopped

Line three baking sheets with parchment paper.

Sift together the almond flour and the confectioners' sugar. Set aside.

In a stand mixer fitted with the whisk attachment, beat the egg whites and cream of tartar on medium-high speed until foamy. Turn the speed to low and slowly sprinkle in the granulated sugar over the whites. Turn up the speed to medium-high and beat the whites until they reach medium peaks. Add in the vanilla and

food coloring (if using). Continue beating until you've reached stiff, glossy peaks.

Remove bowl from the mixer and sift one-third of the almond meal mixture over the meringue. Use a rubber spatula to fold the mixtures together, until just combined. Repeat with another third of the almond mixture, folding to combine. Fold in the last of the sifted almond mixture. The batter will be quite thick after it is all added.

Do the macaronage: Spread the batter up the sides of the bowl—you'll see that it will cling onto the bowl without slumping into the middle. Scrape the batter back to the bottom of the bowl. Continue to spread the batter up the sides and scrape it back to the bottom until it begins to slowly slump down on its own. This will take about six times, but it may be more or fewer times depending on the strength of your meringue. Lift some of the batter up and drizzle it over the rest of the batter in a ribbon, it should sit on top and then melt back into itself after 10 to 12 seconds, then you're ready to pipe.

CONTINUED

Fill an 18-inch pastry bag fitted with a round Ateco brand #804 tip with half the macaron batter. Pipe the batter, holding the piping bag straight up and down, squeezing out a nickel-size round that is ¼ inch / 6mm thick onto the prepared baking sheet, leaving about 1½ inches between them to allow for spreading. If you are new to piping macarons, use a macaron template that slips under the parchment paper to create perfect shapes (you can find macaron templates to print online).

Gently but firmly bang the tray on the counter 3 or 4 times to work out some of the air bubbles and flatten the macarons to about ⅛ inch / 3mm thick. If there are any bubbles, pop them with a toothpick. Repeat the piping and banging with the remaining baking sheets until all the batter is used.

Let the baking sheets sit, uncovered, at room temperature until the tops of the macarons are dry to the touch. This will take about 30 minutes, but it will depend on the environment. If it is particularly humid, this can take considerably longer. In dry climates, it can take half the time. Be sure to bake them in the order you piped, so they are at the right stage of drying out when they go in the oven.

Meanwhile, preheat the oven to 320°F / 160°C with the rack in the top third of the oven.

Bake the sheets, one at a time, for 10 to 12 minutes. When they're done, they'll have puffed up, developed a "foot" at the base, and look dry. If they are not set and done, then rotate the tray and bake for an additional 1 to 2 minutes. Overbaking will result in a hard shell. If they are set, remove the tray from the oven. The macarons should lift as one unit and have some give to them when pressed, but not be brittle. The timing may be slightly different depending on your oven.

Cool completely on the baking sheet. Flip over every other shell. Try to match up same-sized shells.

Make the ganache (if using): In a medium microwave-safe bowl, heat the chocolate and cream in 10 second intervals until the chocolate is warm and can be whisked smooth. The amount of time needed will depend on your chocolate. Allow to cool until thick enough to pipe, about an hour. The ganache can be made ahead and left at room temperature for a day.

Fill your macaron shells with ganache or whatever filling your heart desires! Sandwich the macarons and store in the refrigerator for several hours or overnight to hydrate them, before serving. If you skip the hydrating step, the macarons will be hard and may shatter when you bite into them. The filled cookies last for a few days covered in the refrigerator and can be wrapped and frozen for several weeks.

BAKER'S NOTES

Maturing the egg whites is a trick I learned from Ginger Elizabeth, owner of the eponymous macaron shop in California, to strengthen the meringue. Place 5 or 6 egg whites in a container and leave them out on the counter, uncovered, for 12 hours, to allow some of the water to evaporate from them. When you are ready to make your macaron batter, weigh out the 134g of whites from the container. This will result in a stronger meringue and a better shape and texture in the final macaron. About 8 grams of water can evaporate from the eggs as they sit.

If you want a different flavor, add ¼ teaspoon lemon, mint, or orange extract at a time to the batter before the macaronage stage, until you get the desired flavor.

Lacy Oat Crisps (Florentines)

Florentines are one of the first cookies I made beyond Toll House chocolate chip cookies. When I was in middle school, I found a recipe in the Time-Life cookbooks at school, and I made them for a school project. It was for French class because, despite their name, they are thought to be French in origin and are not really from Florence, Italy. I remember being fascinated by the very thin, almost glass-like consistency of the cookie, which seemed so fancy compared to anything else I had baked. The honey perfumes the lacy cookie and caramelizes around the mixed candied fruit and pecans. Make them as an elegant addition to your holiday desserts or anytime you want to impress.

Makes about 12 cookies

Cookie Academy Review
- Using a Portion Scoop, see page 43
- Batch Baking, see page 56

½ cup / 110g unsalted butter, at room temperature

¼ cup / 80g honey

1 cup / 120g confectioners' sugar

⅓ cup / 40g all-purpose flour

1 cup / 100g rolled oats

¼ tsp kosher salt

1 tsp ground cinnamon

½ cup / 80g finely chopped candied fruit (optional)

½ cup / 60g finely chopped pecans (optional)

BAKER'S NOTE

To shape the cookies into cookie cups, drape them over a small ramekin while they are still hot and flexible. If they harden before you drape them, you can pop them back in the 325°F / 165°C oven for a minute and they will soften again.

Preheat the oven to 325°F / 165°C. Line two baking sheets with silicone baking mats or lightly greased parchment paper.

In a large bowl, cream together the butter, honey, and confectioners' sugar with a stiff rubber spatula. Add the flour, rolled oats, salt, and cinnamon, and stir until well combined. Add candied fruit and nuts (if using).

Scoop the cookie dough using a #60 (1-tablespoon) portion scoop onto the prepared baking sheets. Evenly space six cookie balls on each. Using wet fingers, pat the balls of dough into disks ¼ inch / 6mm thick.

Bake in the middle of the oven, one sheet at a time, for 12 to 14 minutes, until the cookies are evenly caramelized.

Remove from the oven and allow to rest on the baking sheet for about 3 minutes. If you lift them too early, they will break apart. Using an offset spatula, lift the cookies from the sheets (see Baker's Note) and allow to cool on cooling racks.

Store in a cool, dry place, separated by sheets of wax paper.

Honey Tuile

Tuile means "tile" in French, and these light wafers are named after the shape of Parisian tiled roofs. Traditionally, after baking for just a few minutes they are draped over a rolling pin to give them their unique curved shape. The delicate cookies are the secret weapon of many restaurant pastry departments, where they are rolled into tubes or cones and filled with mousse or pastry cream, formed into bowls for ice cream, or used as garnishes for desserts.

If you want to get a little fancy, you can buy or easily make tuile stencils and add some color. Some design options could be stenciling on simple modern geometric shapes or adding writing and intricate details in contrasting colors. I use plastic lids of large yogurt containers to cut out designs with an X-Acto blade to create my stencils. (If you want something larger, you can use a sheet of heavy-gauge vinyl from a crafting store.)

Makes about 24 four-inch cookies

Cookie Academy Review
Batch Baking, see page 56

3 Tbsp / 45g unsalted butter, at room temperature

½ cup / 60g confectioners' sugar

2 Tbsp honey

1 egg white, at room temperature

½ cup / 60g all-purpose flour

1 pinch of kosher salt

Food coloring (optional)

In a small bowl, using a stiff rubber spatula, mix together the butter and confectioners' sugar until smooth. There should be no lumps. Stir in the honey and mix until well incorporated. Blend in the egg white. Stir in the flour and salt until you have a smooth paste. You can use the cookie batter right away, refrigerate it for up to 5 days, or store in the freezer for up to 1 month. See Baker's Note to add color to the mix.

Preheat the oven to 325°F / 165°C. Line a baking sheet with a silicone mat or parchment paper.

Use an offset spatula to spread a thin coat of the batter evenly over a stencil. The thickness of the tuile will match the thickness of your stencil. Carefully peel the stencil off the baking sheet, leaving the shaped batter. Repeat with as many cookies as you'd like or will fit on the sheet. If you choose to use more than one stencil, you'll need to bake in multiple batches to keep like-size cookies together. All of the cookies should be the same size and shape so they can bake evenly.

Bake in the middle of the oven for about 5 minutes, until they are evenly golden and set. If you want to form the tuile into a shape, allow it to cool for no longer than a minute so that you can safely lift it off the baking sheet, and so that it is still flexible. Use an offset spatula and drape over a form or twist it into a tube around a dowel. If the cookies harden before you've had a chance to form them, return them to the oven and bake for another minute, then try shaping again.

These cookies can be stored in an airtight container for a couple of days. If it is very humid, they will soften, so bake and reshape (see previous step) just before using.

BAKER'S NOTES

If you are baking the tuiles on parchment paper, try doubling up the baking sheets to insulate the cookies, which makes them bake more evenly.

To add color or cocoa, divide the batter into bowls (if you want multiple colors) and add a bit of food coloring or 1 tsp of cocoa to get the desired color. Once you have spread the batter with your stencils, you can also put some of the batter into a parchment piping bag, to add a more exacting design.

Alfajores

Alfajores are South American cookies with dulce de leche. I all but forgot about these impossibly delicate shortbread-like cookies until I was judging the Silos Baking Competition where one of the bakers, Julia Perugini, made them. The cookie is so tender, it seems to melt away like magic. The secret is the high ratio of starch in the dough. I use potato starch and confectioners' sugar to get that texture. The sandwich cookie is held together with a caramel made from sweetened condensed milk that has been boiled in the can for hours at a time. The result is dulce de leche, a super-rich, decadent, caramel-colored, spreadable filling that is the perfect match for the lightly almond-scented cookies. You can certainly buy premade dulce de leche, but the homemade version is darker and deeper in flavor. I always boil two cans, just to have one on hand in the pantry. Try it in the Rice Crispy Bars (page 221) or on Graham Crackers (page 86).

Makes about 30 sandwich cookies

Cookie Academy Review
- Freezing the Dough, see page 45
- Rolling the Dough, see page 52
- Batch Baking, see page 56

---

1 cup / 120g all-purpose flour

¾ cup / 140g potato starch (see Baker's Note)

1 tsp baking powder

¼ tsp baking soda

½ tsp kosher salt

½ cup / 110g unsalted butter, at room temperature

¾ cup plus 1 Tbsp / 100g confectioners' sugar, plus extra for dusting on top

2 egg yolks, at room temperature

1 Tbsp rum (dark or spiced)

1 tsp almond extract

1 tsp pure vanilla extract (page 16)

One 14-oz / 396g can dulce de leche, store-bought or recipe follows

In a medium bowl, whisk together the flour, potato starch, baking powder, baking soda, and salt. Set aside.

In a stand mixer fitted with the paddle attachment, cream the butter and confectioners' sugar on medium speed until light and fluffy, about 2 minutes. Add the egg yolks and mix on medium speed until combined. Scrape down the bowl. Mix in the rum and almond and vanilla extracts. Add the flour mixture and mix on low speed until just combined.

On a sheet of plastic wrap, form the dough into a rectangle ½ inch / 1.3cm thick. Wrap and refrigerate for at least 1 hour, or up to 3 days. It can also be frozen for about 1 month.

Preheat the oven to 350°F / 175°C. Line two baking sheets with parchment paper.

Place the chilled dough on a silicone mat or piece of parchment paper. Cover it with plastic wrap and roll it into a rectangle ⅛ inch / 3mm thick. Place the rolled-out dough in the freezer for at least 10 minutes to set firm.

Using a 2-inch / 5cm round cookie cutter, stamp out the cookies. You can press the scraps together and reroll once.

Lay the cookies on the prepared baking sheets about 1 inch apart, leaving room for them to spread slightly.

Bake, one sheet at a time, in the middle of the oven for 12 to 15 minutes, until they are just slightly golden on the bottom (they are meant to stay very light in color). Allow to cool on the baking sheet completely before filling.

When you are ready to fill, spoon the cooled dulce de leche into a piping bag fitted with a round tip (Ateco #803) and pipe a ¼-inch / 6mm layer over half the cookies. Top with remaining cookies. Dust with confectioners' sugar.

BAKER'S NOTE

Potato starch and potato flour are not the same, so be sure to use the starch for this or your cookies will not have the intended texture.

MY HOME-EC COOKIE EVOLUTION

▨ Nut-Free　▨ Gluten-Free

Dulce de Leche

This decadent caramel made from sweetened condensed milk is easy to make, it just requires some time. I typically make it on the stove top, which can take hours before it achieves the desired deep caramel color and flavor. If you have a pressure cooker it will cut down the time substantially. I give both methods and the results are equally delicious. Because it takes time, I usually make at least two cans, since they will last indefinitely as long as you don't open the can.

Makes one 14-oz / 396g can

One 14-oz / 396g can sweetened condensed milk (I use Carnation and Eagle brands)

▨ **TO MAKE ON THE STOVE TOP**

In a large pot, cover an unopened can of sweetened condensed milk with water and bring to a boil. Allow to boil for about 3½ hours, making sure the can is completely submerged the whole time. You may need to add more water as it cooks. If you let the water boil off, the can may explode. After 3½ hours, remove the can and let it cool *completely* before opening. If you open the can before it cools, it may explode. Once you open the can, it will last about a week, covered, in the refrigerator.

▨ **TO MAKE IN A PRESSURE COOKER**

Place a trivet or basket in the inner pot of an Instant Pot. Remove the label from the can of sweetened condensed milk and wrap the unopened can completely in foil. Place the can in the center of the trivet and fill the pot with water to completely cover the can. Don't go beyond the fill line. Set the manual cooking setting to 45 minutes. The entire cook time will take slightly longer, because the pressure cooker will take a bit of time to get to temperature. Once the pressure cooker has cooked and cooled (*do not* manually release the pressure) according to the manufacturer's directions, remove the can and allow it to cool *completely*! If you open the can before it cools, it may explode. Once you open the can, it will last about 1 week, covered, in the refrigerator.

Speculoos (Biscoff-ish)

Speculoos, the cinnamon-spiced Belgian biscuit, became well known and much loved in my family due to the Lotus Biscoff cookies that are often served mid-flight. I don't usually take my inspiration from airplane snacks, but these are a phenomenon. You too may have nibbled on one while you were miles high in the air. Or you may have sampled "cookie butter," the wildly popular spreadable version of the rich, caramelly cookie, which would also be amazing spread on these cracker-like cookies. The cookies get their snap and rich flavor from a combination of almond and wheat flours. I've added a few more spices to the mix than is traditional and shape them into a brick before slicing them into dunk-able rectangles. It's simple, and they taste just divine.

Makes about 48 cookies

Cookie Academy Review
▧ Freezing the Dough,
see page 45
▧ Batch Baking, see page 56

1¾ cups / 210g all-purpose flour

½ cup / 60g almond meal or flour (see page 19)

¼ tsp baking soda

¼ tsp kosher salt

1¼ tsp ground cinnamon

¼ tsp ground ginger

⅛ tsp ground cardamom

⅛ tsp ground cloves

⅛ tsp ground nutmeg

½ cup plus 2 Tbsp / 140g unsalted butter, at room temperature

1 cup / 200g lightly packed brown sugar

2 tsp light or dark molasses (not blackstrap)

1 egg yolk, at room temperature

In a small bowl, whisk together the flour, almond meal, baking soda, salt, cinnamon, ginger, cardamom, cloves, and nutmeg. Set aside.

In a stand mixer fitted with the paddle attachment, cream the butter, brown sugar, and molasses on medium speed until light and fluffy, about 2 minutes. Mix in the flour mixture on low speed until just combined.

On a sheet of plastic wrap, form the dough into a 6 by 3-inch / 15 by 7.5cm brick, using a bench scraper to form neat sides. Wrap and refrigerate for at least 1 hour, or up to 3 days. You can also freeze it for about 1 month.

Preheat the oven to 350°F / 175°C. Line two baking sheets with parchment paper.

Using a very sharp knife, cut the chilled dough along the short side into slices ⅛ inch / 3mm thick and 3 inches / 7.5cm long. Lay the slices on the prepared baking sheet. They won't spread much, so they can be placed close together.

Bake, one sheet at a time, in the middle of the oven for about 15 minutes, until they are a caramel-brown color. Allow to cool on the baking sheet completely.

BAKER'S NOTE

If they lose their snap, you can re-bake them at 350°F / 175°C for 5 minutes.

Russian Tea Cakes
(Mexican Wedding Cookies)

These little powdery orbs are interchangeably called Russian tea cakes, Mexican wedding cookies, Viennese sugar balls, Italian butterball cookies, snowballs, and snowdrops, and I've probably missed a few. They have an honored place on many a holiday cookie tray. You've no doubt popped one in your mouth and left a little snow shower of powdered sugar on your holiday sweater. You were too busy enjoying the melt-in-your-mouth treat to care! Luckily, these tender, nutty treats are incredibly easy to make. My secret trick is to brown the butter and toast the nuts to amp up the flavor. You won't be sorry you took the time to do so. My favorite variations include swapping out the pecans for walnuts.

Makes 55 to 60 cookies

Cookie Academy Review
▓ Using a Portion Scoop, see page 43
▓ Batch Baking, see page 56

1 cup / 113g pecans (or walnuts), lightly toasted and cooled

2 cups / 240g confectioners' sugar, divided

2 cups / 240g all-purpose flour

½ tsp kosher salt

1 cup / 224g brown butter (page 41), at room temperature

2 tsp pure vanilla extract (page 16)

½ tsp almond extract

Preheat the oven to 350°F / 175°C, with the racks at the top and lower third of the oven. Line two baking sheets with parchment paper.

In a food processor, pulse the pecans and ½ cup / 60g of the confectioners' sugar until they are a fine meal.

In a large bowl, whisk the nut mixture, flour, and salt.

In a stand mixer fitted with the paddle attachment, cream the brown butter and ¾ cup / 90g of the confectioners' sugar on medium speed until light and fluffy, about 4 minutes. Mix in the vanilla and almond extracts. Add the flour mixture and mix on low speed just until the dough forms a ball, about 30 seconds.

Scoop the cookie dough using a #70 (2½-teaspoon) portion scoop onto the prepared baking sheets. You can make the cookies larger or smaller, but it will affect the baking time. Roll them in your palms to create round balls. Position them on the lined baking sheet so they have about 1½ inches / 4cm between them.

Bake in the oven with one sheet on the top rack and the other on the lower rack for 12 to 14 minutes, rotating the trays and switching from top to bottom and front to back, halfway through the baking, until the bottoms are golden and the tops set, but pale. The tops may crack slightly.

Allow the cookies to cool completely before you roll them in 1¼ cups / 150g confectioners' sugar. If you roll them too soon, the sugar will melt and get clumpy.

Dip them again right before you pack or serve them.

Dairy-Free

Chocolate Biscotti

These biscotti are loaded with chocolate, hazelnuts, dried cherries, and candied oranges, and I bake them regularly as holiday gifts. Biscotti are ideal for gifting because they last for weeks at room temperature, freeze well, and look like they're studded with jewels. Some recipes call for butter, but you'll notice I leave it out. Butter softens everything, and I prefer the characteristic crunchy biscotti that holds up well when you dunk it in coffee or tea (or wine, if that's how you fancy it!). These rich and chocolaty biscotti are an easy and satisfying after-dinner treat. Or crumble some on top of vanilla ice cream to add delicious flavor and a satisfying crunch.

Makes about 30 to 40 biscotti

Cookie Academy Review
- Batch Baking, see page 56
- Melting Chocolate, see page 59

1⅔ cups / 200g all-purpose flour

⅓ cup / 40g Dutch-processed cocoa powder, sifted if lumpy

1 tsp baking soda

1 tsp kosher salt

3 eggs, at room temperature

1 cup / 200g granulated sugar

2 tsp pure vanilla extract (page 16)

6 oz / 170g bittersweet chocolate, chopped

1 cup / 120g whole hazelnuts or another nut

1 cup / 135g dried tart cherries

⅓ cup / 50g coarsely chopped candied citrus peel or candied ginger

4 oz / 112g bittersweet chocolate, melted (optional)

Dried edible rose petals (optional)

Flaky sea salt (optional)

Preheat the oven to 350°F / 175°C. Line a baking sheet with parchment paper.

In a stand mixer fitted with the paddle attachment, mix together the flour, cocoa, baking soda, and salt on low speed, until just combined, about 15 seconds. Add the eggs, sugar, and vanilla, turn the speed up to medium, and mix until it just comes together into a thick but wet dough, for about 1 minute. Mix in the chocolate, nuts, dried cherries, and candied citrus until just combined.

You may need to stir with a rubber spatula to make sure they are evenly distributed.

Form the dough into two equal logs 3 inches / 7.5cm in diameter and 8 inches / 20cm long and place on the lined baking sheet. Leave about 3 inches / 7.5cm between them, so they have room to spread.

Bake in the middle of the oven for 30 to 35 minutes, just until the dough is set but still soft.

Allow the logs to cool, just until they are cool enough to handle, 10 to 15 minutes. With a sharp serrated knife, cut the logs into slices ½ inch / 1.3cm thick. Keep the oven on.

Lay the slices on the baking sheet and bake again for 10 minutes. Flip the cookies over and bake for about 10 more minutes, or until crisp.

Cool on baking sheet and store in an airtight container. These cookies last for weeks. Before serving, drizzle with melted chocolate and sprinkle with rose petals and a few flakes of salt (if using). Refrigerate for a few minutes until the chocolate is set.

Triple Almond "Biscottini"

These biscotti spread quite a bit during their first bake, making them thinner by their last bake. My trusted recipe tester, Sara, nicknamed them "biscottini!" Little is sometimes better. Almond is such a classic flavor for biscotti, and I absolutely love it, so I generally pack my biscotti with as much almond as I can, using paste, nuts, and extract to get the richest flavor possible. Along with the crunchy nuts, these thin biscottini are dotted with almond paste and mini chocolate chips, which add a little chewy texture. They're great with morning coffee or for dunking in white wine or champagne on a summer evening. For a burst of color and flavor, try the pistachio "biscottini" variation with apricots.

Makes about 36 biscottini

Cookie Academy Review
Batch Baking, see page 56

1⅓ cups / 160g all-purpose flour

½ tsp baking powder

¼ tsp kosher salt

6 Tbsp / 80g unsalted butter, at room temperature

½ cup / 100g granulated sugar

2 large eggs, at room temperature

2 tsp pure vanilla extract (page 16)

1 tsp almond extract

½ cup / 100g roasted, salted whole almonds

½ cup / 100g almond paste, chopped into ¼-inch / 6mm cubes

½ cup / 100g mini semisweet chocolate chips or small chunks

Preheat the oven to 325°F / 165°C. Double up a baking sheet and line with parchment paper.

In a small bowl, whisk together the flour, baking powder, and salt.

In a stand mixer fitted with the paddle attachment, cream the butter and sugar together on medium-low speed, about 1 minute.

Add the eggs, one at a time, mixing well and scraping the bowl between additions. It may not look smooth but will come together when the flour is added.

On low speed, stir in the vanilla and almond extracts, and then add the flour mixture. Mix until just combined, about 1 minute.

Add the almonds, almond paste, and chocolate, stirring to just combine.

Using wet hands, form the dough into two logs each 2 inches / 5cm in diameter and 11 inches / 28cm long. Be sure to leave 3 inches / 7.5cm of space between them so they can spread.

Bake in the middle of the oven for about 20 minutes, just until the dough is set but still soft. They will spread quite a bit.

Allow the logs to cool for about 5 minutes. Use a very sharp serrated knife to cut them into slices ¼ inch / 6mm thick. If the dough sits for too long, it gets brittle. Keep the oven on.

Lay the slices on the doubled-up baking sheet and bake again for about 15 minutes, until just golden crisp. You may want to flip the cookies over halfway through if they are not baking evenly.

Cool on the baking sheet and store in an airtight container. These cookies last for weeks.

VARIATION: PISTACHIO "BISCOTTINI"

Replace the almonds with pistachios and replace the chopped almond paste with chopped apricots.

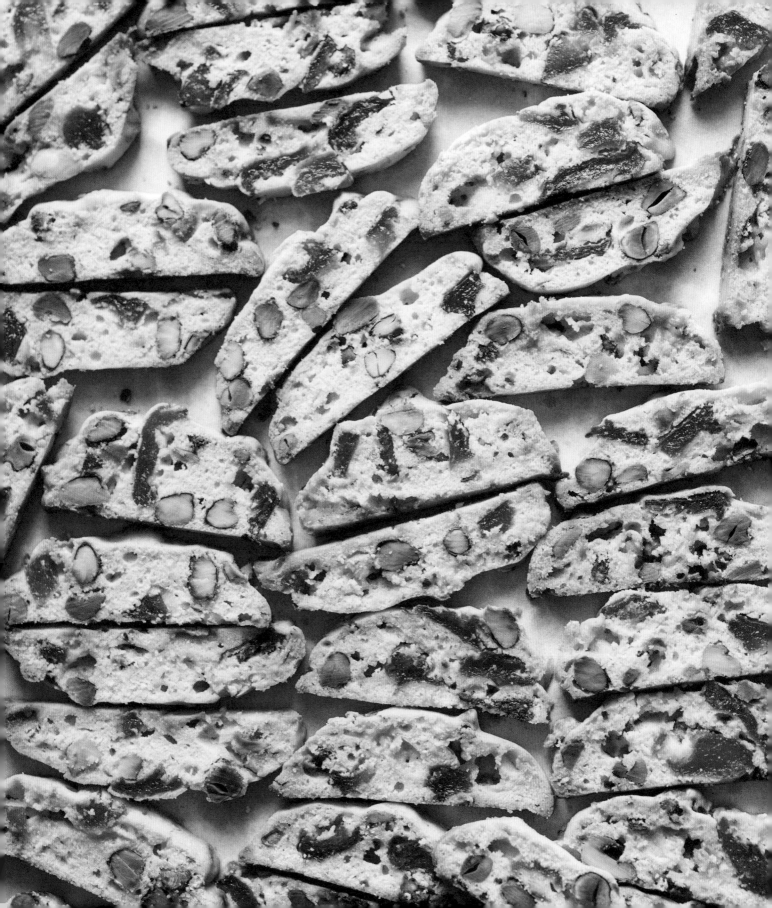

Italian Rainbow Cookies

More like tiny cakes or petit fours than cookies, these rainbow cookies take a little bit of work but are so worth it. The almond paste and extract—don't skimp on either of these—give them a beautiful richness. My friend Stephen Tedesco took me to one of his hometown favorite Italian bakeries, Mozzicato De Pasquale, in Hartford, Connecticut, where these colorful almond treats were my hands-down favorite. As we ate them, Stephen suggested they may be good with a bit of sambuca. So, when I got home, I experimented by brushing a layer of sambuca on before adding the jam, and the anise flavor soaked into the cake, balancing out the flavors and giving the air of a party.

Makes about 48 cookies

Cookie Academy Review
▦ Melting Chocolate,
see page 59

1 cup / 200g granulated sugar

8 oz / 226g almond paste (be sure it is soft)

1¼ cups / 275g unsalted butter, at room temperature

4 eggs, at room temperature, separated

¼ cup / 60ml whole milk

2 tsp almond extract

2 cups / 240g all-purpose flour

Red and green food coloring (page 15)

¼ cup / 60ml sambuca, rum, or brandy (optional)

½ cup / 110g raspberry preserves

1½ cups / 340g bittersweet chocolate, melted

Preheat the oven to 350°F / 175°C.

Line the bottom of three 9 by 13-inch / 24 by 36cm pans with greased parchment paper.

In a food processor, pulverize the sugar and almond paste. Add the butter a few tablespoons at a time and blend well, making sure the mixture is smooth before adding the next few tablespoons. Scrape the sides of the bowl to make sure it is all blended evenly.

Add the yolks, one at a time, until evenly blended. Add the milk and almond extract. Add one-third of the flour (⅔ cup / 80g) and pulse until just combined. Repeat with the remaining flour (1⅓ cups / 160g).

In a stand mixer fitted with the whisk attachment, beat the egg whites until they are just holding stiff peaks. Add one-third of the whipped whites to the almond paste mixture and pulse to incorporate. Pour the mixture out of the food processor bowl and into the bowl of egg whites and fold everything together. Divide the batter into three bowls. Color one bowl with the red food coloring, another with the green, and leave the last bowl without color.

Spread the red batter in a prepared pan. Repeat with the green batter in the second pan, and natural-colored batter in the third pan. Bake in the top and bottom thirds of the oven for 12 to 15 minutes, until set. Check after 10 minutes to make sure they are baking evenly and rotate top to bottom and back to front if needed. Allow to cool completely in the pan.

To assemble: Brush the sambuca over the baked red layer, still in the pan, and then cover it with half of the raspberry preserves, making sure to spread it all the way to the edges. Invert the natural-colored layer over the raspberry-topped red layer (be sure to remove parchment paper once it is in place), and cover with the remaining preserves. Invert the final green layer on top of the raspberry-topped natural-colored layer. Press the three layers gently together, then peel off the top parchment paper from the green layer.

Spread half of the chocolate evenly over the top. Using a serrated knife or a fork, draw squiggly lines in the chocolate to create a wavy pattern. Refrigerate the layers until the chocolate is well set, about 30 minutes. Flip the layers over onto a cutting board or sheet of parchment paper, remove the parchment paper from the red layer, spread with the remaining melted chocolate, and create the wavy pattern again. Refrigerate until set, about 30 minutes.

Using a thin, sharp knife dipped in hot water to prevent the chocolate from cracking, trim the edges, so you have a clean, even edge. Cut the layers into small pieces—I went with 1 by 2 inches / 2.5 by 7.5cm, but it's totally up to you.

MY HOME-EC COOKIE EVOLUTION

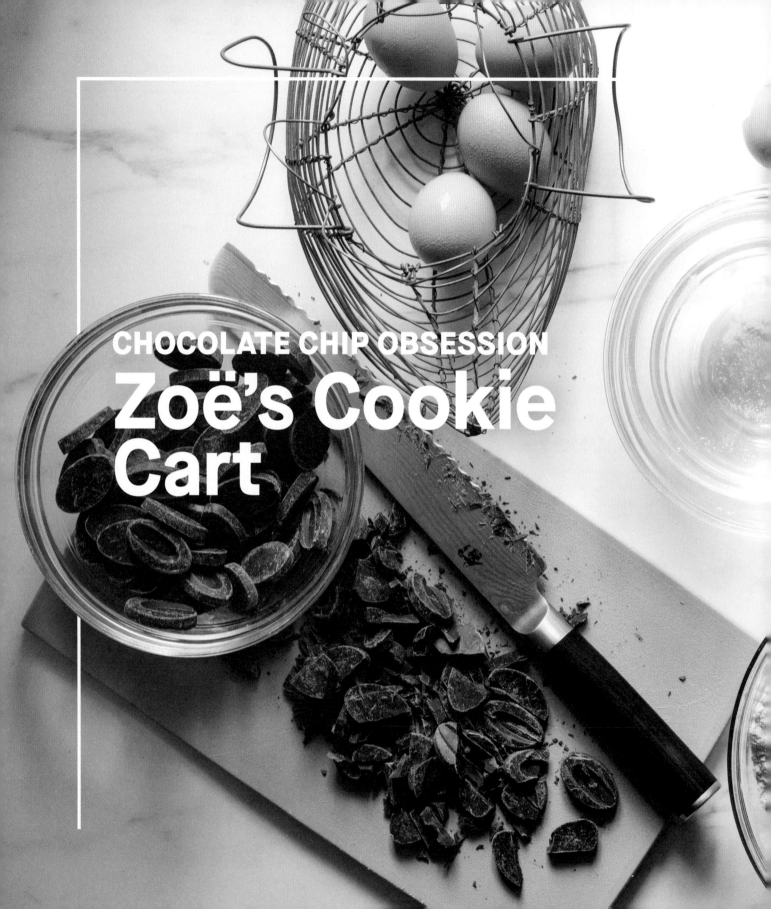

CHOCOLATE CHIP OBSESSION
Zoë's Cookie Cart

The cookie cart business I started in college was inspired by my obsession with chocolate chip cookies. Back then I was riffing off of the recipe on the bag of Nestlé chocolate chips, mixed with some inspiration from the gourmet cookie craze of the 1980s. Some of the cookies seemed amazing back in the day, but over the years, as I've learned more and my palate has become more discerning, I've ended up experimenting endlessly with the recipes (you can see some of that process in Chocolate Chip Cookie Lab, page 46). In this chapter you will find all of my favorites from my perfect go-to chocolate chip cookie (page 181) to my super-thick Smash Cookies (page 182). This is also where you will find the ultradecadent brownies and blondies. If you are a fudgy brownie lover or someone who likes a cakier crumb, they're all here. There is something for everyone and every mood.

Zoë's Perfect Chocolate Chip Cookies

My favorite cookie from the 1980s has evolved over time as I've amped up my skills and perfected my tips and techniques. This version is my perfect chocolate chip cookie. The beauty of this recipe is that it is meant to change according to your mood. I've even changed it since it appeared on my TV show and blog. It's the perfect example of how fluid baking can be, which is exactly what makes it so fun and exciting!

See Chocolate Chip Cookie Lab (page 46) for all my experiments, tricks, and tips.

Makes about 20 cookies

Cookie Academy Review
▦ Using a Portion Scoop, see page 43
▦ Freezing the Dough, see page 45
▦ Chocolate Chip Cookie Lab, see page 46
▦ Batch Baking, see page 56

2⅔ cups / 320g all-purpose flour

1¼ tsp baking soda

1½ tsp kosher salt

¾ cup / 170g unsalted butter, at room temperature

¼ cup / 57g shortening

1 cup / 200g granulated sugar

1½ cups / 300g lightly packed brown sugar

1½ tsp pure vanilla extract (page 16)

2 eggs, at room temperature

8 to 12 oz / 225 to 340g bittersweet chocolate, chopped in largish chunks (about ¼ inch / 6mm; see Baker's Note)

Flaky sea salt for finishing

In a medium bowl, whisk together the flour, baking soda, and salt. Set aside.

In a stand mixer fitted with the paddle attachment, cream the butter, shortening, granulated and brown sugars, and vanilla on medium speed until creamy, about 3 minutes.

Add the eggs, one at a time, beating on medium speed until incorporated. Add the flour mixture all at once and mix until just incorporated. Mix in the chopped chocolate pieces. You may need to give the bowl a couple of swipes with a rubber spatula at the end to make sure the chocolate is evenly distributed.

Line a baking sheet with parchment paper. Scoop the cookie dough using a #20 (3-tablespoon) portion scoop onto the baking sheet. You can make the cookies larger or smaller, but it will affect the baking time.

Refrigerate the dough balls for at least 30 minutes; but if you have the time, they improve if you let them sit for 24 to 36 hours. After they are chilled, you can bake them or freeze the dough balls for baking later.

Preheat the oven to 375°F / 190°C. Line a baking sheet with parchment paper.

Evenly space six chilled cookie balls on the prepared sheet and sprinkle them with flaky sea salt. Bake in the middle of the oven for about 12 minutes or until golden brown and slightly puffed. Repeat with as many batches as you need.

Allow the cookies to cool slightly on the baking sheet, until you can move them without them falling apart, about 5 minutes. Then move them to a cooling rack to finish cooling.

BAKER'S NOTE

My husband likes a cookie with more dough and fewer pools of chocolate, so I make some with less chocolate for him and then dump the rest in for me. You can adjust to how much you like.

▦ **VARIATION: CHOCOLATE CHIP COOKIES WITH BACON BITS**

This is a cookie I made for my family while vacationing at a cabin. We'd just had a big breakfast and there was bacon fat left over. Instead of throwing it away, I used it in a batch of cookies. Holy moly were they good! Replace the amount of butter and shortening in the recipe with ½ cup / 110g bacon fat + ½ cup / 110g unsalted butter, and add in ¼ cup / 55g crispy bacon pieces when you add the chocolate. Bake as directed.

ZOË'S COOKIE CART

Smash Cookies

I was inspired by the Levain Bakery cookie craze in New York City to create a *big*, thick, chocolaty pile of deliciousness. These gigantic cookies are best served warm and slightly underbaked, so you get the feel of toasty, just shy of raw, cookie dough.

As I was creating my version of this wildly popular cookie, something a little unexpected happened, and they turned into smash cookies. The dough mixes together like a crumb topping you'd put on a fruit crisp or crumble, which I then press together into a ball. I chill the dough balls, bake them big and round, then smash them flat when they come out of the oven. This way the inside stays soft, but the outside has a toffee-like flavor and slight crispiness. The secret to this recipe lies in the giant balls of dough; if you make them smaller, they won't have the same consistency.

Makes about 12 large cookies

Cookie Academy Review
▓ Freezing the Dough, see page 45
▓ Batch Baking, see page 56

3½ cups / 420g all-purpose flour

1 tsp baking powder

1 tsp baking soda

1¼ tsp kosher salt

¾ cup plus 2 Tbsp / 200g unsalted butter, melted and slightly cooled

2¼ cups / 450g lightly packed brown sugar

2 tsp pure vanilla extract (page 16)

2 eggs, at room temperature

5 oz / 140g bittersweet chocolate, finely chopped or chips

1 cup / 140g toasted pecan pieces (or walnuts, macadamia nuts, coconut, dried cherries, M&Ms, or whatever you can think to jam in there)

In a medium bowl, whisk together the flour, baking powder, baking soda, and salt. Set aside.

In a large bowl, whisk together the melted butter, brown sugar, and vanilla until uniformly mixed. Add the eggs, one at a time, whisking until they are incorporated. With a wooden spoon mix in the flour mixture all at once until just incorporated. It should be quite thick, but not dry. Add the chopped chocolate and nut pieces.

Line a baking sheet with parchment paper. Press together roughly shaped 4.25-ounce / 120g dough balls. Don't flatten them; the dough balls should be the shape of a baseball.

Refrigerate the dough balls on the prepared baking sheet for at least 1 hour; if you have the time, the cookies will be even thicker if you let them sit for 24 to 36 hours. After they are chilled, you can bake them or freeze the dough balls for baking later.

Preheat the oven to 375°F / 190°C *convection* heat (or 400°F / 205°C flat heat). Double up two baking sheets and line with parchment paper. The double sheets will prevent the bottoms from overbrowning in the hot oven.

Evenly space six chilled dough balls on the prepared doubled baking sheets. Leave 2 inches / 5cm between them so they can be smashed after baking. Bake, one sheet at a time, in the middle of the oven for about 12 to 14 minutes or until they are golden brown on the outside, but still soft in the center. Remove the sheets from the oven and while they are still hot, gently smash the cookies with a metal spatula so they are 1-inch / 2.5cm thick disks.

Allow the cookies to cool for about 5 minutes on the baking sheets, then move to a cooling rack. Enjoy slightly warm or at room temperature.

▓ **VARIATION: BROWN BUTTER SMASH BLONDIES**

Replace the butter with brown butter (page 41), and mix as directed above. Smash the dough into a 9 by 13-inch / 24 by 36cm pan, lined with a lightly greased parchment-paper sling. Bake at 375°F / 190°C for about 12 minutes, or until the edges are golden brown. Allow to cool completely in the pan before removing and cutting.

Chocolate Hazelnut Cookies

The richness of hazelnuts is the perfect match for bittersweet chocolate; it is no wonder this marriage of flavors has inspired countless desserts. They blend together flawlessly. The hazelnut flour in this recipe not only adds a deep, decadent flavor, but it also creates a luxurious texture. Adding in the Nutella gives it an extra hit of flavor and *pow!* My husband said this cookie is his new favorite, and I'm keeping track of how many make that list! ;)

I love the more earthy flavors of pistachios and tahini in the variation, which remind me of the halva (sesame fudge) that I used to have as a child. These have a more old-world flavor and I think my Bubbe Berkowitz would have been a big fan.

Makes 20 cookies

Cookie Academy Review
- Using a Portion Scoop, see page 43
- Freezing the Dough, see page 45
- Chocolate Chip Cookie Lab, see page 46
- Batch Baking, see page 56

2½ cups / 340g all-purpose flour

1 cup / 100g hazelnut flour or meal (see Baker's Note)

½ tsp baking soda

2 tsp baking powder

1½ tsp kosher salt

1 cup / 226g unsalted butter, at room temperature

1½ cups / 300g lightly packed brown sugar

1 Tbsp pure vanilla extract (page 16)

2 eggs, at room temperature

12 oz / 340g bittersweet, semisweet, or milk chocolate, chopped

Flaky sea salt for finishing (optional)

In a small bowl, whisk together the all-purpose and hazelnut flours, the baking soda, baking powder, and salt. Set aside.

In a stand mixer fitted with the paddle attachment, cream the butter, brown sugar, and vanilla on medium speed until creamy, about 3 minutes.

Add the eggs, one at a time, beating on medium speed until incorporated. Add the flour mixture all at once and mix until just incorporated. Mix in the chopped chocolate pieces. You may need to give the bowl a couple of swipes with a rubber spatula at the end to make sure the chocolate is evenly distributed.

Line a baking sheet with parchment paper. Scoop the cookie dough using a #16 (¼-cup) portion scoop onto the prepared baking sheet. You can make the cookies larger or smaller, but it will affect the baking time.

Refrigerate the dough balls for at least 30 minutes; if you have the time, they improve if you let them sit for 24 to 36 hours. After they are chilled, you can bake them or freeze the dough balls for baking later.

Preheat the oven to 350°F / 175°C. Line as many baking sheets as you need with parchment paper. (You will need four baking sheets to bake the entire batch.)

Evenly space six chilled cookie balls on each sheet and sprinkle each with flaky sea salt (if using). Bake, one sheet at a time, in the middle of the oven for 12 to 15 minutes, until golden brown on the bottom and just set on top.

Allow the cookies to cool for a few minutes on the baking sheets, then move to cooling racks.

BAKER'S NOTE

To make your own hazelnut flour: In a food processor, pulse together ¾ cup / 100g lightly toasted hazelnuts and ¼ cup / 30g of the all-purpose flour called for in the recipe until the nuts are very finely ground and the consistency of cornmeal.

VARIATION: PISTACHIO TAHINI COOKIES

Replace the hazelnuts with pistachios and make the flour in the same way as instructed above. Mix in 1 Tbsp tahini (black or white) to the batter with the butter. Just before scooping the cookies, drizzle 2 Tbsp melted tahini over the batter. Scoop, refrigerate, and bake as written above.

Triple Chocolate Chunk Cookies

The intensity of the cocoa powder is the perfect backdrop for white, milk, and bittersweet chocolate chunks. These are for the most enthusiastic chocolate fans and deliver in every bite. The cookie itself is lighter than it looks and has a slightly soft texture. They will leave your fingers unapologetically covered in chocolate if you eat them slightly warm.

Makes about 30 cookies

Cookie Academy Review
▨ Using a Portion Scoop, see page 43
▨ Freezing the Dough, see page 45
▨ Chocolate Chip Cookie Lab, see page 46
▨ Batch Baking, see page 56

2 cups / 240g all-purpose flour

½ cup / 50g Dutch-processed cocoa powder, sifted if lumpy

¼ tsp baking soda

1 tsp baking powder

1 tsp kosher salt

1 cup / 220g unsalted butter, at room temperature

1½ cups / 300g lightly packed brown sugar

1 tsp pure vanilla extract (page 16)

1 egg, at room temperature

3 oz / 85g white chocolate, chopped into chunks

3 oz / 85g milk chocolate, chopped into chunks

3 oz / 85g bittersweet chocolate, chopped into chunks

Flaky sea salt for finishing (optional)

In a small bowl, whisk together the flour, cocoa powder, baking soda, baking powder, and salt. Set aside.

In a stand mixer fitted with the paddle attachment, cream the butter, brown sugar, and vanilla on medium speed until creamy, about 3 minutes.

Add the egg, beating on medium speed until incorporated. Add the flour mixture all at once and mix until just incorporated. Mix in the chopped chocolate. You may need to give the bowl a couple of swipes with a rubber spatula at the end to make sure the chocolate is evenly distributed.

Line a baking sheet with parchment paper. Scoop the cookie dough using a #40 (1½-tablespoon) portion scoop onto a baking sheet. You can make the cookies larger or smaller, but it will affect the baking time.

Refrigerate the dough balls for at least 30 minutes; if you have the time, they improve if you let them sit for 24 to 36 hours. After they are chilled, you can bake them or freeze the dough balls for baking later.

Preheat the oven to 350°F / 175°C. Line as many baking sheets as you need with parchment paper. (You will need six baking sheets to bake the entire batch.)

Evenly space six chilled cookie balls on each sheet and sprinkle them with flaky sea salt (if using). Bake, one sheet at a time, in the middle of the oven for 12 to 15 minutes, until the cookies crackle a bit on top and no longer look wet.

Allow the cookies to cool for about 5 minutes on the baking sheets, then move to cooling racks.

Crisp Chocolate Chip Cookies

When both my mom and aunt asked for a crisp, buttery cookie, I knew I needed to come up with something really special to satisfy their sweet tooths. The butter and sugar unite in the oven to create a toffee-like cookie that supports the large chunks of bittersweet chocolate. Adding a few salt flakes perks up all the flavors and brings out the caramel flavor of the cookie. I normally go for a chocolate chip cookie with some chew, but I fell hard for these crispy delights.

Makes about 36 cookies

Cookie Academy Review
▌ Using a Portion Scoop, see page 43
▌ Chocolate Chip Cookie Lab, see page 46
▌ Batch Baking, see page 56

2¼ cups / 270g all-purpose flour

1¼ tsp baking soda

2 tsp kosher salt

1 cup / 220g unsalted butter, at room temperature

1½ cups / 300g granulated sugar

½ cup / 100g lightly packed brown sugar

1½ tsp pure vanilla extract (page 16)

2 eggs, at room temperature

12 oz / 340g bittersweet, milk, and/or white chocolate, chopped in largish (about ¼-inch / 6mm) chunks

Flaky sea salt for finishing (optional)

Preheat the oven to 350°F / 170°C. Line baking sheets with parchment paper or a silicone mat.

In a small bowl, whisk together the flour, baking soda, and kosher salt. Set aside.

In a stand mixer fitted with the paddle attachment, cream the butter, granulated and brown sugars, and vanilla on medium speed until creamy, about 3 minutes.

Add the eggs, one at a time, beating on medium speed until incorporated. Add the flour mixture all at once and mix on low speed until just incorporated. Mix in the chopped chocolate pieces. You may need to give the bowl a couple of swipes with a rubber spatula at the end to make sure the chocolate is evenly distributed.

Scoop the cookie dough using a #40 (1½-tablespoon) portion scoop and arrange six dough balls evenly spaced on the prepared baking sheets. Sprinkle them with flaky sea salt (if using). You can make the cookies larger or smaller, but it will affect the baking time. Plan to bake the cookies right away, so they spread even more and are super crispy.

Bake, one sheet at a time, in the middle of the oven for 12 to 15 minutes, until caramelized and quite crispy. Repeat with the remaining cookie dough.

Allow the cookies to cool for about 5 minutes on the baking sheets, then move to a cooling rack.

Rye White-Chocolate Macadamia Nut Cookies

This cookie is a nod to the most iconic 1980s Mrs. Fields flavor, the white chocolate and macadamia nut cookie, but with even more depth of flavor using rye flour. I remember the first time I had Mrs. Fields's version. I'd never had a macadamia nut before that cookie, so I was blown away by its buttery texture and how it blended perfectly with the white chocolate. It's such a classic combination, but I think both of those flavors are so rich, the cookie needed a bit more flavor to carry them into a more modern realm. The bit of rye flour is just the right note.

Makes about 20 cookies

Cookie Academy Review

▨ Using a Portion Scoop, see page 43

▨ Freezing the Dough, see page 45

▨ Chocolate Chip Cookie Lab, see page 46

▨ Batch Baking, see page 56

1⅓ cups / 155g all-purpose flour

½ cup plus 1 Tbsp / 80g rye flour

½ tsp baking soda

½ tsp baking powder

½ tsp kosher salt

½ cup / 110g unsalted butter, melted

1¼ cups / 250g lightly packed brown sugar

½ cup / 100g granulated sugar

1½ tsp pure vanilla extract (page 16)

1 egg, at room temperature

4 oz / 112g white chocolate, chopped into small chunks

3 oz / 85g macadamia nuts, chopped into small pieces

Flaky sea salt for finishing

In a small bowl, whisk together the all-purpose and rye flours, baking soda, baking powder, and salt. Set aside.

In a large bowl, mix the melted butter, brown and granulated sugars, and the vanilla until uniformly blended. Add the egg, stirring until incorporated. Add the flour mixture all at once and mix until just incorporated. Mix in the chopped chocolate pieces and nuts. You may need to give the bowl a couple of swipes with a rubber spatula at the end to make sure the chocolate and nuts are evenly distributed.

Line a baking sheet with parchment paper. Scoop the cookie dough using a #40 (1½-tablespoon) portion scoop onto a baking sheet. You can make the cookies larger or smaller, but it will affect the baking time.

Refrigerate the dough balls for at least 30 minutes; if you have the time, they improve if you let them sit for 24 to 36 hours. After they are chilled, you can bake them or freeze the dough balls for baking later.

Preheat the oven to 350°F / 175°C. Line as many baking sheets as you need with parchment paper. (You will need four if you plan to bake the entire batch.)

Evenly space six chilled cookie balls on each sheet and sprinkle each with flaky sea salt. Bake, one sheet at a time, in the middle of the oven for 10 to 14 minutes, until caramel brown along the bottoms.

Allow the cookies to cool for a few minutes on the baking sheets, then move to cooling racks.

Zoë Bakes "Anything Goes" Brownies

One time, I was putting together a care package for my youngest son, Charlie, and his college roommates, who all wanted their own flavor. Instead of making four separate pans of brownies, I mixed up one batch but topped them four different ways, to suit all four boys. It was a *huge* success, and the boys loved them. The key to these dense, fudgy, over-the-top brownies is to not overbake them. If you want them a bit cakier, which is a legit choice, you can bake them for an extra 5 minutes. Also, you must let them cool completely before cutting, so the chocolate has a chance to set up. If you don't wait, they're more like pudding—but if that's how you like them, have at it!

Makes 32 brownies

Cookie Academy Review
▨ Parchment-Paper Sling, see page 39
▨ Clean Cut Bars, see page 58

2⅔ cups / 280g cake flour

½ cup / 45g Dutch-processed cocoa powder, sifted if lumpy

1 tsp kosher salt

2 cups / 452g unsalted butter

12 oz / 340g bittersweet or semisweet chocolate, chopped

7 eggs, at room temperature

3 cups / 600g granulated sugar

2 tsp pure vanilla extract (page 16)

Toppings—these are what Charlie and his friends picked, but you can get creative with how you top the brownies.

Peanut Butter & Oreos (optional)

Nutella & Hazelnuts (optional)

Chocolate on Chocolate (optional)

Preheat the oven to 350°F / 175°C. Grease and line a 9 by 13-inch / 24 by 36cm baking pan with buttered parchment paper that goes up the long sides to create a sling.

In a medium bowl, whisk together the flour, cocoa powder, and salt. Set aside.

In a medium saucepan over medium-low heat, melt the butter and bring it to a simmer. Remove from the heat and add in the chopped chocolate. Swirl the pan to cover the chocolate and allow it to sit for 3 minutes. Gently whisk until smooth.

In a bowl of a stand mixer fitted with the whisk attachment, whip together the eggs, sugar, and vanilla on medium-high speed until light and fluffy, about 5 minutes. Turn the speed to low and slowly add in the melted chocolate mixture. Add the flour mixture and stir until just combined. Pour into the prepared pan.

Make your desired toppings.

▨ IF MAKING PEANUT BUTTER & OREOS

Warm 2 tablespoons of peanut butter in the microwave for a few seconds to make it spreadable. Add it to ¼ of the prepared pan, swirl it with a skewer, then poke 10 Oreos broken in half into the top of the brownies.

▨ IF MAKING NUTELLA & HAZELNUTS

Warm 2 tablespoons of Nutella in the microwave for a few seconds to make it spreadable. Add it to ¼ of the prepared pan, swirl with a skewer, then sprinkle on ⅔ cup / 85g of toasted hazelnuts.

▨ IF MAKING CHOCOLATE ON CHOCOLATE

Measure out a 3-ounce / 85g mix of white, milk, and dark chocolate chunks. Poke half into ¼ of the batter and top with the remaining half.

The last ¼ of the brownies can be left plain and simple or you can add another flavor here.

Bake in the middle of the oven for 35 to 40 minutes, or until a tester comes out with moist crumbs. If you like your brownies dense and gooey, bake them until the sides puff, but the center is still fudgy when tested, about 30 minutes. If you want them cakier, add a few more minutes and the tester should come out with dry crumb, about 45 minutes.

Cool completely in the pan before using the sling to lift the brownies out of the pan and cutting.

Betty LeRoy's Chocolate Chews

I found the recipe for this treat in my Granny's recipe box, faded and well worn. Betty was one of the four "Roselawn Girls," a group of my granny's friends who lived on Roselawn Street in Detroit. They met in kindergarten and stayed close friends their entire lives. Barbara (my Granny), Betty, Marion, and another Betty often exchanged recipes and family gossip, sometimes together on one stained card.

This recipe is called "Chocolate Chews," and I kept the name out of respect for Betty. But for the life of me, I can't figure out where the chew comes from. Like so many old recipes, I just have to guess at Betty's methods. Whipping the eggs makes for a light and delicate cake-like texture that is lovely and delicious.

Makes about 12 brownies

Cookie Academy Review
▯ Parchment-Paper Sling, see page 39
▯ Clean Cut Bars, see page 58

½ cup / 110g unsalted butter

1 Tbsp coconut oil (or vegetable oil)

2 oz / 60g unsweetened (baking) chocolate

2 eggs, at room temperature

1 cup / 200g granulated sugar

⅛ tsp kosher salt

1 tsp pure vanilla extract (page 16)

½ cup / 60g all-purpose flour

4 oz / 112g bittersweet chocolate, finely chopped

2 oz / 55g pecans, chopped and toasted (optional)

1 generous pinch of flaky sea salt for top (optional)

Preheat the oven to 350°F / 175°C. Line a greased 8-inch / 20cm baking pan with greased parchment paper that goes up the sides to create a sling.

In a medium saucepan over low heat, melt the butter, coconut oil, and chocolate, stirring continuously until blended. Remove from the heat.

In the bowl of a stand mixer fitted with the whisk attachment, whip together the eggs, sugar, salt, and vanilla on medium-high speed until light and fluffy, about 5 minutes. Turn the speed to low and slowly add in the melted chocolate mixture. Using the whisk attachment or a rubber spatula, fold the flour into the chocolate mixture by hand, until just combined. Pour the batter into the prepared pan and sprinkle chopped chocolate, pecans, and sea salt over the top, if desired.

Bake in the middle of the oven for 18 to 20 minutes, until a tester comes out with moist crumbs and the brownie is puffed and set.

Cool completely in the pan before removing from the pan and cutting. Chilling the brownies gives them more of a "chew."

Cocoa Nutella Brownies

This brownie has a chew to it that I am in love with. I make them with a dark Dutch-processed cocoa powder, so the flavor and color is super-intense. You can go a step further and use some black cocoa. There is no melted chocolate, so it's more like what you would expect from a great boxed brownie. I like the richness the brown sugar adds, but the real magic is the Nutella and hazelnuts swirled into the batter.

Makes 16 brownies

Cookie Academy Review
▨ Parchment-Paper Sling, see page 39
▨ Clean Cut Bars, see page 58

1 cup / 120g all-purpose flour

½ cup / 50g Dutch-processed cocoa powder, sifted if lumpy (see Baker's Note)

¼ tsp baking powder

¼ tsp kosher salt

4 Tbsp / 57g butter, melted

3 Tbsp vegetable oil

1¼ cups / 250g lightly packed brown sugar

2 eggs, at room temperature

1 tsp pure vanilla extract (page 16)

4 oz / 112g bittersweet chocolate chips or chunks

2 tablespoons Nutella

2 oz / 57g chopped hazelnuts, toasted (optional)

Preheat the oven to 350°F / 175°C. Line a greased 8-inch / 20cm square cake pan with greased parchment paper that comes up the sides to create a sling.

In a small bowl, whisk together the flour, cocoa, baking powder, and salt.

In a large bowl, whisk together the butter, oil, brown sugar, eggs, and vanilla, until just combined. Fold in the flour mixture. Stir in the chocolate chips. Spread the batter into the prepared pan.

In a small, microwave-safe bowl, warm the Nutella in the microwave until it liquefies, about 10 seconds. Drizzle the Nutella in stripes over the batter and sprinkle the hazelnuts (if using) over the top. Drag a knife through the batter to distribute the toppings and create a marble pattern.

Bake in the middle of the oven for about 20 minutes, until set on the edges and on the top.

Allow to cool completely before removing from the pan and cutting.

BAKER'S NOTE

Replace a couple tablespoons of Dutch-processed cocoa with black cocoa for color and intensity.

■ Nut-Free

Bourbon Biscoff Brownies

This is a simple brownie doused in bourbon and dressed up in black tie. You can leave off the fancy toppings, and you'll have a delicious bourbon-scented treat. Add the extra layers and it's a real party. My friend Stephanie March, an authority on all things bourbon, described these brownies to me, and I set out to re-create her concept. The booze bakes out of the brownie, but then I brush the tops with more bourbon, per Stephanie's description, as they come out of the oven, so it flavors, moistens, and gives them a hearty kick. But, that's not all—the buttercream has a hit of bourbon, too, plus I've added Biscoff cookie butter to make them even more delicious and complex. The thin chocolate glaze is there for its elegant shine; no one has ever complained about more chocolate in a brownie!

Makes about 16 brownies

Cookie Academy Review
■ Parchment-Paper Sling, see page 39
■ Clean Cut Bars, see page 58

1 cup / 120g all-purpose flour

¼ cup / 25g Dutch-processed cocoa powder

½ tsp baking powder

¼ tsp kosher salt

6 Tbsp / 80g unsalted butter

¾ cup / 150g granulated sugar

1 tsp pure vanilla extract (page 16)

½ cup bourbon, divided

12 oz / 340g bittersweet chocolate, finely chopped, divided

2 large eggs, at room temperature

1 cup / 80g chopped pecans (optional)

Bourbon Buttercream

½ cup / 110g unsalted butter, at room temperature

1 cup / 120g confectioners' sugar

¼ cup / 65g Biscoff cookie butter

1 Tbsp bourbon

Chocolate Glaze

3 oz / 85g semisweet chocolate chips

3 Tbsp unsalted butter

Preheat the oven to 350°F / 175°C. Line a greased 8-inch / 20cm square cake pan with greased parchment paper that goes up the sides to create a sling.

In a small bowl, whisk together the flour, cocoa powder, baking powder, and salt. Set aside.

In a medium-size saucepan over low heat, bring the butter, sugar, vanilla, and ⅓ cup of the bourbon to a simmer. Remove from the heat, whisk until smooth, and add in 8 oz / 224g of the chopped chocolate. Swirl the pan to cover the chocolate and allow it to sit for 2 minutes.

Whisk until there are no chunks of chocolate left. Whisk in the eggs, one at a time, mixing until incorporated.

Fold in the flour mixture with a rubber spatula. Stir in the pecans (if using) and remaining chopped chocolate. Spread the batter evenly in the prepared pan.

Bake in the middle of the oven for 20 to 24 minutes. The brownies should be puffed but still a bit wobbly in the center. Be careful not to overbake these, otherwise they won't have the outrageous fudge quality. As soon as you take them from the oven, use a pastry brush to gently brush the remaining bourbon over the top.

Cool completely in the pan before topping.

Make the buttercream: In a medium bowl, beat the butter and confectioners' sugar until smooth and fluffy with a stiff rubber spatula. Add the Biscoff cookie butter and bourbon. Use a small offset spatula to smooth the buttercream over the cooled brownies. The smoother the surface, the more elegant the finished brownies will be. Refrigerate for about 30 minutes or until the buttercream is firm.

Make the chocolate glaze: In a small microwave-safe bowl, microwave the chocolate and butter for about 30 seconds. Stir until smooth and let cool slightly. Spread evenly over the chilled buttercream. Return to the refrigerator and chill for at least 30 minutes to set.

Run the tip of a knife dipped into hot water around the edge of the pan. Use the parchment-paper sling to carefully remove the bars from the pan. Use a very thin knife, dipped into hot water, to cut the bars into whatever size or shape you'd like. Serve at room temperature or chilled.

State Fair and Other Favorites

I didn't quite understand how serious people could get about baking cookies until I moved to Minnesota and went to the state fair. People from all over the state bring their baked sweets to the acre-long barn to be judged by their peers. The rules are intense, and people spend the better part of the year practicing their winning bakes. Marjorie Johnson is our local blue ribbon champion with thousands of wins to her name. At 101 years old she said, "I'm a cockeyed optimist. I always think only wonderful things are going to happen. And you know, they do. I don't know how it works out that way, but it's wonderful." I think this is a great philosophy for life and for baking. Only wonderful things can come from blending butter and sugar.

These recipes are inspired by some of the classics I was introduced to here in Minnesota; not only do we host one of the largest state fairs, but it's also home to Betty Crocker, another woman, albeit fictitious, who knows a thing or two about cookies.

Bars are a layered dessert baked in a pan resembling a brownie (or cookie or pie) and can be made with fruit, caramel, chocolate, or anything else your pantry contains. Once they're out of the oven and cooled, they are cut into neat bars. I was first introduced to this concept when I moved to Minneapolis in 1993 from Vermont. Bars are generally served on a buffet table with lots of Crock-Pots and "hot dish" (aka casserole for non-Minnesotans). Every family has their own bar recipes that are usually a tightly held secret, but the results are shared with neighbors, friends, family, and in church basements.

▓ Nut-Free

Chocolate Wafers

The classic Famous Chocolate Wafer cookie was recently discontinued and left a hole in the cookie aisle. I love baking up a scratch version with Dutch-processed cocoa, which ensures the signature dark color and rich, deep chocolate flavor. Eat them plain or stuff with a dollop of buttercream frosting sandwiched between two cookies to create a delicious and totally dunk-able version of the iconic Oreo. It's such an easy and nostalgic dessert.

You can also make a variation of these chocolate wafers by adding mint extract and coating them in chocolate. They're reminiscent of the famed thin, minty Girl Scout cookie!

Makes about 80 cookies or 40 sandwiches

Cookie Academy Review
▓ Batch Baking, see page 56

Chocolate Wafers

1 cup / 110g cake flour

½ tsp baking soda

½ tsp kosher salt

½ cup / 40g Dutch-processed cocoa powder, sifted if lumpy

½ cup / 110g unsalted butter, at room temperature

1 cup / 120g confectioners' sugar, sifted

2 tsp pure vanilla extract (page 16)

Buttercream (Use the Bourbon Buttercream on page 198, but omit the bourbon; optional)

Make the chocolate wafers: In a small bowl, whisk together the cake flour, baking soda, salt, and cocoa powder.

In a stand mixer fitted with the paddle attachment, mix the butter, confectioners' sugar, vanilla, and the flour mixture on medium-low speed until evenly mixed, 1 to 2 minutes.

On a sheet of plastic wrap, form the dough into a log 1½ inches / 4cm in diameter. Wrap and refrigerate until firm, at least an hour. It can also be made the day before or frozen for several weeks.

Preheat the oven to 350°F / 175°C. Line two baking sheets with parchment paper.

Using a sharp knife with a thin blade, slice the log into coins, about ⅛ inch / 6mm thick. Arrange on the prepared baking sheet, leaving about ½ inch / 1.3cm of space between each cookie.

Bake, one sheet at a time, in the middle of the oven for about 8 minutes, until set and no longer shiny. Allow to cool completely on the parchment before filling with the buttercream (if using).

If making sandwich cookies, once cool, spread a ⅛-inch / 3mm layer of buttercream on one cookie and sandwich with another one. Store in an airtight container in the refrigerator for a few days or freeze.

▓ **VARIATION: CHOCOLATE-MINT THINS**

These cookies are reminiscent of the famous mint Girl Scout cookies. They are the chocolate wafer dipped in minty chocolate, no stuffing needed. Add ¼ teaspoon mint extract to the dough. Bake the cookies as directed and cool completely. In a medium-size, microwave-safe bowl, melt 8 oz / 225g of bittersweet chocolate and 1 teaspoon of vegetable oil. Gently stir in ¼ teaspoon mint extract until smooth. Allow to cool for about 5 minutes or until it is thick enough to cling to the cookies. Use a fork to lower a cookie into the chocolate, then gently shake off the excess coating and wipe the bottom of the fork against the bowl. (If the chocolate mixture is too thick, reheat the chocolate to thin it out.) Place the dipped cookie on a silicone mat or parchment paper. Repeat with each cookie. Drizzle leftover chocolate over the tops to decorate.

■ Nut-Free

Snickerdoodles

I think snickerdoodles sometimes have the unfair reputation of being dull or old-fashioned, likely because they're so ubiquitous, especially in the Midwest. When my son Henri requested I make some—and a friend of mine chimed in that the store-bought versions remind her of school functions—I was determined to create and master an awesome snickerdoodle recipe. This version of the popular classic still has that characteristic excited puff and slight tang from the cream of tartar, but what sets these apart is the extra coating. The trick to a thick cinnamon and sugar top is to double dip in sugar. After an initial roll in the sugar mix, I dip them in heavy cream and back again in the cinnamon sugar. This creates a lovely thick crust surrounding a fluffy cookie that will make you love those school functions or any other occasion.

Makes about 28 cookies

Cookie Academy Review
■ Using a Portion Scoop, see page 43
■ Batch Baking, see page 56

2¾ cups / 330g all-purpose flour

1¼ tsp cream of tartar

1 tsp baking soda

½ tsp kosher salt

1 cup / 220g unsalted butter, at room temperature

1¼ cups / 250g granulated sugar

¼ cup / 50g lightly packed brown sugar

1 tsp pure vanilla extract (page 16)

2 eggs, at room temperature

Topping

¼ cup / 60ml heavy whipping cream

½ cup / 100g granulated sugar

1 Tbsp ground cinnamon

In a medium bowl, whisk together the flour, cream of tartar, baking soda, and salt.

In a stand mixer fitted with the paddle attachment, cream together the butter, granulated and brown sugars, and vanilla on medium speed until light and fluffy, about 2 minutes. Scrape down the sides of the bowl with a rubber spatula. Mix in the eggs, one at a time, until well incorporated. Scrape down the bowl again.

Add the flour mixture all at once and mix on low speed just until it all comes together. Scrape down the bowl, turn the speed to medium, and mix for 15 seconds.

Line a baking sheet with parchment paper.

Scoop the cookie dough using a #40 (1½-tablespoon) portion scoop onto the prepared baking sheet. Roll each dough ball in the palm of your hand to make a round sphere.

Make the topping: Fill a shallow bowl with the cream. In a medium bowl, stir together the sugar and cinnamon. Roll the cookies in the cinnamon and sugar mixture, covering them completely. Then dip just the top half in heavy cream and dip that back into the sugar mixture, so the tops are double dipped.

Freeze the dough balls for about 15 minutes, so they are very firm but not completely frozen or refrigerate them for at least 30 minutes. You can also leave them refrigerated and covered overnight.

Preheat the oven to 400°F / 205°C. Line two baking sheets with parchment paper.

Place the dipped cookies onto the prepared cookie sheets, leaving 3 inches / 7.5cm of space between each cookie. They will spread.

Bake, one sheet at a time, in the middle of the oven for 8 to 10 minutes, until golden brown on the bottom (see Baker's Note). The cookies will puff wildly while baking, then flatten out just a bit when they come out. If some of the sugar slips to the pan and caramelizes, cut it off with a round cookie cutter or a knife while it's still hot.

Cool completely on the baking sheet.

BAKER'S NOTE

The way you bake these will change the texture. If you like them a little chewier, take them out of the oven a couple of minutes early, so the inside is just a bit underbaked.

Peanut Butter–Maple Sandwich Cookies

Peanut butter lovers rejoice! This cookie is an ode to my favorite childhood spread. The crispy peanut butter cookie is filled with a creamy—you guessed it—peanut butter frosting. These sandwich cookies are packed with peanut butter, and the maple in the frosting beautifully balances it out. They're inspired by Nutter Butter cookies, but I like to cut them out in maple leaf shapes to indicate the star ingredient in the frosting. I grew up eating freshly ground peanut butter, but these are best with Skippy or Jif, because of their melting qualities. Save the natural stuff for your sandwiches.

Number of cookies depends on cutter size

Cookie Academy Review
▥ Freezing the Dough, see page 45
▥ Rolling the Dough, see page 52
▥ Batch Baking, see page 56

Cookie Dough

1⅔ cups / 200g all-purpose flour

½ tsp baking soda

¼ tsp kosher salt

5 Tbsp / 70g unsalted butter, at room temperature

⅓ cup plus 1 Tbsp / 100g creamy peanut butter (Skippy or Jif)

½ cup / 100g lightly packed brown sugar

½ cup / 100g granulated sugar

1 large egg, at room temperature

1 tsp pure vanilla extract (page 16)

Peanut Butter–Maple Frosting

½ cup / 130g creamy peanut butter

½ cup / 60g confectioners' sugar

1 Tbsp pure maple syrup

2 to 4 Tbsp heavy cream

Make the cookie dough: In a medium bowl, whisk together the flour, baking soda, and salt. Set aside.

In a stand mixer fitted with the paddle attachment, cream together the butter, peanut butter, and brown and granulated sugars on medium speed until light and fluffy, about 2 minutes. Scrape down the sides of the bowl with a rubber spatula. Mix in the egg until well incorporated. Mix in the vanilla. Add the flour mixture all at once and mix on low speed just until it all comes together. Scrape down the bowl, turn the speed to medium, and mix for 15 seconds.

Divide the dough into two disks, wrap them in plastic, and refrigerate until firm, at least an hour. The dough can also be made a couple of days ahead or frozen for up to 3 weeks.

Preheat the oven to 350°F / 175°C. Line baking sheets with parchment paper.

Roll one of the disks of dough out between two pieces of parchment paper to a rectangle ⅛ inch / 3mm thick. The dough may crack slightly along the edges. You can work them back together with your hands, but don't fret too much, because the results will still be amazing.

Use a cookie cutter to create fun shapes out of the dough. You can gather the scraps, refrigerate, and reroll once before the dough gets too tough. Place the cut cookies on the prepared baking sheet, leaving about ¾ inch of space between them. If your dough starts to get warm and sticky, return it to the refrigerator. Warm dough will be difficult to work with.

Bake, one sheet at a time, in the middle of the oven for 8 to 12 minutes, until the bottoms turn light golden brown. The baking time will vary based on the size of the cookie.

Allow to cool completely before filling. The cookies can be made a few days before and stored in an airtight container or wrapped and frozen for up to 1 month.

Make the frosting: In a medium bowl, cream together the peanut butter, confectioners' sugar, maple syrup, and enough cream to make the filling pipeable, but thick enough to stay in place. Fill a piping bag fitted with a medium star tip (Ateco #821) and pipe the filling on half the cookies. (In a hurry? Use a knife to spread it on instead.) Sandwich another cookie over the filling.

Chocolate Peanut Butter Cookies

Each year, I happily support the Girl Scouts by buying stacks of boxes, and for years, I've been thinking about how to reverse engineer my personal favorites: the peanut butter patties (aka Tagalongs). I use a dark chocolate shortbread for the base, add a dollop of peanut butter filling, drizzle them in chocolate, and add a sprinkling of crushed peanuts. They end up just as addictive as the ones in the box, but with a touch more sophistication for the adults in the room. One of my very young taste testers even said they are his "new most favorite cookie *ever*!" Can't beat that review.

Makes about 50 sandwich cookies

Cookie Academy Review

▥ Freezing the Dough, see page 45

▥ Rolling the Dough, see page 52

▥ Batch Baking, see page 56

▥ Melting Chocolate, see page 59

Chocolate Shortbread Cookie Base

2 cups / 240g all-purpose flour

2 Tbsp Dutch-processed cocoa powder, sifted if lumpy (see Baker's Note)

½ tsp baking powder

⅛ tsp baking soda

½ tsp kosher salt

½ cup / 110g unsalted butter, at room temperature

3 Tbsp shortening

¾ cup / 150g lightly packed brown sugar

1 tsp pure vanilla extract (page 16)

1 egg, at room temperature

Peanut Butter Frosting

½ cup / 110g unsalted butter, at room temperature

1¼ cups / 325g creamy peanut butter (Skippy or Jif)

1¼ cups / 150g confectioners' sugar

1 tsp pure vanilla extract (page 16)

Topping

4 oz / 112g bittersweet chocolate, melted

4 oz / 1 cup / 112g roasted and salted peanuts, crushed into small pieces

Flaky sea salt for topping

Make the cookie base: In a medium bowl, whisk together the flour, cocoa, baking powder, baking soda, and salt.

In a stand mixer fitted with the paddle attachment, cream together the butter, shortening, brown sugar, and vanilla on medium speed until light and fluffy, about 2 minutes. Scrape down the sides of the bowl with a rubber spatula. Mix in the egg until well incorporated. Add the flour mixture all at once and mix on low speed just until it all comes together. Scrape down the bowl, turn the speed to medium, and mix for 15 seconds.

Press the dough into a rectangle, wrap it in plastic, and chill for at least an hour. This can also be made the day before rolling or can be frozen for up to 1 month.

Preheat the oven to 350°F / 175°C. Line baking sheets with parchment paper.

On a lightly floured surface, roll the dough into a rectangle ⅛ inch / 3mm thick.

Use a 1½-inch / 4cm round cutter to cut out the cookies and place them about 1 inch apart on the prepared baking sheet. You can gather the scraps, refrigerate, and reroll them once before they get too tough.

Bake, one sheet at a time, in the middle of the oven for 10 to 12 minutes, until the cookies are set and no longer look wet. Let them cool on the parchment paper completely before filling.

Make the frosting: In a medium bowl, cream together the butter and peanut butter with a stiff rubber spatula until creamy.

Stir in the confectioners' sugar and vanilla until smooth. Using a knife or offset spatula, spread an ⅛ inch / 3mm thick layer of peanut butter frosting on each cookie.

Drizzle with the melted chocolate, then sprinkle with peanuts and sea salt flakes.

BAKER'S NOTE

This recipe will work with natural cocoa, but the color and intensity of the Dutch-processed is my go-to. You could really punch up the flavor by using a black cocoa powder.

Chocolate Peanut Butter Bars

This classic pairing is a bit of an obsession for my best friend, Jen. I try to come up with new and different ways to present her with chocolate and peanut butter desserts for any and all occasions. Layering the chocolate and peanut butter dough and baking them into one delicious bar turned out to be a new favorite. The creamy chocolate frosting with the little crunch and saltiness of the chopped peanuts on top intensifies the flavors.

Makes 16 bars

Cookie Academy Review
- Parchment-Paper Sling, see page 39
- Clean Cut Bars, see page 58
- Melting Chocolate, see page 59

1 cup / 120g all-purpose flour

½ tsp baking powder

1 pinch of kosher salt

½ cup / 110g unsalted butter, melted

⅓ cup / 90g creamy peanut butter (Skippy or Jif)

¾ cup / 150g lightly packed brown sugar

¼ cup / 50g granulated sugar

1 egg, at room temperature

1 tsp pure vanilla extract (page 16)

2 oz / 56g bittersweet chocolate, finely chopped

Chocolate Frosting

4 oz / 112g bittersweet chocolate, finely chopped

2 Tbsp unsalted butter

1 cup / 120g confectioners' sugar

¼ cup / 60ml heavy whipping cream

⅓ cup / 40g salted peanuts, chopped (optional)

Preheat the oven to 350°F / 175°C. Line a greased 8-inch square cake pan with greased parchment paper that goes up the sides to create a sling.

In a small bowl, whisk together the flour, baking powder, and salt.

In a large bowl, combine the butter, peanut butter, brown sugar, granulated sugar, egg, and vanilla.

Stir the flour mixture into the peanut butter mixture, just until combined. Divide the mixture equally into two bowls.

Melt the chocolate and stir it into one of the bowls with the peanut butter mixture. Press the chocolate dough mixture into the prepared pan. Freeze for about 5 minutes to set the layer. Once it is set, press the remaining peanut butter mixture evenly over the first chocolate layer. Bake in the middle of the oven for 25 to 30 minutes, until set. Cool to room temperature.

While the bars are cooling, make the frosting: In a large bowl, heat the chocolate and butter in the microwave, just until melted, about 1 minute. Stir until smooth. Add the confectioners' sugar and use a handheld mixer on low speed to mix, while drizzling in the heavy cream. Mix until combined, then turn up the speed and mix until smooth. If the mixture seems grainy or separated, add a teaspoon of cream. Repeat until smooth. Spread it evenly over the cooled bars.

Sprinkle the top with chopped peanuts (if using). Refrigerate for about 20 minutes to set the frosting before removing from the pan and cutting.

Miso Caramel Chocolate Bars

This is a play on Twix, one of my favorite candy bars with its layers of shortbread, caramel, and chocolate. The bar version is often called the millionaire bar. I've added a bit of miso, a fermented soybean paste used in Japanese cuisine to add umami to a dish. It is salty and earthy, which is a terrific addition to the rich, sweet caramel. I chose to use a traditional aged red miso, which has a pretty strong flavor and just a hint of funk (in the best way). To give the base even more depth of flavor, the shortbread has five spice added to it.

Makes about 16 bars

Cookie Academy Review
- Parchment-Paper Sling, see page 39
- Making Pressed Dough Crust, see page 54
- Clean Cut Bars, see page 58
- Ganache SOS, see page 59

Crust

1 cup / 120g all-purpose flour

⅓ cup / 38g confectioners' sugar

1 pinch of kosher salt

½ tsp five spice powder (optional)

½ cup / 110g unsalted butter, at room temperature

Miso Caramel

1¼ cups / 250g granulated sugar

1 tsp light corn syrup

¼ cup / 60ml water

One 14-oz / 396g can sweetened condensed milk

1½ Tbsp miso

4 Tbsp / 55g unsalted butter

¼ tsp kosher salt (the amount of salt you use may vary depending on the kind of miso you use)

Bittersweet Chocolate Ganache

4 oz / 112g bittersweet chocolate, finely chopped

2 Tbsp heavy whipping cream

Preheat the oven to 350°F / 175°C. Line a greased 8-inch / 20cm square cake pan with greased parchment paper that goes up the sides to create a sling.

Make the crust: In a medium bowl, mix the flour, confectioners' sugar, salt, five spice (if using), and butter with a wooden spoon until it comes together into a rough dough.

Evenly spread the dough into the prepared pan, cover it with plastic, and press it tightly using your fingers or the bottom of a glass. Freeze for 10 to 15 minutes, until solid.

Bake in the middle of the oven for about 20 minutes, until golden brown along the edges. Allow to cool completely before adding the filling.

Make the miso caramel: In a medium pot, combine the sugar, corn syrup, and water. (Try not to get any sugar crystals on the sides of the pot.) Cook the sugar mixture over high heat, without stirring or moving the pot, until it starts to turn amber along the edges; this can happen as quickly as a couple of minutes, so stay close. Once it starts to caramelize on the edges, swirl the pot so it caramelizes evenly. Continue to cook until the caramel starts to smoke slightly and is a dark caramel color; this will help intensify the flavor. Remove the pot from the heat and whisk in the condensed milk, miso, butter, and salt. Attach a candy thermometer to the pot, return it to the stove, and cook over medium-low heat until the mixture reaches 220°F / 105°C, stirring continuously with a rubber spatula to make sure the sides of the pan get wiped down.

Pour the caramel mixture over the baked crust and allow to cool to room temperature, about 1 hour.

Make chocolate ganache: In a microwave-safe bowl in the microwave, heat the chocolate and cream together for 30 seconds, then gently stir. If the chocolate hasn't melted, continue to heat in 10-second intervals, gently stirring after each time until the ganache is smooth.

Spread the ganache over the chilled caramel layer and allow to set until the ganache is firm, about 30 minutes.

Run the tip of a knife dipped into hot water around the edge of the pan. Use the parchment-paper sling to carefully remove the bars from the pan. Use a very thin knife, dipped into hot water, to cut the bars into whatever size or shape you'd like. Serve at room temperature.

"Big Game Day" Bars

I am admittedly only interested in the Super Bowl for the snacks and the halftime music show. All the salty snacks that I don't typically eat any other time are on the big game day menu. I wanted a treat that was befitting of this national holiday of sorts and that could travel well. They're gooey, salty, sweet, crunchy, and chewy all at the same time. My recipe tester, Sara, said, "I don't even understand what these are, but I just *love* them and can't stop eating them!" That's exactly what I was going for. You have full permission to make them for any occasion.

Makes about 16 bars

Cookie Academy Review
▦ Parchment-Paper Sling, see page 39
▦ Making Pressed Dough Crust, see page 54
▦ Clean Cut Bars, see page 58

Crust

1½ cups / 200g graham cracker crumbs (store-bought or homemade, page 86), crushed

¼ cup / 55g unsalted butter, melted

Filling

One 14-oz / 396g can sweetened condensed milk

1 Tbsp espresso powder

1 tsp pure vanilla extract (page 16)

1¼ cups / 226g semisweet mini chocolate chips

2 cups / 100g mini marshmallows

1 cup plus 2 Tbsp / 110g loosely packed sweetened shredded coconut

1 cup / 128g salted roasted peanuts

Topping

¼ cup / 60ml heavy whipping cream

2 Tbsp light corn syrup

2 tsp pure vanilla extract (page 16)

4 oz / 112g bittersweet chocolate, finely chopped

2 oz / 57g potato chips (2 small lunch box–size bags), crushed

¾ cup / 57g lightly crushed pretzels

Preheat the oven to 350°F / 175°C. Line an 8-inch / 20cm square cake pan completely with foil, then create a sling with greased parchment paper that comes up over the sides of the pan.

Make the crust: In a medium bowl, combine the crushed graham crackers and butter. Cover with plastic wrap and use a glass to press the cookie crust very tightly into the bottom of the prepared pan.

Bake for about 10 minutes, or until it is lightly toasted. Allow to cool while making the filling.

Make the filling: In a small saucepan over medium heat, bring the condensed milk to a simmer. Remove from the heat and mix in the espresso powder and vanilla.

Scatter the chocolate chips, marshmallows, coconut, and peanuts over the baked crust.

Pour the condensed milk mixture over the top of the bars. Bake the bars for about 25 minutes, until the edges start to bubble and the center is set. Allow the bars to cool to room temperature.

Make the topping: In a small saucepan over low heat, heat the cream, corn syrup, and vanilla to a gentle simmer. Remove from the heat and add in the chocolate. Swirl the pan to cover the chocolate and allow it to sit for a couple of minutes. Gently stir the mixture until completely combined. Pour over the bars and spread to cover evenly. Sprinkle the crushed potato chips and pretzels over the top.

Refrigerate just until the chocolate topping is set, about 30 minutes.

Run a hot knife around the edge of the pan. Use the parchment-paper sling to carefully remove the bars from the pan. Use a very thin knife, dipped into hot water, to cut the bars into whatever size or shape you'd like. Serve and freeze any leftovers for a couple of weeks.

Caramelita Bars

A version of these bars won the Pillsbury Bake-Off Contest in 1967, the year I was born. The winning baker was from Minnesota, and the recipe became synonymous with the state. My best friend, Jen, is a Duluth, Minnesota, native and her mom, Eileen Carlson, has made her own "secret" version on every special occasion for the past five decades. They hold a special place in the hearts of everyone who tries them. Like any good family recipe, we make them our own. The original 1967 version used oleo, another name for margarine, and caramel ice cream sauce or caramel candies individually wrapped in plastic. I riffed on the classic and came up with a version I hope makes Eileen proud. I've swapped the oleo for brown butter and created a quick caramel goop to use in place of the ice cream sauce or candies. Using bittersweet chocolate tempers the sweetness, but you can use semisweet chocolate chips as they did in 1967. As Jen says, these are a messy, two-napkin bar, and there's still probably going to be some caramel and chocolate on your fingertips.

Makes 16 bars

Cookie Academy Review
- Parchment-Paper Sling, see page 39
- Making Pressed Dough Crust, see page 54
- Clean Cut Bars, see page 58

Oat Crust

½ cup / 110g unsalted butter, melted

1 cup / 120g all-purpose flour

1 cup / 100g rolled oats

¾ cup / 150g lightly packed brown sugar

½ tsp baking soda

½ tsp kosher salt

Caramel Goop

¼ cup / 80g sweetened condensed milk

¼ cup / 80g corn syrup or Lyle's Golden Syrup

½ cup / 100g lightly packed brown sugar

2 Tbsp unsalted butter

½ tsp kosher salt

2 tsp pure vanilla extract (page 16)

6 oz / 170g bittersweet chocolate, chopped

½ cup / 60g chopped walnuts or pecans, lightly toasted

Preheat the oven to 350°F / 175°C. Line a greased 8-inch / 20cm square cake pan with greased parchment paper that goes up on the sides to create a sling.

Make the oat crust: In a large bowl, mix the butter, flour, oats, brown sugar, baking soda, and salt until it comes together. Pour two-thirds of the mixture into the pan, cover with plastic wrap, and press the dough with a glass into the bottom of the prepared pan.

Bake in the middle of the oven for about 20 minutes, until golden brown.

Make the caramel goop: Meanwhile, in a small pot, warm the sweetened condensed milk, corn syrup, brown sugar, butter, salt, and vanilla over medium heat, stirring until it comes to a simmer and the butter melts, about 3 minutes.

Once the crust is baked, pour the caramel mixture over the hot crust. Cover it evenly with the chopped chocolate, walnuts, and sprinkle the remaining third of the oat mixture over the chocolate.

Bake in the middle of the oven for 15 to 18 minutes, until the oat mixture is golden brown and caramel is bubbling on the edges. Allow to cool completely before lifting it out of the pan and cutting. This can also be made days ahead and refrigerated or frozen for months.

Rhubarb Blondies

This is the perfect pairing of a sweet, rich, brown butter blondie and the tartness of rhubarb crisp. I grow one thing in my garden that is edible and it is rhubarb. I have several varieties and the best one for this recipe is the kind that is thin and red throughout the stalk. Its green cousin will certainly deliver on the flavor, but for the pretty specks of red in the bars, I like the red. If you live in a part of the country where rhubarb doesn't grow, you may want to move; but if that's not an option, then make these wonderful blondies with fresh or frozen sour cherries, tahini and halva, or chocolate chunks for a more traditional take.

Makes 16 bars

Cookie Academy Review
▦ Parchment-Paper Sling, see page 39
▦ Making Pressed Dough Crust, see page 54
▦ Clean Cut Bars, see page 58

1½ cups / 180g all-purpose flour

½ tsp baking powder

½ tsp kosher salt

6 Tbsp / 85g brown butter (page 41), melted

1¼ cups / 250g lightly packed brown sugar

1 egg, at room temperature

1 tsp pure vanilla extract (page 16)

¾ cup / 100g thinly sliced rhubarb

Oat Topping

3 Tbsp butter, melted

¼ cup / 30g all-purpose flour

¼ cup / 25g rolled oats

¼ cup / 50g lightly packed brown sugar

⅛ tsp baking soda

¼ tsp kosher salt

Preheat the oven to 350°F / 175°C. Grease and line an 8-inch / 20cm square cake pan with parchment paper that comes up the sides to create a sling.

In a small bowl, whisk together the flour, baking powder, and salt.

In a large bowl, whisk together brown butter, brown sugar, egg, and vanilla until just combined. Using a wooden spoon or stiff rubber spatula, stir in the flour mixture. The batter will be very thick.

Spread the batter into the prepared pan and press evenly with your fingers. Lay the rhubarb out evenly over the batter.

Make the oat topping: In a small bowl, combine the butter, flour, oats, brown sugar, baking soda, and salt until it comes together in a crumbly topping. Distribute the oat mixture evenly over the rhubarb.

Bake for 20 to 25 minutes, until the rhubarb is tender and the edges and top crusts are golden brown.

Allow to cool completely before removing from the pan and cutting.

▦ VARIATION: SOUR CHERRY BLONDIES

Swap out the rhubarb for equal amounts of fresh or frozen sour cherries. If you use frozen cherries, let them thaw and strain out the juices before adding them to the recipe.

▦ VARIATION: TAHINI & HALVA BLONDIES

Swap out the rhubarb and oat topping for 2 teaspoons tahini, white or black, and 3 oz / 85g crumbled halva. Drizzle the tahini over the batter. Sprinkle the halva over the top. Drag a knife through the top in a zigzag pattern to distribute the tahini and halva.

▦ VARIATION: TRADITIONAL BLONDIES

Replace the rhubarb and oat topping with ½ cup / 85g bittersweet chocolate chips or chunks and ⅔ cup / 85g toasted walnut or pecan pieces by mixing them into the batter before spreading into the pan for a more traditional blondie recipe.

■ Gluten-Free   ■ Nut-Free

Rice Crispy Bars

I first made brown butter rice treats in 2011 when I visited Flour Bakery in Boston. The esteemed pastry chef, Joanne Chang, improved on a childhood favorite by adding one of my all-time favorite flavors: brown butter. I was smitten. My favorite rice bars are both crispy from the cereal and soft and chewy from the marshmallows. The trick is to barely cook the marshmallows, otherwise they harden as they cool, almost like a candy. I don't want a stiff, brittle bar, unless I'm trying to sculpt with it. Once I was asked to make a dragon head out of cereal for a giant edible Viking ship. It took twenty bags of marshmallows and eight family-size boxes of cereal, plus a sleepless night of figuring out how to mold the cereal into a beast. I give some suggestions in the Baker's Note if you want to try it yourself—maybe on a smaller scale.

Makes 9 bars

Cookie Academy Review
■ Clean Cut Bars, see page 58

¼ cup / 56g unsalted butter
or brown butter (page 41)

¼ tsp kosher salt

5 cups / 284g mini-
marshmallows
(see Baker's Note)

2 tsp pure vanilla extract
(page 16)

5 cups / 130g crisp rice
cereal

Lightly butter an 8-inch / 20cm square cake pan.

In a large heavy pot over medium-low heat, bring the butter and salt to a simmer. Turn off the heat and add the mini-marshmallows.

Stir until the mixture is smooth. Try not warm it up any more, or your bars will end up hard. If the marsh-mallows are not fully melted, cover the pot and let them sit a minute. Stir in the vanilla, add the rice cereal, and mix until thoroughly incorporated.

Pour the mixture into the prepared pan. Allow to set at room temperature for about 30 minutes before cutting.

■ **VARIATIONS**

Other Cereals. Experiment wildly and use your favorite! I have tried many, but not all. The larger the cereal bits, the less cereal you need.

Dulce de Leche. Add 3 Tbsp of dulce de leche (page 168) to the melted marshmallows.

Pumpkin Pie Spice. Add 1 tsp of pumpkin pie spice to the melted marshmallows.

Peanut Butter. Add ¼ cup / 65g of peanut butter to the melted marshmallows. Use Skippy or Jif here; this is not the place for natural peanut butter, as the oil will throw the recipe off. You can also add ⅓ cup semisweet mini chocolate chips at this stage for something even more fun.

Strawberry. This variation is inspired by the photo on the box of cereal. Add ½ cup of freeze-dried strawberries (or other berries) with the cereal.

Rainbow Sprinkles. Add ¼ cup / 45g rainbow or chocolate sprinkles after cereal is added.

BAKER'S NOTES

Mini-marshmallows melt faster and require less heat than large marshmallows, so they don't get overcooked and hard. If you can only find large marshmallows, stir them in the butter, then cover the pot for 30 seconds and stir again. Repeat until melted.

If you want a stiffer rice treat that holds a shape (let's say a dragon head for a friend), cook the marshmallow mixture for an extra minute or two before adding the rice. Increase the rice cereal by 1 cup.

STATE FAIR AND OTHER FAVORITES

Lemon Bars

I love a lemon dessert. The brightness of the tart juice—tempered by just the right amount of sweet—baked into a soft, custardy layer that sits on top of a shortbread cookie crust is divine. The shakes of bitters in the recipe come from my husband; he's never made a lemon bar, or any bar for that matter, but whenever we make lemonade, he always adds a few drops of aromatic bitters to the mix. His family is from Trinidad, the home of Angostura, so it goes into rum cocktails and just about everything else to give it a little something extra. Its subtle herbaceousness, spices, and orange notes are just lovely with the lemon.

Makes about 16 bars

Cookie Academy Review
- Parchment-Paper Sling, see page 39
- Making Pressed Dough Crust, see page 54
- Clean Cut Bars, see page 58

Crust

1 cup / 120g all-purpose flour

⅓ cup / 40g confectioners' sugar, plus more for top

¼ tsp kosher salt

½ cup / 110g unsalted butter, at room temperature

Lemon Filling

3 eggs, at room temperature

2 egg yolks, at room temperature

1½ cups / 300g granulated sugar

¼ cup / 30g all-purpose flour

¼ tsp kosher salt

2 lemons, zested

¾ cup / 175ml fresh lemon juice (about 4 large lemons)

5 shakes of aromatic bitters

Preheat the oven to 350°F / 175°C. Line a greased 8-inch / 20cm square cake pan with greased parchment that goes up the sides to create a sling.

Make the crust: In a medium bowl, mix the flour, confectioners' sugar, salt, and butter with a wooden spoon until it comes together as a rough dough.

Press the dough into the prepared pan. Lay a piece of plastic wrap over the top and then rub it smooth. Freeze the dough for about 10 minutes, then lift the plastic wrap off.

Bake in the middle of the oven for 18 to 20 minutes, just until it is light golden brown. Allow the crust to cool while you prepare the lemon filling.

Make the lemon filling: In a large bowl, whisk the eggs, yolks, sugar, flour, salt, zest, lemon juice, and bitters until well combined.

Reduce the oven temperature to 325°F / 165°C. Pour the lemon filling over the still warm crust. Drape a piece of foil over the top of the pan, making sure it doesn't touch the filling. Bake for 20 to 25 minutes, until the center of the lemon filling is wobbly and set.

Cool to room temperature and then refrigerate to fully set, about an hour. Lift the lemon bars out of the pan using the parchment sling and cut using a sharp knife dipped in hot water. Dust with confectioners' sugar.

VARIATION: KEY LIME BARS OR PASSION FRUIT JUICE BARS

When making the filling, swap the lemon juice for equal parts key lime juice or passion fruit juice! Neither are as tart as lemons, so I like to decrease the sugar by a few tablespoons. If you can get fresh passion fruit, it's lovely with or without the seeds. They give the curd a fun spotted look and add a bit of crunch. If you want the smooth texture, strain the passion fruit before adding the juice to the filling. If you are using frozen juice, be sure it is 100 percent passion fruit and not loaded up with a bunch of sugar.

Blueberry Pie Bars

Blueberries are Minnesota's state berry, and they are taken very seriously. Finding a wild blueberry patch is like striking gold, and you never share that secret location with friends or even family members! My best friend, Jen, and I used to take our young boys to a few blueberry patches when they were in season, and it all reminded me of *Blueberries for Sal*, my favorite children's book. I almost expected to find bears picking berries over every hill. We never saw bears, but we picked a whole bunch of sweet, juicy, tart berries. The boys ate them, and whatever we didn't finish, we made into blueberry pie bars. These bars are made with a lemon thyme shortbread that is fragrant and just right with the berries. It's layered with a zippy cooked blueberry filling, made with fresh ginger and lemon, then topped with a beautiful lattice made with a cream cheese dough. The flavors all play so well together and are sophisticated for the adults and sweet enough to satisfy the kids.

Makes 16 bars

Cookie Academy Review
- Parchment-Paper Sling, see page 39
- Making Pressed Dough Crust, see page 54
- Clean Cut Bars, see page 58

Cream Cheese Dough

4 oz / 112g cream cheese, chilled

6 Tbsp / 84g unsalted butter, at room temperature

⅓ cup / 40g confectioners' sugar

1⅓ cups / 160g all-purpose flour

¼ tsp kosher salt

Shortbread Cookie Crust

½ cup / 60g confectioners' sugar

1½ cups / 180g all-purpose flour

¾ cup / 170g unsalted butter, cold and cut into small pieces

¼ tsp kosher salt

1 Tbsp lemon thyme leaves, finely chopped (optional)

Blueberry Filling

6 cups / 890g fresh or frozen blueberries (see Baker's Note)

½ tsp lemon zest

1 tsp very finely chopped peeled fresh ginger

½ cup / 100g granulated sugar

2 Tbsp cornstarch

Egg wash (1 egg mixed with 1 tsp water)

Granulated or sparkling sugar, to sprinkle on top crust

Make the cream cheese dough: In the food processor, cream together the cream cheese, butter, and confectioners' sugar until combined. Add the flour and salt, and pulse the dough several times until it comes together in a soft ball. On a sheet of plastic wrap, flatten the dough into a square and refrigerate it for at least 1 hour; the dough can be made the day before.

Preheat the oven to 350°F / 175°C. Grease an 8-inch / 20cm square cake pan with butter. Line the pan with a piece of parchment paper with two sides overhanging the edges of the pan to create a sling.

Make the shortbread crust: In a food processor, combine the confectioners' sugar, flour, butter, salt, and lemon thyme (if using). Process until it forms a dough; this may take a few minutes.

Press the dough into the prepared pan. Lay a piece of plastic wrap over the top and then rub it smooth. Lift the plastic wrap off. Bake in the middle of the oven for about 20 minutes, just until it is light golden brown. Allow the crust to cool while you prepare the blueberry filling.

Make the blueberry filling: In a medium-large saucepan, combine the blueberries, zest, and ginger. In a small bowl, whisk together the sugar and cornstarch, then add it to the blueberries. Cook over low heat until the blueberries thicken and reduce by about half. When the blueberries are cooked down, you should have about 2½ cups / 590ml of blueberry filling. Set aside to cool while you prepare the lattice.

CONTINUED

BLUEBERRY PIE BARS, CONTINUED

Assemble the blueberry bars: Once the cream cheese dough is chilled, roll it out on a well-floured surface until it has a thickness of about ¼ inch / 6mm. Use a pastry wheel to create strips. You can make them thick or thin, depending on what look you are going for. I cut mine so they are about ½ inch / 1.3cm wide.

Line a baking sheet with parchment paper. Lay out half the strips on the prepared baking sheet, with some space between the strips. Starting at the middle, fold up every other strip and lay one of the remaining strips across those still laid flat, unfold the strips over the perpendicular strip. Repeat by folding up the strips that had laid flat, laying the next strip across. Keep repeating with the next rows until you reach the bottom. Start back at the middle and do the same on the other side. Transfer the baking sheet to the freezer to stiffen, 15 to 20 minutes.

Once the lattice is chilled, pour the blueberry filling over the thyme shortbread crust. Remove the stiff lattice from the freezer and use a pastry wheel or knife to trim the lattice to fit the inside dimensions of the pan (you can always trim more after you place it on the filling). Brush the lattice with the egg wash (doing this before you place it on the filling will prevent the blueberries from staining the lattice).

Carefully transfer the stiff lattice onto the filling. If the lattice is chilled well enough, this should be a very easy task. If it is too soft, return it to the freezer until it is harder. Trim off any excess. Sprinkle with sugar.

Bake in the middle of the oven for 45 to 50 minutes, until the crust is golden and the filling is bubbling.

Allow the bars to cool completely before running a knife around the edge and lifting it out of the pan. Trim the edges and cut into sixteen equal pieces. They can be stored at room temperature for 1 day and then covered and refrigerated or frozen.

BAKER'S NOTE

Swap the blueberries for raspberries, blackberries, a mix of berries, or sour cherries in equal amounts.

Chocolate Ginger Marbled Cheesecake Bars

Here, in the Midwest, any sweet cut into a square is called a "bar." It changes this rather sophisticated flavor combination from a plated dessert into an after-school treat. I have to say, the rich chocolate ganache mixed with the ginger cheesecake batter sitting on top of a dark chocolate and crystallized ginger crust is a real winner. Marbling the two flavors and cutting them into bars makes them pure fun! I shared these chocolate ginger cheesecake bars with several neighbors to keep me from eating the entire batch.

Makes about 16 bars

Cookie Academy Review
- Parchment-Paper Sling, see page 39
- Making Pressed Dough Crust, see page 54
- Marbling, see page 55
- Clean Cut Bars, see page 58

Chocolate Cookie Crust

1½ cups / 200g crushed Chocolate Wafers (page 202) or Graham Crackers (page 86)

2 Tbsp Marcona almonds (or any toasted almonds)

2 Tbsp brown sugar

¼ cup / 56g unsalted butter, melted

2 Tbsp finely chopped crystallized ginger

Cheesecake

1 pound / 450g cream cheese, at room temperature

½ cup plus 2 Tbsp / 125g granulated sugar

¾ cup / 160g sour cream, at room temperature

2 extra large eggs, at room temperature

1 Tbsp peeled and very finely grated fresh ginger (use a Microplane; see Baker's Note)

Finely grated zest of 1 lemon

½ tsp fresh lemon juice

Ganache

1 oz / 30g bittersweet chocolate, finely chopped

2 Tbsp heavy cream

Preheat the oven to 350°F / 175°C. Line an 8-inch / 20cm square cake pan with parchment paper that comes up the sides of the pan to act as a sling.

Make the crust: In a food processor, pulverize the wafers with the almonds, brown sugar, butter, and crystallized ginger until you have well-ground crumbs. Pour it into the prepared pan. Cover with plastic wrap and press the crumbs into an even, packed layer with your hands or the bottom of a glass.

Remove the plastic and bake in the middle of the oven for 10 minutes, until the edges are golden. Remove from the oven and allow to cool while you make the cheesecake batter.

Reduce the oven temperature to 300°F / 150°C.

Make the cheesecake: In a stand mixer fitted with the paddle attachment, beat the cream cheese on medium speed for about 1 minute. Scrape down the sides of the bowl with a rubber spatula and mix for another 30 seconds. Add the sugar and continue mixing on medium speed for about 1 minute; the mixture will get thinner once the sugar is added. Mix in the sour cream. Mix in the eggs, one at a time, scraping down the bowl after each addition. Mix in the ginger, zest, and lemon juice. Set aside while you make the ganache.

Make the ganache: In a medium microwave-safe bowl, heat the chocolate and cream in 10 second intervals until the chocolate is warm and can be whisked smooth. The amount of time needed will depend on your chocolate. Allow to cool for a few minutes.

Once the ganache is cooled, add about ⅓ cup of the ginger cheesecake batter to the bowl of ganache and gently whisk together. Transfer the mixture to a measuring cup or small pitcher. Set aside.

Pour the remaining ginger cheesecake batter over the cooled crust and pour the chocolate batter in thin stripes over it. Very gently tap the cheesecake on the counter to get out any air bubbles.

CONTINUED

STATE FAIR AND OTHER FAVORITES

Using a chopstick or skewer, draw a zigzag line through the stripes in the cheesecake batter. Don't go too deep or you will disturb the crust.

Bake for about 25 minutes, or until the cheesecake is just set. It will jiggle like Jell-O when it is ready. Be sure not to overbake, or the cheesecake will crack. A few cracks are normal for a cheesecake not baked in a water bath, but we want to limit the amount of them.

Remove the pan from the oven and immediately run a knife around the outside edge of the cheesecake. This will also prevent the cheesecake from cracking more. Let it cool to room temperature, then refrigerate it for at least 2 hours before cutting.

Using the parchment sling, gently lift the cheesecake from the pan. If it doesn't easily lift out, very quickly, just for a few seconds, wave the pan over the burner of the stove to heat the bottom of the pan and try again.

Using a very thin sharp knife dipped in hot water, cut the cheesecake into bars.

BAKER'S NOTE

Use fresh ginger that has a smooth tight skin. If it is shriveled and dried out, the ginger will be too fibrous and hard to grate, and the flavor won't be as intense.

Nut-Free

Blueberry Gooey Butter Bars

This is the love child of the famous St. Louis gooey butter cake and a blueberry oat crisp. The shortbread crust is the foundation for the super-rich and gooey filling, which has a nice balance of sweet and tanginess from the blueberries. The oat topping makes this feel like you could reasonably serve it at breakfast as the most delicious way to start your day, or you could serve it with a scoop of ice cream for dessert. It is also super-tasty when made with sour cherries. I made the cherry variation on *Zoë Bakes* and brought them to a Lutheran Church event, where they all disappeared. That's the greatest compliment of all!

Makes about 16 bars

Cookie Academy Review
- Parchment-Paper Sling, see page 39
- Making Pressed Dough Crust, see page 54
- Clean Cut Bars, see page 58

Shortbread

½ cup / 110g unsalted butter, at room temperature

½ cup / 60g confectioners' sugar

1 cup / 120g all-purpose flour

¼ tsp kosher salt

Oat Topping

¾ cup / 75g rolled oats

½ cup / 60g all-purpose flour

¾ cup / 150g lightly packed brown sugar

6 Tbsp / 83g unsalted butter, melted

1 pinch of kosher salt

Gooey Layer

3 Tbsp unsalted butter, melted

3 Tbsp cream cheese, at room temperature

¼ tsp kosher salt

½ cup / 100g granulated sugar

1 Tbsp Lyle's Golden Syrup or honey

2 tsp pure vanilla extract (page 16)

1 large egg, at room temperature

2 cups / 300g wild blueberries, fresh or frozen

Preheat the oven to 350°F / 175°C. Line an 8-inch / 20cm square cake pan completely with foil, then create a sling with greased parchment paper that comes up over the sides of the pan.

Make the shortbread: In a medium bowl, mix together the butter, confectioners' sugar, flour, and salt, until it comes together in a uniform dough. Press the dough evenly into the prepared pan. Press it down with your hands or with the bottom of a glass to pack it tightly into the pan.

Bake in the middle of the oven for about 15 minutes, until golden and set. Cool to room temperature. Keep the oven on.

Make the topping: Using the same bowl you used for the crust, mix together the oats, flour, brown sugar, butter, and salt with your fingers, so the mixture forms small clumps. Set aside.

Make the gooey layer: In a medium bowl, whisk together the butter, cream cheese, salt, and sugar until smooth. Mix in the Lyle's syrup, vanilla, and egg. Pour the gooey mixture over the baked crust. Scatter the blueberries evenly over the filling and then add the topping in an even layer.

Bake for about 45 minutes, until the top is light caramel-brown and the fruit is bubbling.

Allow to cool completely in the pan. You can remove it from the pan and cut it into bars or refrigerate it and serve chilled.

VARIATION: CHERRY GOOEY BUTTER BARS

Replace the blueberries with 2 cups / 272g of pitted sour cherries.

STATE FAIR AND OTHER FAVORITES

Cherry Cheesecake Bars

My husband, Graham, planted a sour cherry tree in our backyard when we bought our house. It's still young and produces only enough fruit for a single pie or these delicious bars. If I am going to bake our limited supply of cherries into something, it has to be worthy, and this one certainly is. Adding sour cherry juice to the sour cream topping was the pink magic these bars needed to make them a showstopper for a summer party, but they're still rustic enough for a backyard picnic. The luscious, creamy cheesecake is just the perfect frame for the tart cherries. Someday we'll grow enough cherries to make a double batch, but until then, I supplement with frozen sour cherries.

Makes about 16 bars

Cookie Academy Review
▥ Parchment-Paper Sling, see page 39
▥ Making Pressed Dough Crust, see page 54
▥ Clean Cut Bars, see page 58

Crust

⅓ cup / 60g brown butter (page 41), melted

½ cup / 100g lightly packed brown sugar

1 cup / 120g all-purpose flour

⅛ tsp kosher salt

Cheesecake

1 pound / 450g cream cheese, at room temperature

⅔ cup / 130g granulated sugar

¼ cup / 60g sour cream, at room temperature

2 eggs, at room temperature

2 tsp pure vanilla extract (page 16)

¼ tsp kosher salt

2½ cups / 454g sour cherries, pitted (fresh or frozen, thawed and drained, juice reserved), coarsely chopped

Sour Cherry Topping

¾ cup / 180g sour cream

4 tsp granulated sugar

2 Tbsp reserved cherry juice if using frozen fruit (optional)

Preheat the oven to 350°F / 175°C. Line a greased 8-inch / 20cm square cake pan with greased parchment paper that goes up the sides to create a sling.

Make the crust: In a medium bowl, mix the brown butter, brown sugar, flour, and salt with a wooden spoon until it comes together in a uniform dough. Press the dough evenly into the prepared pan. Press it down with your hands or the bottom of a glass container to pack it tightly into the pan.

Bake in the middle of the oven for about 15 minutes, until golden and set. Cool to room temperature.

Reduce the oven temperature to 325°F / 165°C.

Make the cheesecake: In a stand mixer fitted with the paddle attachment, beat the cream cheese on medium speed for about 1 minute. Scrape down the sides of the bowl with a rubber spatula and mix for another 30 seconds. Add the sugar and continue mixing on medium speed for about 1 minute; the mixture will get thinner once the sugar is added. Mix in the sour cream. Mix in the eggs, one at a time, scraping down the bowl after each. Add the vanilla and salt, and mix for 30 seconds.

Pour half the cheesecake batter over the baked crust. Evenly scatter the chopped cherries over the cheesecake batter. Pour the remaining cheesecake batter over the cherries. Using an offset spatula or the back of a spoon, spread it evenly over the cherries.

Bake in the middle of the oven for about 30 minutes, until just set in the middle.

Make the topping: About halfway through the baking, in a medium-size bowl, stir together the sour cream, sugar, and cherry juice, if using, until smooth.

Remove the cheesecake from the oven and gently spoon the topping over the top, one tablespoon at a time, so it doesn't break the surface of the cheesecake. Spread it smoothly over the top. Return to the oven and bake for another 5 minutes.

Remove the cheesecake from the oven and allow to cool to room temperature in its pan on a cooling rack, then refrigerate for at least 1½ hours, preferably overnight, before removing from the pan, using the parchment sling to lift it out.

Use a sharp knife dipped in hot water to cut the bars.

Basque-Style Cheesecake Berry Bars

A Basque cheesecake is traditionally served crustless and with no berry adornments, but I promise you're going to fall in love with this rebellious version. I layer it with a cookie crust; I really like the spice in the Speculoos (Biscoff-ish) cookie and bright berries, which just make the mahogany top and lusciously smooth texture sing. You'll notice the ingredients—like the cream cheese—are cold rather than at room temperature, so it won't overbake in the hot oven as the top browns.

Makes about 16 bars

Cookie Academy Review
■ Parchment-Paper Sling, see page 39
■ Making Pressed Dough Crust, see page 54
■ Clean Cut Bars, see page 58

Crust

1½ cups / 200g cookie crumbs (use Speculoos [Biscoff-ish], page 169; Ginger Snaps, page 105; or Graham Crackers, page 86)

¼ cup / 50g lightly packed brown sugar

¼ cup / 55g unsalted butter, melted

1 pinch of kosher salt

Fruit Layer

½ cup / 100g granulated sugar

1 Tbsp cornstarch

3 cups / 400g mixed berries (fresh or frozen, thawed and drained; see Baker's Note)

Cheesecake

1½ pounds / 680g cream cheese, chilled

¾ cup / 150g granulated sugar

2 eggs

2 egg yolks

½ cup / 120g sour cream

2 tsp pure vanilla extract (page 16)

3 Tbsp all-purpose flour

¾ tsp kosher salt

Preheat the oven to 475°F / 245°C *convection* (or 500°F / 260°C flat heat). Line an 8-inch / 20cm square cake pan with parchment paper that comes up the sides of the pan to act as a sling.

Make the crust: In a food processor, pulse to combine the cookie crumbs, brown sugar, butter, and salt. Pour the mixture into the prepared pan, cover with plastic wrap and press with a glass to an even layer.

Bake in the middle of the oven for 10 minutes, until it starts to look well toasted. Set aside to cool.

Make the fruit layer: In a small bowl, whisk together the sugar and cornstarch. In a small pot, cook the berries and sugar-cornstarch mixture together over medium heat until the juices are thick and clear, 3 to 5 minutes. Remove from the heat.

Make the cheesecake: In a stand mixer fitted with the paddle attachment, beat the cream cheese on medium speed for about 1 minute, until smooth. Scrape down the sides and mix for another 30 seconds. Add the sugar and mix for about 1 minute, scraping down the sides of the bowl. Mix in the eggs and yolks, one at a time, scraping down the sides after each. Add the sour cream and vanilla and mix for 30 seconds, until incorporated.

In a medium bowl, combine the flour and salt. Add about 1 cup of the cream cheese mixture to the flour and whisk until smooth. Transfer this mixture back into the bowl of cream cheese and mix until uniformly blended.

Spread the cooled berries evenly over the baked crust. Gently pour the cream cheese batter over the berries, making sure the fruit isn't pushed to the top.

Bake in the middle of the oven for 20 to 25 minutes. The cheesecake will still be soft, but the top will be a deep brown mahogany color.

Let it cool to room temperature, then refrigerate for at least 2 hours before cutting.

Use the parchment-paper sling to carefully remove the bars from the pan. Use a very thin knife, dipped into hot water, to cut the cheesecake into bars.

BAKER'S NOTE

You can use any berries for this, and you can even use sour cherries. If you use strawberries or any other larger fruit, be sure to chop them up a bit, so they create an even layer on the bottom.

Sources

You will find links to all the products I use for my cookies on my website, ZoeBakes.com.

Ateco:
nycake.com/ateco-usa

Cake turners and decorating supplies

Bob's Red Mill:
bobsredmill.com

Specialty flours and other dry ingredients

Emile Henry Cookware:
emilehenryusa.com

Cookware and ceramic dinnerware

Kerrygold:
kerrygoldusa.com

European-style butter

King Arthur Flour:
kingarthurflour.com

Flour, specialty cake ingredients, and baking supplies

KitchenAid:
kitchenaid.com

Mixers and small appliances

Nordic Ware:
nordicware.com

Bundt pans and other baking equipment

OXO:
oxo.com

Cookie scoops and other kitchen supplies

Penzeys Spices:
Penzeys.com

Spices

Seed+Mill:
seedandmill.com

Halva and tahini

S.O.S.:
sos-chefs.com

Dehydrated fruit powder, spices, and dried edible roses

Vermont Creamery:
vermontcreamery.com

Butter and other fine dairy products

Valrhona Chocolate:
valrhona-chocolate.com

Chocolate and cocoa powder

Williams Sonoma:
williams-sonoma.com

Baking sheets

Wilton:
wilton.com

Baking and decorating supplies

Acknowledgments

Thank you, Graham, this book would simply not exist without your constant, unconditional love, tech support, photo filing, and hearty appetite. Henri and Charlie and Sarah, thank you for eating all the cookies and being so generous with your honest criticism. Your feedback always makes for a better book. I know the sacrifice was real, but at least there were always cookies!

Thank you, Jane Dystel, for being my champion over the last two decades. Ten books later and I am so grateful for your wisdom and guidance.

Thank you to my editor at Ten Speed Press, Claire Yee, for having the patience of a saint. The book took much longer to come to life than I'd planned but we got there and I'm in love with it! Betsy Stromberg, thank you for having the vision to create beauty out of the jumble of photos and recipes. Thank you to the whole Ten Speed team: production editor Ashley Pierce, production designers, Mari Gill and Faith Hague, production manager and prepress color managers Jane Chinn and Claudia Sanchez, copyeditor Andrea Chesman, proofreader Rita Madrigal, publicist Lauren Chung, and marketer Andrea Portanova.

To my friends, family, and colleagues, it takes a village to write a book and I have the best one. Jen Sommerness, thank you for being my cheese. Thanks to ALL my neighbors for opening your doors when I come with MORE cookies; Craig and Patricia Neal (my folks), thank you for taste testing 300 versions of the same cookies; Lorrain Neal (my mom), thank you for keeping me sane, testing recipes and telling me stories of the Bubbies. Thanks to my late grandmothers, Sarah Berkowitz and Barbara Neal, whose family recipes inspired much of this book; Jay and Tracey Berkowitz, thank you for digging up old photos of the Bubbies; Marion and John Callahan; Adam Cohn, thanks for teaching me to read contracts; Barb and Fran Davis, thank you for always supporting me; Todd France and Liz Arum, thanks for letting me stuff cookies in your freezer; Anna and Ewart François, you're what I aspire to; Kristin Neal, your love of baking set me on a path to sweets; Sally Simmons and David van de Sande, your love means the world to me; Carey and Heather, you knew I'd teach Victoria and Bennett to use a blow torch eventually! Stephen Tedesco, thank you for being my trusted navigator and suffering through endless B&W cookies; and Amy Vang, thank you for making my workspace shine.

Matt, Tom, Adam, Madeline, Brooke, Trish, Gillian, Andrea, Fatima, Dusti, the Patricks, Andrew, the entire team at Intuitive Content, and Joanna and Chip Gaines from Magnolia Network for creating Zoë Bakes, where I got to workshop some of these recipes; Blue Star Appliances, your beautiful oven baked all the cookies; Michelle Gayer; Rose Levy Beranbaum, Dorie Greenspan, Claudia Fleming, Deb Perleman, David Lebovitz, Molly Yeh, Kerry Diamond, Brian Hart Hoffman and all the bakers who shaped my ways in the kitchen; Lady Brainers, thanks for pushing me to be my best, bravest self (Stephanie Meyer, Stephanie March, Kim Kolina, Molly Hermann, Kellee O'Reilly, Ali Kaplan, Eliesa Johnson); Ginger Elizabeth, thanks for your macaron wisdom; Valrhona, thanks for all the chocolate; Kerry Diamond, your support means the world; my NY dining club, Jessie Sheehan, Hetty McKinnon, Susan Spungen, Jill Fergus, and Judy Kim.

Kate Childs, Nikki Goldfarb, Matthew Horowitz, Jordan Soloman, Kip Ludwig, and the whole team at CAA who helped keep my head on straight while shooting the show and writing a book.

Thank you, Dr. Montezuma, Dr. Hou, and Dr. Costillo, who gave me sight when things were dark!

Thank you, Liz Rolfsmeier and Joy Summers, for helping me put my stories on the page. Sarah Kieffer, you're always ready with a gif to make me laugh when I want to cry and thank you for taking photos of me, especially with the poodles. Sara Bartus, your recipe testing and extensive notes are the essential last step before I put the cookies into the world with joy and confidence. Finally, Stephani Johnson, there aren't enough words to express my gratitude for all you do to make my work/life better and way more fun. I couldn't have done this without you. xo

About the Author

ZOË FRANÇOIS is the author of ten cookbooks, including the 2022 IACP Best Baking Cookbook, *ZOË BAKES CAKES*, and co-author of the best-selling *Artisan Bread in Five Minutes a Day* series. She is also the host of *Zoë Bakes* on the Magnolia Network. Zoë studied art at the University of Vermont and then baking and pastry at the Culinary Institute of America (CIA) in New York. Since then, she has been a pastry chef at several Twin Cities restaurants, taught baking and pastry nationally, and her work has been featured in many publications, including *The New York Times*, *Washington Post*, *Better Homes & Gardens*, and more. Zoë's portfolio of work can be found on her website, ZoeBakes.com, Instagram (@zoebakes), and her Zoë Bakes Substack Newsletter. She lives in Minneapolis with her husband, Graham, and poodle, Rafman. Her two sons, Henri and Charlie, are off in the world, hopefully baking!

Index